T0339845

NOTES FROM THE OTHER CHINA

NOTES FROM THE OTHER CHINA

ADVENTURES IN ASIA

Troy Parfitt

Algora Publishing
New York

ISBN-13: 978-0-87586-582-9 (trade paper)
ISBN-13: 978-0-87586-583-6 (hard cover)
ISBN-13: 978-0-87586-584-3 (ebook)

Library of Congress Cataloging-in-Publication Data —

Parfitt, Troy, 1972—
    Notes from the other China : adventures in Asia / Troy Parfitt.
        p. cm.
    ISBN 978-0-87586-582-9 (trade paper: alk. paper) — ISBN 978-0-87586-583-6 (hard
cover: alk. paper) — ISBN 978-0-87586-584-3 (ebook) 1. Asia—Description and travel. 2.
Taiwan—Description and travel. 3. Parfitt, Troy, 1972—Travel--Asia. I. Title.

    DS10.P38 2008
    915.04'43—dc22

                2007033587

Front Cover: Taipei, the world's new tallest building, towers over a busy street in
Taipei. Image: © Louie Psihoyos/Corbis

Printed in the United States

For my mom and dad.

Acknowledgments

I would like to thank the following people for their generous assistance, kind support, sustaining feedback, and handy tips during the preparation of this book: Tom Bishop, Emma Chou, Robert Dobie, Helen Hsu, Linda Hung, Andrew Johnston, Scott Lawson, Noel Merlino, John Ross, and David Wilson. Most of all, I would like to extend a special thank-you to my friend and former colleague Chris Smith for helping me to see that I had this in me.

"The use of travel is to regulate imagination by reality, and instead of thinking how things may be, to see them as they are."

Samuel Johnson

Table of Contents

Chapter 1. From Hope Restored to the Hermit Kingdom

I come from Saint John, New Brunswick, Canada. Now you can say you've heard of someone who does. No one outside of Canada seems to have heard of the province of New Brunswick, while Canadians themselves can't seem to associate much of anything with it, save for perhaps an unremarkable drive they took through it in order to reach the more appealing provinces of Nova Scotia, Prince Edward Island, and Newfoundland on a summer holiday. In point of fact, New Brunswick, whose motto is Hope Restored, is a beautiful place filled with heaps of friendly and colorful people, but it is obscure, not to mention painfully conservative, and by the tender age of 14 I was making plans to leave it behind.

This had to do with a long held desire to be able to step outside my door and *be* somewhere, and for the longest time that somewhere was Britain. The plan, as untenable as it was, was to head down to the dock one day and board a ship bound for England, a country I reckoned to be a sort of Heaven on Earth; home to an endless array of comedy programs, soccer matches, pop music, good beer, literary figures, history, castles, and people who employed words like bumbershoot, cock-up, and higgledy-piggledy in dead earnest. Over time, however, my interest in things British dwindled and dissolved.

Then, somehow, I started to think about moving to Asia. Japan, specifically. It looked decidedly modern on TV and in pictures, and I figured that what with it being the world's second largest economy, the people there had to be doing something right. Staring out the window one day from my grade twelve classroom at Canada's oldest cemetery on a typically bleak and blustery March morning, I made up my mind that I would go there for a couple of years to teach English if things didn't work out for me at home. And work out, they didn't.

Five years later, while in the process of looking for a teaching position on the new fangled Internet, I heard about a goodbye party for an old high school friend of mine named Dave McGuire. Dave was going to Seoul to teach. Upon telling him that I was working on going to Japan, he said he'd see if the school that hired him needed any extra teachers. A month later, I followed him over. It would be good to have a friend on my adventure, and after finishing my contract I could do an additional year in, say, Tokyo.

The night before I was slated to leave, my mother informed me that her brother-in-law had called and had wanted to tell me something about Korea. I wasn't in at the time.

"What did he say?" I asked.

"Well, he said he had a buddy who was there."

"And?"

"And according to this buddy of his, Korea is an awfully muddy place. He said he'd never seen the likes of it."

"Muddy?"

"Well, he was there during the *war*, dear."

"Oh, right. And that's it? That's what he called to tell me?"

"Yes, I think so. Do you have everything you need, dear? Maybe you'd better take a pair of rubber boots from the basement."

The people who were supposed to pick me up at the Kimpo International Airport were five hours late and by the time they got around to retrieving me, it was past the point where anyone felt like making the long haul out to the suburbs to where I'd be working. Instead, they took me to another branch of the school in downtown Seoul, after which they put me up for the night in a nearby hot-sheet hotel. On the dresser, there was a mountain of used tissues smeared with lipstick while in the bathroom there stood a mountain of sand that was nearly a meter tall. I stared at it for a minute or more, wondering dully what it could possibly be doing there.

Famished, I ventured outside in search of a restaurant and within seconds I was passed by a silver Hyundai. This wouldn't be particularly noteworthy if it weren't for the fact that it passed me on the sidewalk. I never saw that before. But, in retrospect, this was child's play. For the next twenty months, I would observe vehicles perform feats I had only previously witnessed on *The Dukes of Hazard*.

Too intimidated to try Korean food, I settled on an American steak house where I ordered a salad and two Miller beers and was charged the equivalent of

26 $CAN. Somewhere in between staring at the bill, gaping out the window at the blinking Korean script, and recalling that my hotel could be rented by the hour and had a replica of one of the Pyramids next to the toilet, it dawned on me that I was truly a long way from home.

The language school I signed on with was called ECC and was located in the municipality of Anyang, just south of Seoul proper. Dave and I lived in an apartment we dubbed "the hovel." We survived on jokes, CDs, crackers and peanut butter, and no small amount of beer. Teaching proved to be fairly straightforward and I got on well with my coworkers, Canadians and Koreans. The students were generally a pleasure, too.

After two or three months of getting my bearings and wondering just where in the heck I was, I unknowingly entered the first stage of culture shock: the Honeymoon Phase. Suddenly, it all seemed so appealing; the tremendous size and pace of Seoul, the rugged mountains looming everywhere, the "work hard, play hard" mentality of the people, the spicy and incredibly tasty food, and the million and a half Korean *won* that ended up in my bank account every month. In the span of just a few weeks, I had gone from being a pitiable student to being a millwonaire, a thought that thrilled me to no end. My student loans started to disappear before my very eyes and the remainder I wisely invested in books, compact discs, and nights on the town. After a couple more months, I began studying *Hangugeo*, or Korean, and would make a pretty serious go of it as long as I was there.

Korea is extraordinary in its degree of Korean-ness. When I was there, a ban was in place on anything Japanese and the sighting of an American car merited a comment. Shops and department stores were everywhere, thoroughly modern, and spotless, and yet finding anything in them that was made abroad was virtually impossible. I was stunned to learn that items like cheese and wine were considered exotic to the point where they could only be procured in one or two specialty shops in downtown Seoul, or else on the black market. Like most foreigners, I frequented the black market, although I have to say that I never grew totally accustomed to whispering, "Pssst! Got any mustard," while nervously glancing around for the cheddar police. This, I thought, was hardly befitting of a huge international city. Seoul proper has more than 10 million residents and Greater Seoul a hefty 23 million, making it the second most populous metropolitan area in the world. Only Tokyo ranks higher. But although Seoul is big, it is anything but international. Like the rest of the country, it is 100% pure Korean, or at least it was in 1996. Protectionism was the unofficial state religion. The reason why I only occasionally saw a foreign car was that driving one was considered to be the ultimate mark of a traitor.

Not long before I arrived in Korea, an American chocolate company had tried to break into the Korean market. Government regulations stipulated that their product had to be tested for quality assurance, a process which took a little over a year. In the end, the authorities deemed the candy coated chocolates to be harmful, claiming that they "hurt Korean people's stomachs." In the end, it was ruled that they couldn't be sold. A few months later, a local version of the candy hit the shelves; it was nearly identical in taste, packaging, and name. There are quite a few similar cases. Guinness beer was once banned because it wasn't carbonated enough (hence failing a freshness test), never mind that stout beer generally has a low level of carbonation. My favorite such anecdote has to do with the Philip's Softone light bulb. The coated bulb, in a Korean television report, was judged to be too dim and therefore unsuitable for the Korean consumer.

Before I left for Seoul, my mother's hairdresser and her husband had tried to get me to sign up with Amway in the hopes that I would spend my lunch hours knocking on strangers' doors and pedaling tile cleaner. I tried my utmost to avoid them, but they ended up cornering me anyway. By way of a sales pitch, the husband smiled a lot, kept repeating the phrase, "Troy, this is a *tremendous* opportunity," and showed me a dozen or so photos of the founding members' mansions.

It's a good thing he wasn't very convincing, because Amway had only recently come under serious attack from the *chaebol*, or Korean conglomerates, for having the nerve to sell a superior product on the free market, never mind that they had been given the green light to do so in 1991. A collection of rival companies got together and began a smear campaign citing that Amway's products were a major source of water pollution. A government agency then formed an anti-Amway committee, and any newspapers found defending the US based business were threatened and accused of taking bribes. The company president, an American, was even jailed for nine days with his hands bound while his local counterparts were roughed up by the police. Parenthetically, you'll be happy to know that any water pollution issues had been taken care of by the time I arrived there. I know this because of a full page government ad I read in the newspaper one day saying, "Seoul Water — Safe Enough to Drink for the Rest of Your Life."

In a nutshell, I had gone from living in one of the most culturally diverse countries on the planet to one of the most homogeneous. Far from being some wayward tribe of Chinese, the Koreans are actually ethnically and linguistically distinct from anyone else, a fact that they haven't quite gotten over yet. Their geographically imposed isolation has resulted in the existence of a race, history, culture, language, and worldview that are unique, dissimilar even to any of their Asian neighbors. A major upshot of this is a degree of national pride that, for a foreigner living there, is just a wee bit difficult to overlook.

"Korea is number one!" taxi drivers and people on the street would habitually inform me. "Korea has 5000 years of history." "Korea has four seasons." I didn't know how to break it to them that even Canada has four seasons, so I would always just smile and nod. Men would routinely convey that Korea had a gender imbalance. "In Korea, we have a man/woman problem," they would impart solemnly: "51.5 percent of Koreans are men but only 48.5 percent are women." "And the remainder?" I always inquired. The obligatory dramatic pause was accompanied by a standard follow up. "So...many Korean men cannot find a wife." This was always followed by another pause and then usually questions regarding whether I had a girlfriend or if I found Korean women attractive. Korea's gender imbalance is a phenomenon which is very real; it is the result of selective abortion.

A far more pressing "man/woman problem" as far as I could see had to do with domestic abuse. Several times during the night Dave and I were woken to the sound of a woman screaming, apparently being beaten by her husband. One of our coworkers said he had confronted a man in his building about beating his wife, and one of our Korean colleagues casually informed us that it was perfectly legal in Korea to slap one's spouse around. On the subway one day, I saw a man punch his girlfriend in the face and sat there quite astonished to note that no one did the slightest thing about it. On the contrary, most of the passengers quickly resumed what they had been doing all along, which was, by and large, staring at me.

This was another factor that I hadn't bargained for in a city as large as Seoul. People would gawk at, mock, and taunt Westerners as a matter of course. The Korean word for foreigner is *waegug saram* and it was something I heard daily. Other phrases which I heard far too often for my liking included, "Hello American!", "American, go home!" and "Puck you!" There is no "f" sound in Korean, so it is usually rendered as "p" or "b."

Korean people are wonderful once you get to know them. They will invite you into their home, lavish you with food and drink, fire up the karaoke unit, and do everything they possibly can to make you feel welcome. When it comes time to go, they will call and probably even insist on paying for a cab. They will press some kind of parting gift into your hand and then they will ring you up in an hour to make sure you made it home OK. But it's the 47.5 million Koreans that you don't know that you have to worry about.

You're not Korean, and that's something that they never stop reminding you of. The level of xenophobia became impossible to ignore and proved to be the determining factor in causing me to go from the "Everything is OK" stage of culture shock to the "Everything is Awful" one, and this distressed me enormously as it is supposed to occur the other way around.

Simply put, the Koreans despise everyone, and this has to do with the fact that throughout their history they've been kicked around like the proverbial football by their much larger and much more powerful neighbors, chief among them being Russia, China, Japan, and the United States. They may have 5000 years of history, but they've spent the vast majority of that time being poor, powerless, and subjugated, having been invaded a whopping 800 times. This has resulted in something called *han*, a critical component of the national psyche, which can only be approximately defined as "wrath due to a sense of helplessness" or perhaps "a sublimation of unavenged injustice." It is something which Koreans consider to be beyond the capability of foreigners to fathom. Korea analyst and author Michael Breen has noted that "(t)here is an unusual emphasis on (*han*) in the popular culture."

The predictable outcome of all this pent up angst and resentment is that outsiders are routinely accorded suspicion and treated with disdain. It must be said, though, that the Koreans are fundamentally fair in their discrimination, and by that I mean that they detest everyone more or less equally. Everyone, that is, except for the Japanese, for whom they harbor a special degree of loathing. This, of course, has to do with Korea's annexation and brutal subjugation by Imperial Japan during the first half of the twentieth century. And this usually constituted Point 5 of the "Things to Say when You Encounter a *Waegug Saram*" speech. "Korean people don't like the Japanese. They did terrible things to our country."

As a way of dealing with this I used to imagine myself being back in Canada and telling Korean tourists how Canada was number one, how we had a 130-year history, and that we despised the Germans and Italians because of a war that ended more than half a century ago. As a wrap up, I envisioned saying something like, "Now, you have a nice day and remember to stay away from the womenfolk. Oh, and don't forget what I told ya about the four seasons."

Of further significance is that Korea is unquestionably the single most Confucian country on the planet, no minor accomplishment when you consider that virtually every East Asian country maintains a rigid adherence to his thoughts. Born in China in 552 BC, Confucius grew up during a time of total and utter turmoil owing to a series of regional wars. He was a product of his environment and times, and his big idea was that life could improve by leaps and bounds if people would only educate themselves and be civil to each other. In order to achieve this, the sage opined, society needed to be built around strict hierarchies that yielded complete obedience. A student should obey his teacher, a wife should obey her husband, and a subject should obey his ruler. And this is what you have in Korea today: an austere, top down, patriarchal society. This is not a place where you question the teacher or disagree with your boss.

That Korea is more Confucian than the land of Confucius itself has to do with the fact that once Korean people seize upon an idea, they cannot help but carry it through to its logical (or illogical) extreme. Early one Sunday morning, I was woken up by the sound of marching and chanting. I was always being woken up by something and I would usually go to the window to see just what it was. On this day, it was an entire street of people sporting headbands and matching sashes. They were yelling through megaphones and marching in perfect unison. They were Christians, although, to be certain, not your "weekend bake sale" variety. Incidentally, 26% of all (South) Koreans consider themselves to be Christians. The view from my window at night featured dozens of red, lit up crosses, each denoting a place of worship. However, it wasn't just Christians who dressed and behaved like this. Striking workers, protesting students, sports fans, political supporters, and just about anyone else who wanted to be heard would inevitably form a group, pass around the slogan adorned bandanas, switch on the megaphones, and then do their best impression of an oversized aerobics class. Sometimes it seemed Korea wasn't so much a nation of individuals as it was a giant collective of placard wielding sub-collectives.

Sadly, the only real traveling I did in Korea was to the Demilitarized Zone, or DMZ, the buffer area along the 38th parallel that divides the two Koreas. I did this early one Saturday morning with a Canadian couple from work. There are several tours you can take to the DMZ, but we chose the US military one. It was brief but excellent, and the two guides who gave it (both officers) were informative and entertaining. Only an hour north of Seoul, we reached the truce village of Panmunjom, where we could actually cross into the North, albeit within the confines of a negotiation hall. We also saw a village on the northern side, dubbed Propaganda Village by the Americans. "Now, that there might look like a real fine place to live," drawled one of our guides. "But if you *were* to live there, you'd feel mighty lonely because the whole place is totally empty. At 8:00 at night, they throw a switch and all the lights come on. At 8:00 in the morning, they shut 'em all off." The village also boasts having the world's largest flagpole, standing at an impressive 160 meters. The flag attached to it weighs approximately 270 kilograms and must be lowered the instant it starts to rain lest it rip under its own weight. The construction of the pole was a countermeasure to the erection of the South's pole, which, incidentally, is 100 meters in height.

The DMZ had a kind of otherworldly feel about it. The trees on the northern side were wired up with speakers that were squawking propaganda, while both sides had erected Hollywood type signs on the surrounding green slopes. "That one on their side says, 'Our President is Better than Your President,' while this one here behind us says, 'Everybody in the South Owns a Hyundai Car,'" our guide informed us. I had read that in the past, the South had been fond of blaring Michael Jackson's *Thriller* at the soldiers stationed to the north. Miraculously, this didn't lead to a spike in defections.

When my contract ended, I decided I'd give Korea another shot. Despite the annoyances, I was enjoying myself immensely. Living in a foreign culture (especially one as foreign as in Korea) and learning a new language can be enormously stimulating and during the course of the first twelve months I could hardly recall a time when I had felt bored. I got a new job at another children's school and arranged one for my friend Geoff, who flew over from Canada and moved in with Dave and me. In our free time, Dave and I had various part time jobs and private lessons, and our stacks of CDs and empty beer bottles were piling up accordingly. For a while, I worked for Samsung, where I taught a group of engineers, and later I got a job at the Seoul government teaching ministry officials. This was a welcome change from teaching kids and it offered a fair bit of insight into just what was going on in the country. During my very first class, for example, I learned that there was zero homosexuality in Korea and that foreigners were solely responsible for the spread of AIDS.

The first weekend after Geoff arrived, he and I headed to a nearby district to hit some of the neon bedecked bars. At the first place we went to, I ran into Mr. Kim, a friend of Dave's who operated a huge English school for children named the Massachusetts Institute of Technology. We chatted for a while as Geoff, who was already a bit tipsy, made his way to the otherwise empty dance floor. "MIT-Mr. Kim," (not to be confused with "Gorgeous-Wife-Mr. Kim," or "Knows-No-Human-Language-Mr. Kim"; two of the dozen or so other Mr. Kims that Dave and I knew) wanted to know if I would be interested in teaching a few Saturday classes at his venerable learning academy. I told him my schedule was full, but I would ask around. Just then, I noticed that Geoff was holding a chair above his head and engaging himself in hopping about like a bunny atop the tiny (and still empty) dance floor. Mr. Kim and I sat there staring at him for a few moments before he leaned over and said, "What about him? Does he need any classes?"

Geoff was in a bad way. Latching onto his arm, I suggested we leave, and after grunting his ascent we made our way outside and through scores of people calling out a mocking "Hello" and "How do you do?" While at a taxi stand, three women walked by and Geoff gave one of them a brief yet affectionate rub on the arm. I found this amusing, not to mention completely harmless, but unfortunately my sentiments weren't shared by the fellow they were walking with. Throwing his head back and clenching his fists, he emitted an incredible scream. It was a long, eardrum rattling, primeval battle cry, and it had the instantaneous effect of causing a large crowd to stop and form a circle around us. It was *han* and I was deeply worried. Finished yelling, the man then took off his backpack and pitched it at me. Somehow, I managed to catch it. "Is this a gift?" I joked in Korean, but no one laughed. I handed it back to him and pleaded for calm. "I'm very sorry," I said in Korean. "My friend here is very drunk. I just want to get him home." But the ring of people refused to budge. Noting that a taxi had pulled up to the curb, I grabbed Geoff and made a break for it. We only narrowly escaped and I gave the address to the driver before turning around to see that several people were actually chasing after us. Geoff fell fast asleep, nose pressed against my shoulder.

Instead of turning left at the lights, the driver turned right. Then he pulled the car over and demanded nearly ten times the usual fare. There was no bargaining with him. We exchanged words, but that was all. If he had been prepared for anything more than that or anybody from the crowd had come around the corner, it would have been "game over" because by now, Geoff had metamorphosed into a slobbering sack of potatoes. I hauled him out of the cab and thankfully, after carrying him down a flight of steps, through an underpass, and up a flight of steps, we found a taxi and made it home in one piece.

I would like to say that this was an isolated incident, but it wasn't. Korea is a rough place and has the potential for becoming very dangerous very fast, and of course, most of the conflicts are fueled by alcohol. That night out with Geoff was one of my last. There had been too many close calls and bizarre incidents in the past year and going out and drinking was becoming unsafe, not mention repetitive and bad for my health. This lifestyle change wasn't an easy thing to undertake in a culture that viewed drinking as a kind of social obligation. The Koreans are often dubbed the Irish of the East and I think that is a fitting description. I read a statistic once claiming that 80% of all Korean military accidents were alcohol related.

One of my students at the Seoul government was named Mr. Kim. Of course. Mr. Kim worked for the Ministry of Finance and lived nearby my apartment. After class, we would always take the subway home together and chat. He was a kindly man, but he had a lot of grievances and made a habit of petitioning me with them. He believed, for example, that the United States had attacked North Korea, hence sparking the Korean War, a sentiment that would surely surprise most Americans. Actually, a lot of people I met — even well educated ones — believed this to be so, and would communicate this to me on a remarkably regular basis. Usually, this was accompanied by a statement to the effect that although they didn't like the North, they still respected them and their ideology of *juche*, or self-reliance. Mr. Kim would also complain about the American military presence and what he perceived as an overabundance of American companies operating in his homeland.

Although I didn't share his views, I considered him a friend and enjoyed talking to him both in and out of class. One night, he was telling me about how much his son loved comic books when our train came and the doors opened. After getting on, a grey-haired man noticed me and bellowed out in English, "Welcome to Korea!" "*Kamsahamnida*," I replied. "Thank you," and then I bowed slightly, as you do. In the next instant, I felt a stinging hot pain spreading out across my face. The man had belted me with an open palm. Mr. Kim ushered me off to the next car and apologized for the man's behavior. As mentioned, I met a lot of very nice people in Korea and still have quite a few fond memories of my time there, but, for whatever reason, this is the one that most readily springs to mind. "Welcome to Korea," followed by a slap in the face.

During my first year, the Korean economy was, by all accounts, booming. I had never seen so much evidence of prosperity. Everybody was well dressed, owned a brand new car, lived in a tasteful apartment, and threw cash around like it was going out of style. It seemed that whenever anyone's hand emerged from their pocket, it was clutching a thick roll of crisp bills. Everybody went out big on the weekend, and this usually meant dinner, followed by karaoke, and then onto a disco or pub. On Sunday, everyone went shopping or to a movie and then out to dinner again. When people wanted a new TV, they simply heaved the old one in the garbage even if it was purchased three years ago and still in fine working order. If their new one broke, they hurled it in the garbage too. None of it seemed quite real, and that, you see, is because none of it was.

In the latter half of 1997, rumors began of financial troubles followed by the *won*'s embarkation on a slow but steady downward trajectory. For me, an alarm went off when banks stopped selling the dollar, meaning that it was only available on the black market. What was going on? I had no idea. I had read in the newspaper about the *chaebol* being overextended and that banks were struggling with bad loans, but that didn't tell me much. At the time, I didn't have access to the Internet and didn't understand Korean very well; I was living in something of an information vacuum. Also, when it came to serious subjects, Koreans would often tell you what they thought you wanted to hear, as opposed to what the truth was. Dave, Geoff, and I began exchanging our money at a place disguised as a lingerie shop and debating how low the *won* would have to go before working there became unfeasible.

The Koreans' sense of civic mindedness had never been high, but things went right out the window when the economy started to wane. And right on cue, it felt as if the level of anti-foreigner sentiment was turned up a notch. A group of my American friends was attacked at a pub one night as they sat talking about football and drinking their beer. It turned into an enormous brawl and a couple of them were badly marked up. Then, there was the matter of the telephone booth. At our new apartment we didn't have a telephone, for the simple reason that installing one required a king's ransom. As an alternative, we used pagers and the telephone booth in front of our house. Things reached the stage where we considered ourselves lucky if we made it out and back again without incident. One drunken businessman actually tried to physically remove me from the booth, all the while saying, "Come on! Be a good American!" One night when Dave was using it, someone threw a rock through the window.

Even using public transportation was becoming a hassle. On top of the taunts and gawks, it was as though suddenly everyone wanted to talk to me. To deal with this, I bought a Walkman and wore it whenever I went outside, even though I didn't always turn it on. When people spoke to me, I just pretended I couldn't hear them. It didn't always work, though, and often I would exit the train, walk a few cars down, and then get on it again. It was driving me nutty. One day, I somehow managed to misplace my subway ticket and thus couldn't exit through the turnstile. Taking out the cash equivalent of the fare, I proceeded to the ticket booth only for the man on duty to give me a stern dressing down. Not only did he upbraid me (and did he ever), but he got out of the booth so that he could berate me some more without the inconvenience of the glass divide. He hissed, he sputtered, and then he pointed an accusing finger at my face. Other commuters cast me dirty looks. The fare I owed came to a dollar.

Oh, the memories.

One of my favorite such memories has to do with an episode that occurred only a few days later when a man who was liquored to the gills accused me of stealing a compatriot's bag. Again, on the subway, a man next to me had fallen asleep and had wound up using my bag as a footstool. When I got off, I removed it gently so as not to wake him. Then, Seoul's answer to Sherlock Holmes followed me out of the station and into a CD shop where he alerted a group of shoppers about my crime. The man was a slurring, reeking wreck, yet the crowd emitted a collective, "Oh?" before cornering me to have a look. Luckily, my name and personal information were on the bag. When it became clear that it was mine, there was a sort of disappointed group sniffle followed by a dejected shuffling off.

Another phenomenon that the economic situation seemed to give rise to was a crackdown on English teachers. Although it was technically illegal to moonlight or even teach someone in the privacy of their own home, everybody did it. Strictly speaking, my job with the Seoul government was illegal. But now, apartment building security guards were informing police about any illicit tutorials being given on the premises and officers were being dispatched to subway stations in order to inspect foreigners' bags for copies of *My Happy English Reader*.

An agency I had gotten classes with in the past called me one day to ask if I'd be interested in giving a weekly course. I wavered for a while before giving them a tentative "yes." However, after perusing the dry-as-dust textbook and discovering that the students were "basic level," I changed my mind and suggested that they find someone else. "But you *promised* to teach this class," the female manager said irritably. "I never promised anything," I replied. "I said, 'Probably yes,' but this textbook is terrible and we haven't signed the contract yet." "Oh, you foreigners and your contracts!" she retorted hotly. "You're all the same! You're all so proud! I'm going to call the police!" "Go ahead," I replied, and left. That night, I caught a cold and didn't go to work the next morning. I showed up at lunch, though, only for the staff to inform me nervously that the police had been there looking for me. I had heard stories about teachers being roughed up and even tortured by the police in Korea before being deported, and this, as you might imagine, didn't appeal to me in the least. That night, I called all my Korean friends and students and told them that, unfortunately, I was leaving. The next day, I was on a plane back to Canada.

The day after I arrived home, I went downtown (or uptown, as we call it), bought a newspaper, ordered a coffee, took a nice, long, refreshing sip, and then nearly sprayed it all over the man sitting next to me when I spotted the big, black lettered headline at the top of the page: *Korean Economy Implodes*. The *chaebol*, as it turned out, had become colossal, tottering towers of inefficiency and gross fiscal mismanagement that had been running on the fumes of massive corporate loans that they could never ever repay. Eight of them collapsed, the largest having incurred a debt of more than $5 billion. Indeed, it was estimated that the amount of money owed by Korean corporations to Korean banks was a mind boggling $350 billion. Moreover, the stock market had plummeted to a ten-year low while the currency halved its value in less than a week. Add to this the fact that the nation had accumulated a $150 billion foreign currency debt, and I was relieved indeed not to be riding on the Seoul subway system at that particular moment. It was frigid outside that day in my hometown and beginning to snow. I finished my steaming coffee and stepped out the door. People driving by must have thought it odd to see a man with a newspaper in his hand on top of a snow bank doing a little jig.

Rather than take a good long look at themselves in the mirror, the Koreans blamed the entire catastrophe on a foreign plot. It was, according to the president of one of the big belly-up businesses, nothing short of an international *waegug saram* conspiracy devised and delivered with the express intent of sending the nation back to the days of rice paddies and mud huts. The International Monetary Fund, or IMF, came to the country's rescue with a $58 billion bailout package, and within no time the Koreans were referring to their situation as "having to overcome the IMF." The phrase "Asian Economic Crisis" never entered the Korean lexicon.

Headbands everywhere were promptly tightened, fresh (and locally manufactured) batteries were popped into megaphones, and the nation embarked on a massive gold drive. Couples just back from their honeymoons handed in their wedding bands while retirees pulled out their gold teeth. If everyone gave one piece of gold, the public was told, the country's burden could be reduced by billions. As a direct outcome, the price of gold tumbled to an 18-year low.

"Why are you lined up here today?" asked one reporter to a woman queued up with a golden pendant.

"Because of the IMF," she replied.

In the next few weeks, whenever I ran into someone I knew (an event that occurs once every 53.1 seconds in Saint John, New Brunswick, Canada), they would invariably inquire after my experience abroad. "How was Hong Kong?" "Hey! I heard you were in the Middle East." "So, can you speak any Asian now?" Only one of my friends asked me with any degree of earnestness what Korea had been like. "Muddy," I told him. Actually, I had no idea where to begin.

CHAPTER 2. No Yen for Japan

Seoul's new motto was "Your Seoul, Our Seoul," and although I had been living there for 18 months, it didn't feel like my Seoul at all. The second part of the slogan (said quickly) was more fitting, I thought, and it was in this in frame of mind, tired of all the antagonism and narrow mindedness, that I listened to a colleague of mine who had just returned from a trip to Fukuoka, Japan. He had only glowing reviews of life in the Land of the Rising Sun, so I made up my mind to go there for a couple of days and have a look. It had to be more promising than life in the Hermit Kingdom, the name accorded to Korea by Western explorers in the late nineteenth century due to the perceived inward-looking nature of the country's inhabitants.

My flight to Japan was delayed by a full two hours, and so, being young and foolish, I had a couple of beers in the airport lounge. I had a couple more on the plane, and by the time the red lights of the runway came into view, I was somewhat red and lit up myself. Having been seated at the rear of the aircraft, I was the very last passenger to disembark and was also last in line through customs. Here, I was treated to a lengthy wait followed by an interrogation conducted by two humorless officials in spectacularly garbled English. They asked me to sit down and take off my shoes. After having a pretty thorough look inside them, one held up the left shoe and appraised me disapprovingly. "Zay aw Nikes," he announced loudly, his voice reverberating around the otherwise empty hall. "Yes, they are," I confirmed politely, and he grunted and waved for me to go.

This, I thought, was just a trifle disconcerting. I had read that Japan's law enforcement officials take their job very seriously, having, for example, a 90%

arrest rate for violent crime. More pointedly, although foreigners accounted for only 1% of the population, they made up for 5% of all arrestees. I wondered if these and similar statistics weren't artificially inflated through the jailing of passengers unfortunate enough to be last off their plane.

Outside, I caught a cab downtown and managed to find a very nice (and very expensive) hotel, after which I got freshened up and ventured out to have a look around.

Located on the southwestern island of Kyushu, considered to be the birthplace of Japanese civilization, the city of Fukuoka is little more than a small town by Japanese standards and very much off the beaten track. Indeed, it is twice as far from Tokyo as it is from Seoul, and apart from having produced several of the country's top singers, it isn't really known for very much of anything, apart perhaps from its relative obscurity. But it was nice. In fact, it was very nice. Hemmed in by mountains and hugging the sea, it was impeccably clean and aesthetically pleasing. Before I moved to Korea, I had been fully aware that it wouldn't stand comparison with Japan, but to actually *see* the difference only confirmed what I had been thinking during the past couple of months; namely, that I gone to the wrong country.

I took a pleasant stroll downtown and was delighted to note that nobody stared, nobody cat called, cars stopped at red lights and did not drive on the immaculate sidewalks. Crosswalks were well marked, obviously having been designed with people in mind. In Korea, I had begun to think that they existed for the express purpose of making it easier to run people over. Here, the people seemed friendly and very polite, but I was somewhat surprised to see how conservative — nay, uptight — many of them appeared. If it can be said that the Koreans are the Irish of the East, then perhaps the Japanese are the answer to the Germans. And by that, of course, I mean that they both have an immoderate reverence for order and taking things seriously. Both cultures possess an extraordinary work ethic; between them they produce the world's best cars, they are obsessed with organization and efficiency, and they are world renowned for their advancements in science, technology, and medicine. In Asia, Japan is far and away the big man on campus and this has a lot to do with a massive head start it got when the country opened up and moved toward industrialization in the latter part of the nineteenth century. Realizing that good ideas know no national boundaries, the Japanese borrowed heavily from the West, viewing this as a means of bettering themselves without compromising their cultural integrity. The upshot is that while much of Asia plays catch up, Japan is rich and well in the lead. In Japan, the trains have been running on time for years.

Walking around, one is impressed by the high degree of order and apparent asceticism, then, with a certain sense of dissonance, by the weighty amount of pornography and prostitution on offer everywhere. And I do mean everywhere, despite the young children walking by. Surveying one of the main streets, I counted to myself, "flower shop, brothel, fast food joint, brothel, post office, brothel, sushi bar, brothel, electronics shop..." In front of the shops, right next to the sidewalk, there were signs like those at a drive-through indicating which of the staff was on duty (with a lit up picture and personal stats) along with a list of prices. The sheer number of these places was less shocking than how open it all seemed.

I was shocked again later, on the subway, when I saw a businessman examining an adult magazine as if it were the *Asian Wall Street Journal*, and in a convenience store where I watched a throng of uniformed high school boys drool over magazines of partially-uniformed high school girls. But perhaps this was not so much shocking as I was shockable. It's no wonder I would find all of this difficult to process: on a trip to the province of Prince Edward Island one summer, I couldn't quite get over the fact that people there were only required to affix one license plate to their vehicle as opposed to two. It's a good thing I didn't stumble upon a pornography vending machine on my trip (yes, they really exist; but not in eastern Canada) or it may have overloaded the circuitry entirely.

Pornography is big business in Japan and is believed to have a net worth of nearly $1 billion. But unlike in the US, the industry isn't relegated to the underground. Several porn stars have actually gone mainstream, most notably Iijima Ai, a woman who became the biggest name in the business after making more than a hundred movies by the time she was 20. Miss Ai subsequently made the crossover to television, where she appeared regularly on several variety shows in addition to being featured on an educational program that was aired on NHK. From there, she wrote a rather sordid semi-autobiographical account of her life entitled *Platonic Sex*, and this sold over a million copies before being turned into a TV mini-series and then a full length movie.

That night, I thought I should do something cultural, such as taking in a bit of Kabuki theater or checking out an exhibit of woodblock prints, but in the end I opted for a bar in the entertainment district where I put away several frothy beers and smiled at people I didn't know. Returning to my hotel just after midnight, I dumped a mountain of change on the nightstand and promptly fell asleep. I dreamed that I was a samurai being entertained by a geisha in a traditional style house in the countryside. The wooden abode was surrounded by green ponds filled with idle coi fish and dozens of beautiful *sakura*, or cherry trees. Under a pale sliver of moon climbing through a powder blue sky, the pinkish-white blossoms quivered and fell, littering the manicured lawns like confetti as the geisha read me poetry and filled my cup with sake. Oh, who am I kidding? I dreamed of Iijima Ai.

The next morning, I woke up, groggily recalled where I was, and then remembered that I had to check out by 11:00 as the hotel was booked solid. What I assumed would be a relatively easy matter nearly turned into an all afternoon affair consisting of me walking up and down two sides of a river that were chock-full of hotels. Well, at least I thought they were hotels. That's what they looked like and that's what many of them had written on them in English. However, most of them turned out to be what are known in Asia as "love hotels," and apparently, in Japan, they could only be rented by the hour.

Going into one of these places was always the same. The lobbies were sparsely decorated and dimly lit, and I would approach the counter only to find a black window with a slot at the bottom for passing money and keys, along with a narrower slit in the middle from which a pair of brown eyes would be peering out at me. It was unsettling, and it wasn't exclusive to love hotels. Most of the regular hotels featured this bizarre and wholly impersonal arrangement as well. After three torturous hours, I finally managed to find a hotel where sleeping wasn't just a euphemism, and after paying a staggering amount of *yen* to a pair of almond colored eyes, I deposited my things and then went shopping.

I'm not a big shopper, but after a year and a half of residing in a country that only seemed to sell alcohol, dried squid, and kimchi (pickled cabbage), it was nice to be in Japan. It was October and I found a sharp looking winter jacket that I instantly became taken with and paid the small ransom they were asking to own. I had never seen a jacket quite like it, and was immensely proud of myself for purchasing it. Incidentally, in Japan, you sometimes wonder if they've inadvertently added another digit onto the price, but this is just wishful thinking.

I wanted to drop the jacket off, so I walked back to the hotel. As I was wondering how I should spend my last night there, my keys fell out of the leg of my jeans and jangled onto the ground. Reaching into my pocket, I discovered a sizeable hole so I shifted contents to the other pocket and carried on. When I reached my room, I couldn't find my money. After searching for an hour I had only found a large collection of lint. I had had the equivalent of about $100 in *yen*, but the bills were gone. My credit card was past its limit and the only other money I had was $30 worth of Korean *won*, but it was Saturday and banks were closed. Counting the pile of change I'd collected at the pub the night before, I discovered I had about 10 bucks. A cab to the subway would cost $7 and the subway to the airport would be another $2.50. That would leave me with just 50 cents to give to a begging Buddhist monk along the way. At the airport, I could exchange the Korean *won* and thereby cover the airport tax.

I watched TV until about 10:00, and by then I was starving. Cracking open the honor bar, I had a bottle of water. Then I had a Coke. Then I had another Coke. Then I had a stomachache. Finally, I could take no more and I tore into the bag of mixed nuts. Twelve seconds later, I was licking the salt off my fingers and searching the aluminum crevices for crumbs. After this, I watched a movie and fell asleep, stomach rumbling and in a cheerless condition.

I woke at five a.m. The plan was to set the keys on the counter and briskly head for the exit before anyone realized I hadn't exactly been on my honor, so to speak. Gently pulling the door shut behind me, I crept down the stairs and entered the dark and vacant lobby. To my horror, the eyes were watching me and a bill for $10 had been slipped through the bottom slot. I thought this was amazing, and dimly wondered if they had a camera in the room or some device on the refrigerator. I looked over the bill for a second before mumbling, "Umm, no."

"Palisu payu," said the eyes.

"No money," I clarified, and the eyes got very wide.

"Oh?" they exclaimed. "Uh... justu momentu," and then they disappeared. After about two seconds, I followed suit. After all, it was only a couple of Cokes and I thought that, in this case, the $150 I had paid for the room ought to cover it.

At the Fukuoka Airport, I gave my 50 cents to the monk, prayed that Buddha wouldn't turn me into a gnat in my next life, and then stood in line at the airport bank only to find a dark glass window with a slit in the middle and another set of gazing eyes. "Look, I'm not here for anything illicit," I wanted to say. "I just want to exchange some currency," but instead I just passed the owner of the eyes my Korean *won* and asked for Japanese *yen*. A male voice uttered something in Japanese and passed the money back. I asked him to kindly speak English, but he wouldn't or couldn't, and just kept prattling on. This was absurd. Here I was in an international airport, and not only could I not understand what the bank teller was telling me, but I couldn't *see* him. Fearing that the police would soon be doing a dragnet of the facilities, I ran out of patience and started banging on the adjacent door, demanding to see just who it was who wouldn't change my money. The startled employee appeared, and pointed to a large green sign centered on an otherwise empty white wall. It read, "ABSOLUTELY NO EXCHANGE ON KOREAN WON." Breaking into a cold sweat, I looked back over both shoulders before asking him, "How much is the airport tax?" "Whatu?" he replied. Slowly and deliberately, I said, "This airport — tax — how much money?" He looked at me curiously and then responded, "Zisu airporta hasa no taxu." Well, I could have hugged him, and probably would have had I not spotted another large green

sign on the opposite wall saying, "ABSOLUTELY NO HUGGING BANK TELL-
ERS." Unless that was part of my delirium — I was that relieved.

I got back to my apartment in Seoul at noon to find my roommates battling
it out at computer golf. "How was Japan?" Dave asked. "Nice," I said, "but have I
had one crazy morning." I changed into some fresh clothes and was about to join
them when I looked down to see the $100 in *yen* lying in the middle of my bed-
room floor. The bills must have slipped through the hole in my pocket and then
gotten stuck to the inside of my jeans.

As you know, two months later, I left Korea and returned to Canada. One
of the first things I did when I was there was to go see a hockey game with my
parents. It seemed like every fifth man in the building had on the exact same
jacket as me. At first, I was disappointed by this, but then I thought, "The more
the merrier." After all, if those statistics I read are anywhere near being accurate,
it'll be that much harder to track me down.

CHAPTER 3. DISCOVER THE PHILIPPINES

It's easy to overlook the Philippines when thinking of Asia, and yet, there it is. Catholic, English speaking, and a former colony of both Spain and the United States, the nation takes the form of an archipelago comprised of some 7000 islands, although 11 of these account for 94% of the total landmass. The Philippines is frequently bypassed by the Asia traveler despite a natural splendor that rivals any of its neighbors. This is partly because of its inaccessibility, somewhat owing to its occasional kidnappings and beheadings, and very much due to no one having deemed it necessary to create anything in the way of a tourist industry. Indeed, for many people the lack of sincerity in the welcome manifests itself immediately, at the airport.

I have been to the Philippines four times, and each time has been the same. Men accost you while you're waiting for your luggage or changing your money and pelt you with solicitations. Instead of "Do you need help with anything?" the standard opener is "First time to the Philippines?" I have learned that it's best to say "No," and even better to add an "I live here." Otherwise, you'll most likely be informed that it's a national holiday and that all public transportation has been suspended. A taxi can be arranged, however, even if your destination is a hundred kilometers away. Especially if your destination is a hundred kilometers away.

My first trip to the Philippines was also my first to a subtropical country, and I was pretty chuffed about it. Landing in Manila one sultry and airless evening, I caught a cab through streets lined with pawn shops, discos, and money exchanges and checked into an aging hotel that was popular with foreign tourists.

It offered bus service south to the town of Batangas, from where you could catch a ferry to Puerto Galera on the island of Mindoro. From there, you had several beach resort options.

After breakfast the next morning, I maneuvered my way through a crowd of people peddling bananas and sandals and boarded the bus. Soon, we were underway and slowly winding through the streets of Manila toward the highway running south. I promptly fell asleep and by the time I woke up, we were surrounded by beautiful countryside. Two women were up and distributing drinks and sandwiches. Shortly thereafter, they were up again with notepads and pencils and asking people to pay for their "orders." Everyone had assumed the snacks were complimentary and no one was too pleased about the petty deception. But that was small potatoes compared with what would happen next.

After another couple hours of driving, the bus stopped, without warning. We were apparently at our destination, although no one informed us of this. The driver and his sandwich girls alighted and hastily disappeared. The majority of the passengers (most of whom were Westerners) stood up and confusedly looked around. "Where's the water?" everyone seemed to be thinking. "And where's the ferry?" "And why the hell didn't I go to Thailand?" I looked around as well and noticed that a mob of locals was busying itself unloading the luggage from the storage compartment. A Filipino man already had my bag slung nonchalantly over his shoulder and was firing up a cigarette. We all scrambled off the bus and engaged in a game of "Give Me Back My Bag." No one would tell us where the ferry was. "You just missed the last one, sir," said the man with my bag. "But, no problem. My friend has a boat. Follow me." Judging from my map, the strait looked to be about 35 kilometers across. I wasn't about to try this in someone's canoe. Like train wrecks in India, sinking boats is a way of life in the Philippines, although, having said that, official ferries aren't that much safer. This is a nation with over 100 ferry accidents per year. I didn't know much about the country I was traveling in, but I knew that. A few years later, my roommate and his girlfriend would get conned into taking a "friend's boat" at this very spot and nearly paid their lives. A storm blew up out of nowhere, almost causing them to sink. They thought for certain they were goners, and when, after a couple of hours of bailing and praying, they'd miraculously made it to the other side, they were charged the equivalent of $150 for the near death experience as they'd failed to work out the conversion rate and, by that point, were understandably too distressed to give it much thought. A few expletives later and I was walking with my bag toward the security post of some private pier, followed by a small, badgering mob. However, the two shotgun-wielding guards I asked would not betray their countrymen and point me the way to the terminal. Finally I guessed (correctly) that it must be in the opposite direction everyone was telling me.

Once across the choppy strait, I took a Jeepney to the aptly named White Beach, a creamy stretch of sand dotted with unassuming hotels, tourist shops, restaurants, and dive shacks. The view of the water from the shore was striking and featured stunning sunsets every night. The view of the shore from the water was no less impressive and was dominated by a jutting mountain liberally adorned with craning palms. Its summit was in perpetual possession of a lazy swirl of wispy clouds that clung motionlessly, as if magnetized.

The strip of sand was also littered with beach bars. Rudimentary yet quaint, most of them looked as though they'd been built from a kit that included a set of Rastafarian flags and a copy of *Bob Marley — Legend*. Tranquil places, they offered absurdly cheap cocktails and ice cold San Miguel beers for a trifling 50 cents a bottle. In stark juxtaposition to the Bob Marley bars were the larger, more raucous German hangouts. These were largely patronized by aging, tank topped, beer swilling *Deutsche Touristen*, who, judging by their bronzed hues and distended bellies, long ago gave up on *der Vaterland* — or vice versa. Friendly enough after a few drinks, the Germans were a pretty cold lot during the day, and hellos were often met with icy stares. With Germans, it's all about respect. They don't have time for pleasantries as they believe them to be insincere.

The owner of the hotel where I was staying was also the proprietor of three additional hotels and appeared to be the local kingpin. He was a gargantuan man with all the charisma and personality of Jabba the Hutt, whom he uncannily resembled. To be certain, he was cantankerous, as I discovered firsthand after having lunch one day in the hotel restaurant. Claiming that he couldn't break a 1000-peso bill (about $23), he gave me a brief demonstration in local theater. "What? You think I'm rich?" he asked, opening a drawer that revealed oodles of 100-peso bills. Promptly slamming it shut, he proclaimed he had no choice but to write me an IOU. He then ripped a piece of cardboard off his cigarette package, jotted down "875 pesos," and handed it to me. It was one of those moments when I was simply too stunned to protest. So, I waited until he left and then asked one of the waitresses to kindly reimburse me with legal tender, which she apologetically did. It could have been worse, I suppose. He could have had me frozen for ransom like he did with Hans Solo. Later, I witnessed Jabba, who never shut up, lecturing a German fellow who lived next door with his Filipino wife and child.

"How long have you lived here now?" asked the Hutt.

"Four years," replied the severe-looking European.

"Yeah? And when are you going back to Deutschland?"

"Tomorrow morning," came the deadpan response, causing the waitresses and clientele to snigger.

"Good, I'll be glad to see you gone. Oh, and by the way, seeing as how you Germans are all so rich, why don't you buy your wife a washing machine? I see her everyday washing by hand. When are you gonna stop treating her like a slave?"

"Und why would I want to do zat?" the man shot back, taking a thoughtful drag off of his cigarette. "She is zer best damned washing machine I ever owned."

After nine blissful days of swimming, snorkeling, hiking, boating, reading, drinking, and napping, I traveled back across the strait to Batangas to catch a bus to Manila. Predictably, there was another mob waiting for us at the pier, but this time they were trying to sell fake Rolexes and unidentifiable foodstuffs. During the last week, I had gotten pretty good at shaking these guys. The beach had been crawling with them. One technique I found particularly effective was to try and sell *them* something. "Do *I* want to buy a watch?" I would say. "I was just about to ask if *you* wanted to buy a watch. Here. I'll give you this one (an $80 Swatch) for $800. Whaddaya say?" Surprisingly, they would often just silently appraise it, conclude my price was too high, and then saunter off in search of their next target. Another good one was to say, "Oh, the wife's got all the money. Why don't you go ask her?" and then point to some nearby tourist. They would be off like a shot, and so would I. However, my provincial trickery wouldn't have the same effect back in Manila.

During World War II, the city of Manila was reduced to a smoldering rubble heap as a result of fierce fighting between the Americans and Japanese. In fact, only Warsaw saw more war, as it were, and in addition to the soldiers more than 100,000 Filipinos lost their lives in the capital's bloody exchange. Not a whole lot has been done with the place since. On the way out of the city, I had mostly been asleep, but coming back in I was wide awake, mainly owing to the view from my window.

Running along the highway was a galvanized fence separating the road from a rail line. The fence doubled as a wall for miles and miles of rambling squatters' shacks. But this proved to be only one tentacle of squalor. Manila proper revealed itself to be a cosmic sprawl of eyeball-assaulting architecture, traffic jams, filthy street children, and homeless people. "How did I not see this a week ago?" I wondered. Adding to the incongruity was the predominantly English signage. The street scene looked like some murky and distorted reflection of life as I had known it in North America.

The principal means of public transportation in Manila is the Jeepney, which is a converted US Army jeep that more or less resembles a rectangular mirror ball on wheels. Benches are affixed to the back, a top is welded on, a base coat of silver paint is applied, and then they are, for lack of a better word, decorated. Like boats, they are usually named and the names are usually those of saints or other Catholic icons. This is fitting because even the most pious of atheists would be sure to invoke God's name at least once while gripping one of the handles that hang from the ceiling. Capricious turns, gut-wrenching lane changes, blasting horns, choking exhaust, and the blaring of Filipino pop music are all part and parcel of the Jeepney experience.

I still had half a day, and so after checking into a hotel, I went to check out a famous Spanish cathedral and the ruins of an old Spanish fort. I may as well have had a sign around my neck saying, "MUG ME." Nobody would leave me alone, and I got solicited for virtually everything imaginable, on top of a couple of goods and services I didn't even know existed. I consider myself to be fairly adept at reading maps, but after an hour under the scorching sun, I still hadn't figured out where the church was. No one else seemed to know either. But when you're living in an underpass or a cardboard box, as many people were, it is entirely forgivable not to know where the historical heart of your city lies. Darkness fell and walking became treacherous as some streets were completely unlit and the sidewalks featured some very big and very black holes. Ambling along, I started to get that feeling that sometimes comes to you when walking alone in the woods; the one that causes you to wonder if you aren't being watched. This present sensation differed slightly, however; in the woods, I never felt as though I was about to get rolled. I gave up playing tourist and retired meekly to my hotel.

The chief reason the Philippines is such a shambles and hasn't enjoyed the prosperity of many of its Asian neighbors has to do with the stifling — nay, paralyzing — misrule of just one family: the CIA-backed Marcos family. The reign of Ferdinand and Imelda Marcos set the Philippines back monetarily by decades. Easy to dismiss as just another Third World dictator, Ferdinand Marcos, minus the desire to acquire the bomb or invade his neighbors, was *the* quintessential Third World dictator, and doubtlessly served as a role model for aspiring dictators everywhere. Handsome and highly intelligent (he had a photographic memory), Marcos was the illegitimate son of an extremely wealthy and powerful Chinese businessman. As a young man studying law, Ferdinand was indicted for the murder of one of his adoptive father's political rivals but mysteriously beat the charges. In the Philippines, it is said to be convicted of a crime is to lack influence. Later, he ran for president, as a war hero, with the explicit approval of the United States government and the backing of the CIA who were looking to install someone who could deliver Philippine support for the war in Vietnam. Adorned with medals that he had made for himself, Marcos was in fact a Japanese collaborator as well as a war profiteer who came within a hair of being executed for treason. But, once again, his father intervened.

Having run for president on an anti-corruption campaign, Marcos won through vote buying and general tampering before setting out on his first and only order of business: making himself, his family, and his entourage of cronies and sycophants filthy, filthy rich. He had his hand in every pot, and if he didn't shake down an enterprise, then he simply took it over. After spending millions buying the next election, Marcos deemed the democratic process too costly and time consuming, so he faked a communist uprising, declared martial law, and embarked on a reign of terror and kleptocracy. As the economy ground to a halt and the people languished in poverty and even starvation, Marcos most certainly became the single richest man in Asia, salting away billions in foreign accounts. In addition to bilking local enterprises, he embezzled millions of dollars in aid from the World Bank and spent a considerable amount of time digging up Japanese war gold. It has been estimated that there were thousands of tons of the stuff. His wife's excesses are widely known. On one shopping trip with her daughter to New York in 1968, Imelda spent more than $3 million, and until she got her own private aircraft, she used to travel with an extra jumbo jet just for her luggage. Although best known for her collection of shoes, Mrs. Marcos was in fact a connoisseur of everything from real estate to art, and in the late 1970s she was considered to be the most influential purchaser of jewelry in the entire world.

After 20 years of robbing the nation blind, the Marcos clan was finally sent packing by the legendary movement of "people power," which was orchestrated from New York City through the intriguingly named cardinal of Manila, Cardinal Sin. As a weighty punishment for their misrule and economic plunder, the Marcoses were sheltered, by their US patrons, in Hawaii, where they continued to live a life of opulence and freedom. Those who stormed their former residence discovered 1,200 pairs of shoes and 500 bras, one of which was bullet proof.

In reference to their Spanish and American colonizers, Filipinos had always quipped, "Four centuries in a convent, fifty years in a brothel," but under the Marcos regime this ceased to be a joke. During their tenure, the Philippines were turned into a center for arms trafficking, drug running, gambling, money laundering, prostitution, and child prostitution. The effects of all this can still be seen today. Meanwhile, the Filipino people are unquestionably a friendly lot and the country is quite beautiful.

As I was reading Sterling Seagrave's *The Marcos Dynasty* one day in a Taipei park, two Filipino women (probably maids or factory workers) noticed the cover.

"You are reading about Marcos," one exclaimed.

"Yes, I am."

"Is it any good?" she asked.

"It's pretty interesting," I replied.

"I miss him," she said. "At least with Marcos, we had order. Now everything is chaos."

"Yes," her friend chimed in smilingly. "And he was *so* handsome."

Chapter 4. To the Other China

Just a few days after I returned to Canada, having broken the spell that had exiled me in the Hermit Kingdom, the entire eastern half of the country was hit by the worst winter storm in over a century. Within a week, I had gone from sipping a cappuccino in a Seoul coffee shop and thinking, "Hmm, the *won* lost more ground today," to smashing at ice a foot thick in my father's driveway, with a pick.

Everything was covered in ice. During the day the sky would emit a misty drizzle while at night it would freeze. Day in and day out, it went on like this with inexplicable consistency, the temperature oscillating between negative and positive one degree Centigrade. Before long, telephone poles and tall trees were snapping like twigs and there were power outages nearly everywhere. The result of this freakish weather was a sort of forced hibernation characterized by long spells of total boredom punctuated by protracted phases of utter tedium. I spent an immoderate amount of time just looking out the window and wondering why it was I lived here. When the worst of it was over, the temperature returned to normal, which is to say freezing. And for a change of pace, I would occasionally venture uptown to see how long I could stroll around before frostbite set in.

Canadians will watch a weather report from, say, Detroit, where it'll be minus 15 (or 5 degrees Fahrenheit), and they'll think, "That's pretty cold." However, if another news crew member has the audacity to say, "Don't forget to bundle up if you're headed outdoors today. It's *cold* out there," then the grumbling begins. "Minus 15? They think *that's* cold? Americans. Why don't they try minus 25 on for size? And while they're at it, why don't they learn the metric system?" Yes, in

Canada, arctic weather along with knowing how many decimeters make up a kilometer make for bragging rights. For the first time in my life, I started to see this as strange.

In fact, I started to see many things as strange, and it occurred to me slowly (as most things do) that I was experiencing a mild form of reverse culture shock. I especially had trouble relating to what people tended to talk about. Local politics, the pending mill layoffs, the shortening of moose season.... Since I had returned, I had been debating whether to stay or whether to try another Asian country, and one day I began to lean heavily toward the latter — after having the following conversation with a former schoolmate.

"So, how's things with you? Heard ya were over there in Mongolia or some darned place."

"Korea."

"Oh, Korea. North or South?"

"South."

"Uh-huh. Don't suppose they do much moose huntin' over there?"

"Not really, no."

"They have moose over there?"

"Not that I know of."

"Just sit around eatin' rice, I suppose."

"Pretty much."

"Well, you must be glad to be back."

"Oh, absolutely," I replied.

Why does everyone say that? It was so cold that my eyeballs hurt, there was absolutely nothing to do, the entire city looked like some sort of tree graveyard, the consumer tax was 18.7% (a number arrived at after the taxing of a tax), you had to fake a coronary in order to get noticed at store counters, and public transportation was all but non-existent.

I began looking for teaching jobs in Japan, Singapore, Hong Kong, and Taiwan. Schools in Japan wanted someone who was in Japan already, while ones in Hong Kong and Singapore required a teaching certificate that I didn't have then, although I have it now. A school in Taipei, Taiwan found my university degree and experience in Korea sufficient and informed me that I could begin training in three weeks. Also, they would pay for my flight. I went to a travel agency and bought a ticket.

The plan was to stay in Taiwan for a year. I have been here for nine. I found a good teaching job, made friends, got a girlfriend, learned some Chinese, and, in short, grew attached. Or perhaps I just grew accustomed to it. I'll be the first to admit that Taiwan was an odd choice, though, especially since up until the time I lived in Seoul, I had no idea where or what it was.

In university, I used to study a world map that was in the back of one of my textbooks as the professor lectured, but miraculously, I managed to miss it altogether. Then in 1996 Taiwan made the cover of *Newsweek*. The so-called renegade province, located 160 kilometers (100 miles) off the southeast coast of China, was holding its first presidential election since it split with that country 47 years earlier. China was attempting to influence the vote's outcome by lobbing missiles just off the island's coast. This caused undecided voters to defiantly throw their support behind the man China feared to be an independence advocate in addition to prompting President Clinton to show support by floating two aircraft carrier groups through the Taiwan Strait, thus underscoring the reality that small nations may be proxies in larger contests. The standoff between China and Taiwan, or the People's Republic of China and the Republic of China, has continued up until the present and there is no end in sight.

Taiwan, then, is the *other* China, or what you might call "China Lite." Ninety-eight percent of the population is ethnically Han Chinese, with roughly 70% hailing from the coastal province of Fujian, 10% to 15% being Hakka (a persecuted and wayfaring variety of Chinese often compared to the Jews) and the remainder comprise "mainlanders" (or their offspring) who fled to Taiwan with Chiang Kai-shek's Nationalists, or KMT. Being cut off from the mainland, Taiwan has developed its own unique character and brand of Chinese culture, and "Chinese culture" equates to a thousand and one good things and a thousand and one bad. Although often ignored by the world in general (when not being confused with Thailand), Taiwan is both weird and wonderful, but mostly it is weird. With 23 million people living on an island roughly the size of Tennessee or the Netherlands within a society that is modernizing like mad (it currently constitutes the world's 16th largest economy) and yet remains shackled to the past by the more traditional elements of its culture, this should come as no surprise.

In the following section of Taiwan-related stories, I attempt to paint a picture of what goes on here in this microcosm of East Asia and how things appear to an outsider. The picture is often far from flattering. Living in any foreign country can be extremely trying at times, and Taiwan is no exception. However, despite occasional difficulties and annoyances, Taiwan has kept my attention for nearly ten years and the people are extraordinarily kind. The people living in "the other China" may not be the best organized, most efficient, farsighted, dynamic, or objective people on the planet, but they are trying, and — and this is the key — they are *absurdly* friendly. To be certain, they are infinitely friendlier and more accommodating than their brethren on the mainland. They deserve some consideration when those in Beijing claim it as theirs.

As "the other China" is best known for its politics, I thought we might begin with a little of that.

CHAPTER 5. A RABBI, A GERMAN, AND AN ISRAELI WALK INTO A CHINESE
RESTAURANT

I used to live in a live in a little community in northern Taipei called Tianmu,
which is sort of like the Little America of Taiwan, home to a couple of foreign
schools, foreign shops and restaurants, and even more foreign people. Westerners seem to like the place because, among other things, they can pretty much get
by using only English. My former roommate and friend from Montreal, Tony, for
example, in his two years in Taiwan, made out just fine knowing only Ni hao, or
"hello," zai jian, or "goodbye," and Xitele, which means "Hitler." I taught him the
last one, thinking that he should skip "taxi Chinese" and "restaurant Chinese"
and move on to more pressing subjects, namely "history's-most-evil-person-Chi-
nese." It sounds funny, as the X represents an "Sh" sound, but what's more odd is
the way Nazi Germany and Hitler are viewed in this country.

While exiting the subway station near my school one day, I noticed a new
advertisement for a heater from Germany on the wall near the ticket booth. On it
was a large caricature of Hitler with the company logo substituted for the swas-
tika on his armband. The accompanying English caption read, "Declare War on
the Cold Front!" I brought my camera to take a picture of it a couple of days later
but by then it had already been taken down. Predictably, it upset a few folks from
the German consulate along with a local Jewish group. In its defense, the parent
company had given carte blanche to the local company in regard to advertising and
wasn't aware of the ad. The local company, in typical local fashion, said it was
just trying to emphasize that the heaters were made in Germany, but obviously
none of the employees had been keeping up with the local news, because if they

had, they might have noticed that just a few weeks before a restaurant with a Nazi theme had opened and caused a considerable uproar among the two aforementioned organizations and the foreign community in general.

The Jail was intended to give the patrons the feeling they were eating in, well, a jail. The prison-uniformed staff would lead you handcuffed to your "cell" to dine on overpriced seafood and the like. One of the dining rooms was done in a death camp motif. Not surprisingly, all three of the local English newspapers carried articles about the restaurant with one showing a photo of three bookish-looking Chinese people smiling and giving the peace sign in front of pictures of oversized ovens and bunks of living skeletons staring out blankly at their horrified liberators. As if this weren't enough, the bathrooms were identified by a large wooden sign saying, "Gas Chamber," and were artfully decorated with open pipes and gauges lest anyone fail to grasp the reference. When questioned about their lack of taste, the owners claimed that they had spent months designing the place and that it had never once occurred to them that anyone would take offence.

This isn't the first time this has happened in Taiwan. Numerous local business people have used Nazi iconography to sell everything from athletic shoes to cars. On several occasions, I have seen Chinese men driving along on their scooters with *Vermacht* replica helmets, complete with insignia. And, on another occasion, I spotted a motor scooter entirely decked out in Nazi colors and decals. But while free enterprise may claim to deliver what the consumer wants, the topic rose to a new level when the national government jumped on the *Xitele* bandwagon, too.

Taiwan's present ruling party, the DPP or Democratic Progressive Party, decided to recruit young people by running a TV commercial that opened with a 10-second clip of a Nazi rally featuring Hitler sputtering, spewing, beating his chest, pounding the podium, and rolling his eyeballs into the back of his head. The ad went on to show a scene from Kennedy's inauguration speech, a blip of Fidel Castro, and another one of former Taiwanese president Lee Tung-hui, a man who came to power in 1996 as the first democratically-elected national Chinese leader in history.

Responding to questions about the ad campaign, the director of the party's youth department stated that it was designed to encourage young people to share their ideas with the party. He elaborated by saying that Hitler was chosen as one of the four leaders because he had "dared to speak his mind," adding that the idea was to get youth to "express their views boldly." He went on to say that "this shouldn't be such a big thing" and asked people "not to read into it too much."

In light of vociferous protests from both the Israeli and German consulates along with various Jewish groups and other notable foreign community voices, the DPP did what any morally conscious organization would do: they refused to pull the ad and only modified it slightly, calling their actions a "goodwill response." In the new version, the catchy "dictatorship spawns disasters" was inserted into the Hitler scene, while the rather obvious "democracy requires public participation" was included in the Kennedy clip. Proudly, the party then declared that the new and improved ad offered a "conspicuous contrast between two representative figures of extremely different political ideologies." The protest groups eventually convinced the members of the ruling party to have the ad pulled.

In the following national election, the DPP wisely decided to steer clear of using images of mass murderers to win the people's support and instead ran a "We Want You" style campaign, where Uncle Sam was replaced by a sultry-looking female model wearing a school girl uniform. In Chinese, the slogan said, "It's my first time, and the whole world is watching." Well, it couldn't have meant that it was her first time to vote, because you must be at least 20 to do that in Taiwan. From this, one can only conclude that the ruling party was attempting to woo the country's perverts, or promote sex with the nation's teenaged girls. The public let the party know exactly how it felt about these ads by giving them the majority once again.

In the same election, the nefarious opposition party, the Chinese Nationalists, or KMT, ran an ad comparing the ruling party leader and incumbent president to — can you guess? — Hitler, again. In the KMT ad, voters were called on to end the president's "dictatorship." (Never mind that he was in fact elected; never mind that the KMT had ruled Taiwan under martial law for 38 years.) In response to the new round of protests from the Jewish community, the KMT — can you guess again? — refused to pull the ad, choosing instead to replace the picture of Hitler with one of a stern-looking Buddhist monk. Certainly, you can see the connection.

In an interview for a local paper, the German ambassador to Taiwan said that local people, upon finding out he was from Germany, would often comment favorably on Hitler, citing how powerful he was. But, of course, Nazi Germany was allied with Imperialist Japan, which colonized both Taiwan and China and committed atrocities on a scale to rival those of Europe. Conservative estimates put the Chinese death toll at 10 million. In the city of Nanjing alone, it is estimated that the Japanese army murdered as many as 300,000 unarmed peasants.

In 2007, it came to light that Taiwan has its very own National Socialism Association, a thousand-member-strong group comprised mainly of university students. The organization's stated aims are to strengthen national unity, return to traditional Chinese values, and curtail immigration. The organization's founders deny they are racist and maintain that they are only concerned with sanctioning Hitler's "good points."

However, Taiwan is not alone in this fascination. Hong Kong has been a kind of parallel universe in terms of endorsing Nazism. Pictures in a Karaoke bar depicting German soldiers executing prisoners, a clothing boutique adorned with swastikas, and a television station describing its commercial breaks as "the final solution" are just the tip of the iceberg.

Koreans have also gotten onboard. After all, no one did mass mobilization better than *der Fuehrer*, and Koreans are into mass mobilization in a big way. Adolf Hitler has been used in a gum commercial, and then, of course, there is the unambiguously named Third Reich bar located in a bustling district of downtown Seoul. Inside, you'll find the staff sporting black Nazi uniforms and offering a cocktail called the "Adolf Hitler."

It is tempting to theorize on the implications involved in all of this, to explain just how it relates to Asian education, values, culture, and so on. But without a formal background in either psychology or social-cultural anthropology, I don't feel qualified to do so. And besides, after three ups of Oolong tea, I need to pay a visit to the gas chamber.

CHAPTER 6. ROAD IDIOTS

In 2004, a Taiwanese survey group undertook a study of first-time job seek-ers in order to gauge the amount of knowledge they possessed in regard to in-ternational affairs. The official finding was "not much." Despite the fact that the majority of those surveyed were university or college graduates, 86% failed the questionnaire, which had a pass mark of 60%. Indeed, the average grade was a dismal 35% and masters degree holders fared only marginally better, with a mean score of 47%. To cite a few of the more interesting findings, a whopping 86% of the respondents could not name the president of China (something you might want to know, if you were Chinese) while approximately 40% failed to place Brazil as a South American country. In naming their main sources of information for current global events, most candidates listed textbooks, TV news, and HBO.

At the time this survey was taken, the Olympics was being held in Greece and the people of Taiwan were glued to their TV sets in order to support the na-tional baseball team, only to get trounced by the likes of Italy. The island-nation faired much better in Taekwondo, however, actually winning its first-ever gold medal and, incredibly, a mere 15 minutes later, winning its first-ever second gold medal. Upon their return to Taiwan, the Olympic champions were given a hero's welcome and cash for life, and promptly had their names and images plastered all over the place. Yet according to the survey, 45% of all respondents didn't know where Greece was. What's more, less than 23% of those polled said they would be willing to pay more attention to international events in the future.

But this didn't come as any great surprise to me. After all, I'm an English teacher. There is an unwritten rule which states that each and every English language textbook must contain at least one section on the topic of countries and international travel, and when teaching this section it becomes clear that you are suddenly an authority in an area where you may previously have been considered mediocre.

During my two-year tenure at a Catholic senior high school in downtown Taipei, the curriculum called for the students to learn ten country names and their locations on an extremely simplified world map. The countries were not particularly small or obscure, and included Canada, Russia, the USA, Japan, and Australia, and we spent a considerable amount of time going over them. When test day came, however, the students did horribly, with 34 out of 99 failing to identify China and 11 unable to label Taiwan. It wasn't a language problem. I know this because after the test was finished (they were evaluated individually), I would ask them in Chinese what country I was pointing to, and nearly all of them repeated that they didn't know. In endeavoring to locate their home country, one student pointed to Madagascar and another to Iceland, so at least they are aware they are living on an island.

As a segue into the topic of countries and travel, there's a game I occasionally play with my much more motivated (read: paying) adult classes that's called "map slap." To play "map slap," you simply put the students in two lines and call out a country name, whereupon the person at the head of each line has to find it before his opponent does and "slap" it on a map affixed to the board in order to get a point. Most of them have trouble locating which hemisphere a nation is in, and bear in mind that I only cover perhaps the 30 most commonly known nations. If I were to give them anything even remotely off the beaten track, such as Scotland or Israel, then forget it. They'd be there until sunrise searching in Antarctica.

Chinese people seem to have particular trouble in locating anything in Europe except France and Italy, anything in Asia except Japan and Korea, and the entire Western Hemisphere except for Canada, the United States, Mexico, and Chile. Why they can all identify Chile, I haven't quite worked out yet. You could speculate that it's because of its distinctive shape, but Brazil, Argentina, and Cuba, not to mention, say, Russia all have pretty distinctive shapes as well, but they may as well be the names of distant galaxies. Bear in mind that when I play this game, I omit places like Africa and the Middle East. There just wouldn't be any point.

The final two countries they often have trouble pinpointing are China and Taiwan: the one whose language, history, geography, and culture they learn about in school for years on end, and the other the one in which they live. Indeed, if you think there are lots of Chinese people traveling and living abroad now, just wait until the day they figure out which way the map goes. But that day hasn't arrived yet, and so people here seldom travel independently, preferring instead group travel, claiming that otherwise they'll get lost, mugged, or (heaven forbid) have to learn a smattering of English. It's true that places like Europe and Japan can be pricey, but cost doesn't seem to be the prevailing factor. Even a visit to another Chinese city or town will frequently merit a call to a travel agent, and honeymoon group tour packages are all the rage.

Ask anyone on the street for directions and you are customarily met with one of two responses: "I don't know," or "That way." If you ask for a clarification on the latter, you may given an "On the left," or "On the right," but more often than not the instruction will simply be restated in a higher register. When I teach a class on directions and locations (another obligatory English-language textbook component), the difficulty students face when asked to provide accurate and logically sequential instructions is astounding, and, again, this is not due to a language problem.

As a *finale* to a class on directions and locations, I sometimes use the students' textbooks to create a grid or "town" on the floor. Then I give them each a slip of paper on which to write a street name. Next, they draw a house on another piece of paper and tape it to one of the books (or blocks), and finally we go about "naming the streets" before they practice some English dialogues. In naming the streets, I start the ball rolling by taping the street signs on the floor in rows, doing two or three from north to south, as it were, and then from east to west. Once I've established a pattern, I ask them to complete it. Then I stand back to watch the inevitable unfold. The signs end up all over the place. Seldom do they consult with one another, and no one seems to notice (or speak up about) the fact that streets have been named two or even three times. This is fitting because the Taipei City Government, in its effort to Romanize street signs, does the exact same thing.

In fairness, however, I should add that, when asked if they consider themselves to be good with directions, many of my students will freely admit to being a "road idiot," the Chinese term for someone who has no sense of direction. And more than a few have laughingly disclosed that they pretty much only know how to find their way to work and back again.

When I first came to Taiwan, one of my classes wanted to take me out for lunch so we went to little port town called Danshui just outside of Taipei proper. To get there, you simply take the subway north along a river. When I arrived in Danshui and met my class, they asked me straight away whether I had been there before. When I told them I had been there once, they smiled in relief and asked if it would be possible for me to "lead the way." This was confusing as we were just going to find a place on the waterfront, which was a mere 50 meters away and within view of where we were standing. In fact, that was the only direction we could have gone. To our left was the river, to our right a residential area fringed by mountains, and behind us was the way we had come. I thought they were having a bit of a laugh, but not only did I have to guide them to a café, I had to pilot them the 200 meters back as well. They were mostly university students.

However, in spite of the fact that the people of Taiwan may not be the world's most directionally acute, they are virtual Marco Polos when compared with their brethren on the mainland, or so I surmised from a recent trip there. In attempting to teach a class of university students in Beijing how to speculate in English by using the phrases, "It might be...", "It could be...", "It must be...," and so on, I held up some photos of famous places and asked them where they thought they might be. Much to my dismay, the entire class assured me that Hawaii, Manhattan, the Eiffel Tower, the Statue of Liberty, and a Bavarian castle were all in China. Hawaii was definitely Hainan Island, they said, while Manhattan, the Eiffel Tower, and the Statue of Liberty were all pictures from Shanghai. Furthermore, they seemed to be of the opinion that the western province of Xinjiang was brimming over with German castles and people standing around in front of them playing *ump-pa pa* and dressed in *lederhosen*. A bit taken aback, I just kept asking them if they were certain these places were all in China, and they kept assuring me that there was no question. Shortly thereafter, I asked a female student what country she'd like to travel to and why, and she responded, "Shanghai."

"Oh, could you choose another place?" I prompted politely. "Could you choose a place outside of China?"

"OK. Hainan Island," she said. "There is beautiful."

"Yes, but could you choose another *country*?"

"Oh, uh, England," she said.

"OK, why?" I asked.

"Because people there are very gentle." There was a brief pause and then, "And because so many things there are made in China!"

Granted, this may have been a bit of regurgitated propaganda. The students knew that I taught in Taiwan, and even discussing Taiwan's independence (not that I wished to do that) is sufficient grounds for the death penalty in China. But nevertheless, I got the distinct impression that they genuinely believed those places were in their homeland.

This is all the more puzzling given that people in this part of the world spend a couple of decades studying not only more but much more intensively than their counterparts in the West. The school day can be up to several hours longer, students are subjected to a rigorous schedule of daily tests, they are pushed by their parents and teachers to excel, and they are forced to sacrifice almost all of their free time (including vacations) in order to complete their homework and take extra classes in English, math, or a subject they are deemed to be doing poorly in. The net result of this grand educational scheme is that you have an entire populace walking around without the slightest inkling as to where they are in either space or time. But things weren't always this way, or so I've learned from reading up on the venerable Chinese admiral, Zheng He.

Zheng He was an explorer *cum* diplomat who embarked upon seven voyages that saw China extend its cultural and commercial influence to an estimated 37 countries. The first of these expeditions was begun in 1405. Most notably, the admiral explored India, the Persian Gulf, and East Africa — a colossal undertaking in those days — sailing with a flotilla of 317 vessels including 62 enormous and precision-crafted treasure ships. According to records from the Ming Dynasty, the treasure ships were 122 meters long and 50 meters wide, and, consequently, would have dwarfed their European counterparts. After the admiral's death in 1433, China reinstated its policy of isolationism and the gigantic vessels were either burned by Confucian scholars or simply left to rot. China's latest emperor judged that there was nothing to be gained from consorting with the barbarians. Sadly, the majority of Zheng He's meticulously drawn charts were destroyed as well. The period of isolationism that followed his death would last for the next 500 years.

Although ethnically Chinese, Zheng He was actually a Muslim whose original name was Ma Sanbao. One theory has it that he inspired the legend of *Sinbad the Sailor*, which, if true, almost certainly had to do with his size. He was said to have stood over seven feet tall. And this almost certainly had to do with a hormonal imbalance as a result of having had his goodies cut off as a boy. Admiral Zheng He, you see, was a eunuch.

That the Chinese underwent any kind of age of exploration, let alone one so impressive, is truly remarkable given their inward-looking nature. When the Europeans first landed in the Middle Kingdom, they presented the Chinese with a clock that was regarded merely as an amusing trinket and quickly cast aside. Fatefully, they didn't seem to grasp the implications of being discovered by someone equipped with a vastly superior technology.

I first learned of Zheng He and the treasure ships from a book entitled *1421 — The Year China Discovered the World*, written by Gavin Menzies. In his book, Menzies supplements accepted history to the point where the Chinese circumnavigated the globe a century before Magellan's entourage, charted Australia three centuries years before Captain Cook, discovered the Arctic four centuries prior to the Europeans, and stumbled upon America 70 years before Columbus. Of course, Columbus never actually reached America, but rather the Bahamas, believing until the day he died that he had landed in Asia; and there were already people in Australia when Cook "discovered" it, but there you are. Historians dismiss Menzies's claims as the result of an overactive imagination, but if it weren't for his efforts many in the West would never have known of the Chinese admiral or China's seafaring supremacy.

Coincidentally, just 20 minutes after I bought 1421, I was in a subway station where I spotted one of my students attempting to ascend the down escalator. When he had gotten that sorted out and had made it up to the platform, we got to chatting and I asked him where he was going. "To National Taiwan University" he said, and pointed in the exact opposite direction of its location. National Taiwan University is the country's foremost institute of higher learning. "What book did you buy?" he then wanted to know, but luckily, just then my train came. I think I might have had some trouble explaining.

Chapter 7. A Whale of a Story

It seems as if sometimes you have to move far away in order to appreciate things where you grew up. Take for example my city's New Brunswick Museum, founded in 1842 by geologist Abraham Gesner, who discovered kerosene. The museum constitutes Canada's oldest, and features some pretty absorbing displays of art, zoological specimens, and ship building exhibits. Granted, that may sound a bit run of the mill, but in a city that quite seriously boasts of having the steepest main street in the nation, it is a big deal indeed. Nevertheless, I was never even remotely interested in visiting the place until I returned home for a trip after several years of living abroad.

The reason for my reticence was twofold. First of all, it's local. If the nation's oldest museum were in, say, Toronto, it would doubtlessly seem more enticing and possibly worth a visit if I were to ever find myself in that city and with money enough left over from visiting the Hockey Hall of Fame. Second, I was taken there on an elementary school field trip, and therefore crossed it off my "things to do" list at the ripe age of six.

But this disinterest in things local is universal, or so it would seem. Taiwan's National Palace Museum happens to be ranked fourth in the world, right up there with the Louvre, the British Museum, and the Metropolitan Museum of Art. It houses the world's largest collection of Chinese art, a staggering 700,000 pieces in total. Too numerous an amount to be displayed at any one time, the items are rotated every three months so that you would have to allot 12 years in order to view the entire collection. The artifacts not on display are kept in atmosphere-controlled vaults in the nearby mountains.

No less significant is that virtually every last piece was looted from Beijing's Forbidden City and shipped to Taiwan by Chiang Kai-shek's Nationalists. Hence, the emperors' treasures aren't in Beijing, but rather Taipei, and only about 10 minutes from where I work. Consequently, almost any art you see in China today is a replica, or less than 50 years old. But of course, the only people who find the place at all appealing are Western and Japanese tourists, with locals saying that they went there on field trips in grade school and that they associate their visit with having to write some kind of lengthy report.

It's the same thing with whale watching. When I was 18, a friend of mine rang me up one day and asked if I'd like to go see some whales. At the time, I couldn't think of anything duller, and, if I remember correctly, intimated as much. Now, almost twice that age, I don't know what I was thinking. On Taiwanese TV, I caught a program on whales' migratory paths, with footage of the very place in New Brunswick where my friend wanted to take me. Perhaps it was only the conspicuous contrast to watching guys from Hong Kong kicking each other in the forehead, but suddenly I felt an overpowering urge to get out on the ocean and see some whales.

In Taiwan, the whale watching industry is booming, and although I could have easily caught a bus to a nearby port, the prospect of waking up at daybreak to join a boatload of cute, albeit loud (both vocally and in a fashion sense) Chinese people, who were very likely to croon karaoke at top decibel the entire time, quickly caused me to abandon the idea. Besides, I'd have to buy a new raincoat. Not to prevent from getting splashed mind you, but rather in the event that one of the whales should spontaneously explode. Well, OK, whales don't really blow up; at least, not in the water, they don't. There are, however, two well-documented accounts of exploding whales on land. The first case occurred in Florence, Oregon in 1970, when a dead whale that washed ashore was treated with dynamite in a very flawed and very messy attempt to clear the beach. For two decades this bizarre scene was thought to have been little more than an urban legend, but it had been covered by a local news crew and eventually their footage made it to the Internet. The second exploding whale story occurred here in Taiwan, "weird news capital of the world." In the winter of 2004, a sperm whale 17 meters in length and weighing in at an astonishing 50 tons beached up near the town of Yunlin in the southern part of the island. It was the largest whale ever to have gotten washed up in Taiwan, and in a country where almost any news is big news, it quickly caused a stir. Researchers from the National Cheng Kung University, located in the nearby city of Tainan, arrived on the scene and ordered that the whale be transported to the institute's department of marine biology for examination.

This was no simple task. It took more than 50 men and three large cranes more than 13 hours to get the monster loaded onto the flatbed of a transport truck, after which it embarked on an hour long journey to the city of Tainan. Imagine passing by that on the road. As the truck made its way down the main street of the city, the whale emitted a noise, which according to locals, sounded like, "KAI-BUNG!!!!!" Pent up gasses resulting from decomposition had blown the innards right out of the thing, covering an entire street, including shop windows, parked cars, and pedestrians.

Luckily for the academics involved, enough of the leviathan remained intact to do a study; however, as it turned out, marine biologists weren't the only ones interested in inspecting the mammal. Indeed, it was later reported that more than 100 locals (mostly males) had gone to see the whale (a bull) claiming that they wanted to "experience" its 1.5-meter long reproductive organ.

I should probably mention that prior to and during the effort to load the whale from the beach onto the transport truck, over 600 people came out to observe and a little market was hurriedly set up to sell food and beverages. Chinese people are born capitalists and are extremely adept at turning almost any event or trend into a buck. A Canadian friend of mine who moved to Taiwan over 15 years ago told me that shortly after he arrived, a whale had gotten beached up at a popular resort at the southern tip of the island and on that occasion, too, locals had been quick to act. They held a giant barbecue.

CHAPTER 8. BAD COP, BAD COP

After teaching afternoon classes at the Catholic high school in downtown Taipei, I used to relax for an hour or so in a nearby park, usually with a good book. Located next to a subway station, several gazebos and ponds are set in a pleasant patch of greenery that actually doubles as a memorial. Named 2-28 Peace Park, in commemoration of the February 28th crackdown and subsequent massacre of more than 30,000 civilians at the hands of Chiang Kai-shek's Nationalists in 1947, it is referred to locally as "Gay Park," and if you ever venture through it after sunset you will quickly grasp why. Parenthetically, just down the street from this memorial is the magnificently designed Chiang Kai-shek Memorial Hall, and there, I think, you have "the other China" in a nutshell.

During daylight hours, 2-28 Peace Park is, by and large, just a regular park-type park, and that's when I used to sit in it and read. I use the phrase "by and large" because the festivities don't always wait to commence with the disappearance of the sun, or so I learned one day after making the mistake of falling asleep under one of the gazebos only to awake and discover a man sitting virtually on top of me with a bluntly lustful look in his eye. After that, I stuck to the benches. On another afternoon, while I was relaxing on a bench only a stone's throw from the subway entrance, and engrossed in Frank McCourt's *Angela's Ashes* (a best-seller at the time), two uncommonly focused-looking police officers pulled up on a motorcycle. Scanning the immediate area, I couldn't determine who they could be aiming to talk to, but of course, they were aiming to talk to me.

"Passporto!" one of them barked, striding over. Asian people have a tendency of adding an "a" or "o" sound to the end of English words.

"Sorry, I don't speak Italian," I shot back, knowing that by law I wasn't required to carry my passport. I then gazed back down at my book and waited for their next request, knowing that they would have trouble articulating it in English.

"Your booka iza about whata?" one stammered, so I courteously recounted what I had read so far — from page one — in the hopes that tears of boredom would well up in their eyes and they would leave me alone. Clearly not big fans of character development, they cut me short.

"Are you married?" one asked.

"No," I answered.

"Are you the gay?" was the follow up question. "There's only one?" I thought, but instead replied with, "No, I'm not gay. Why? Are *you*?"

This broke the tension nicely, and we all tittered and tee-heed, relieved in knowing that I preferred to have sex with women. I thought this ironic, seeing as how they were the ones who went around sharing the same motorcycle all day. After they left, it occurred to me just why they had accosted me. The cover of *Angela's Ashes* features a close up of a young boy's face. Some poodle-strolling senior had probably seen this and decided to play concerned citizen. What made this incident all the more unusual was that just a week or two prior, the Taipei police force had been severely reprimanded and issued demerits for harassing patrons of a so-called gay gym. It is not a crime to be homosexual in Taiwan and their ill-conceived actions resulted in the national scandal of the week.

But, even though they were clearly in the wrong, it was nice to see the police harassing someone. This was in stark contrast to their usual role of doing nothing at all in the way of fighting crime or improving public safety, unless, of course, you count a campaign they held to rid the nation of playing cards featuring pictures of naked women on them. Often smiling and friendly, the inefficiency of Taiwan's police force would be difficult to overstate, although one might begin by saying that it can occasionally make law enforcement in Colombia resemble a well-oiled machine.

Taiwanese police, when not hanging around the station smoking, seem to spend the majority of their time driving their routes (with lights flashing), where they are required to stop every third block or so to sign a slip of paper and stuff it into a kind of mailbox to prove that they've been there. This is a serious inconvenience as it means that they have to conduct their other affairs, which include collecting bribes, running gambling houses and brothels, opening pubs that sell narcotics, and abducting prostitutes from China for ransom, all while off duty. Ask any local person what they think of their police force, and they will most likely respond with the word "useless." I would have to concur.

There used to be a local version of *Cops* on TV here, complete with the same "Bad Boys" theme song, and although you could feel your IQ plummeting through the floor while watching it, it was admittedly entertaining. In one episode, I saw a man get pulled over for drunk driving, looking as though he couldn't have driven a fork into a plate of mashed potatoes. He was made to breathe into a paper cup, which three police officers then passed around and sniffed. (Despite the fact that Taiwan produces nearly everything electronic, breathalyzers are a very recent phenomenon here.) After they concluded that he was indeed plastered, the man then began shoving the officers while angrily insisting he had only had one beer. This went on for what seemed like an eternity, but came to an abrupt halt when a cab pulled up and the man was helped into it by the police. Case closed. A subsequent installment of the program featured a Hong Kong action-movie style foot chase through a series of back alleys, over fences, and through some small shops, before finally winding up in someone's home. The police cornered the suspect behind a washing machine, drew their guns, and demanded that he give himself up. After a few tension-filled minutes of shouting and negotiation, a feeble looking octogenarian emerged and surrendered himself.

With a free press, the local media has a field day pointing out the ineptitude of the nation's police force. Once, a local news channel showed a drunken captain suggesting to a crowd of microphone-wielding reporters that they ought to get the hell out of his station. On another occasion, an officer had sex with a high school girl and then tried to brand the words "sex kitten" onto her chest. And then there was the time a uniformed officer who was off duty (and off his rocker) smashed his police scooter into the back of a car at a check point set up to nab drunk drivers. His colleagues rushed him to a nearby hospital, where he was treated for minor facial abrasions and remained for a good night's sleep. The following day, he passed a breathalyzer with flying colors before working out an arrangement with the owner of the vehicle he had hit. No charges were laid. But, at least the officer in question had a valid driver's license. In a county located only an hour from Taipei, it was recently discovered that 31 members of the local police force did not. But as bewildering as these stories are, this next one takes the cake.

A couple of years ago here, a detainee was tortured by three policemen by being beaten, hung upside down, and having a toothpick inserted into his penis. Ostensibly realizing they had gone too far, the police took him to the hospital. But not wanting to arouse suspicion, they checked him in under one of their own names and then went about burning his bloodied clothes. The offending officers were eventually tried and given suspended sentences as the court deemed that they had "administered the torture out of an eagerness to perform their duties well" and that they "ought to be given a second chance to correct their mistakes."

Upset by the police's ineptitude, a Canadian English professor decided to take matters into his own hands. His wife's friend, a Filipino maid, had reported abuse on the part of her employers, but apparently not much was being done in the way of follow up. So, fueled by a sense of justice and good dollop of liquid courage, the good professor walked in the front door of the local cop shop carrying a video camera, whereupon he commenced "gathering evidence" in order to demonstrate how the police weren't fulfilling their duties, a moot point if there ever was one. I can just imagine the cops sitting there smoking and playing poker with the confiscated girlie cards, only to look up and see some tottering foreigner adjusting the zoom. The police wasted little time in getting out their own camera in order to film him filming them. In a video clip taken from a news broadcast and circulated on the Internet, an officer approaches the man and gestures for him to put the camera down. The Canadian responds by delivering a walloping stomach punch that doubles the policeman over. Next, you see five officers tackling him and then the clip stops. When it resumes, the man is sitting handcuffed to a chair, face puffed up, lip ballooning, and sobbing pathetically. For whatever reason, the head of the local community was then called in and informed of his little stunt. A diminutive woman wearing a summer dress, she walks over to the man, and, in Mandarin, says, "OK, you've come to China, so let's handle this the Chinese way," after which she goes about slapping him silly. The video clip then ends by showing a letter from the woman written in broken English apologizing for her actions and attributing them to "cultural differences." Given that the professor's Ph.D. was obtained in Culture and Values in Education, he should have had no trouble in understanding.

This, along with their ability to tow a car in about 30 seconds, is the only thing I have ever seen the police do efficiently. Incidentally, after the police beat him up, they charged him with assault. He's currently facing jail, deportation, or both, but in a way, he's lucky. By all accounts, the station had just run out of toothpicks.

CHAPTER 9. ABOUT FACE

A while back, I decided to move from an apartment in the back of my building to one in the front upon discovering that the adjacent parking lot was to be turned into a skyscraper. In the process, I had to cancel my old phone line and then apply for a new one, with the phone company telling me it would be activated on the following Monday. However, after a couple of weeks of not being able to get a dial tone, I rang them up to see when I could expect one. "You already have a phone line," the woman insisted, despite my claims to the contrary. After verifying she had the correct address, I thanked her, hung up (my cell phone), and decided I'd have to pay a visit to the phone company to find out what was going on.

Christmas fell a couple of days later, and so I ended up using a fistful of phone cards to call my family from the metro station across the street. The conversation was brief and punctuated by bursts of static, beeping sounds prompting me to change cards, arrival and departure announcements, and my parents saying things like, "Now, what's *that* sound?" In fact, it was the very antithesis of one of those fuzzily warm, three-minute AT&T commercials they play during the holiday season back home. ("Gosh son, where are ya callin' from? A Chinese train station?") With this experience fresh in mind, I finally found time to make it to the phone company the following week.

Except for cell phones, there is only one telephone company in Taiwan and although their offices look great, their service — at least in my experience — tends to be anything but. When I inquired as to what happened to the guys who were supposed to come and install my line, a female clerk wearing a neon pink baseball cap informed me that a crew had dropped by only to discover that a line already existed.

"But, I don't have a line," I told her. "That's why I'm here."

"Oh, I don't mean an activated one," she explained. "Our computer shows a Mr. Yang had a line there, but he didn't pay his last bill so we disconnected him." When I asked her what this had to do with me, she stated that according to their regulations, they couldn't install a new line until the previous tenant cancelled his. She then went on to suggest I try and track him down.

"But, I only met him once," I whined. "He's gone." She answered by saying that that was too bad. I then informed her that he had gone off to parts unknown to do his mandatory military service, and she replied by saying that that was too bad too. Anyhow, having come prepared, I then took out a copy of my lease and showed it to her.

"You see?" I said. "I live here now. Not Mr. Yang. If you don't believe me, call my landlady. Her number is right there. I haven't had the Internet or a proper phone for nearly a month. Kindly install my telephone line." But a rule was a rule, she said. We got into a long back-and-forth, eventually drawing a bit of a crowd.

Just for the record, I would like to state that I am not one of those people who thrive on conflict or who enjoys a good blow out every now and again. Honestly, I'm not. But these people can make you loopier than a spool of yarn.

"How do I know he doesn't still live there?" she demanded.

"Because I'm standing here with my lease, telling you he doesn't!" I fumed, and followed up by informing her that she could come by and inspect the place for herself if she didn't believe me. At this point, I'm guessing most people would have conceded defeat, but instead she came back with an improbable, "He could still be living there." "Yes, maybe he's under my bed," I retorted hotly, but this was a mistake, as she gave me a look that said, "So, you admit that he's still there, then."

Not wishing to be memorialized by the headline, *Foreign Man Fights Phone Co., Dies of Coronary*, I sat down in the "customer chair," took a deep breath, and calmly made my request again, adding that I wasn't going to budge until matters were seen to. I had time, I told her. I could wait. Well, that did it. I got the line put in that afternoon, and all for the simple fact that I caused her to lose face.

Any travel book or introduction to Asia and its culture(s) is sure to include an obligatory blurb on the concept of face, without explaining what it equates to in reality. Most sources will attempt to enlighten you with a passage like the following: "Face is a concept of extreme importance in (Asian country's) society. It is infinitely deeper and more mystical than the Western notion of reputation. It is the imperceptible force that binds the Ying and the Yang, the waxing and the waning, the ebb and the flow. It is existence itself. Never ever cause someone to lose face, and this means avoiding confrontation in all cases and at all costs."

Poppycock. Granted, it's not a good thing to have Western tourists traipsing around the globe and stepping on people's toes, but for anyone planning on having anything more than the most cursory of dealings with Asian people, it might be a good idea to elaborate at least a little instead of regurgitating the same old stilted explanation. As for my own explanation, I know that I should probably dress it up through satire or anecdote, but I figure: why not get down to brass tacks?

I once read face described as, "what the Chinese hide behind so they can treat foreigners in a way they would never dream of treating other Chinese," and although this is getting closer, I don't think it has much to do with foreigners. Simply put, the concept of face is just an excuse for people to behave however they darned well please. Full stop. Without confrontation, there is no accountability, and without accountability, there is chaos. Additional and predictable consequences of giving people a blank cheque in terms of how to conduct themselves include widespread incompetence, chronic dishonesty, deeply ingrained distrust, and an extraordinary inability to accept responsibility. When someone actually does get up the gumption to point the finger, the accused seldom admits to wrongdoing, even when confronted with overwhelming evidence, because, you see, that would cause them to lose face. Therefore, face must be preserved at all costs and by whatever means available, and this customarily translates to lying, denial, recrimination, and shifting the blame. And here's the kicker: doing this will often garner respect. Never mind being big about it and saying you're sorry. Just protect your "honor" until the bitter end.

I know of a Western fellow here who lost his cool one day and threw a brick through the window of a car that constantly parked in front of his door, even though he'd asked the owner several times not to. Not surprisingly, a small crowd gathered looking for a confrontation, so he informed his wife (a local) that he was going to go out to apologize and offer to pay for damages. "No, you can't do that!" she told him. "They'll lynch you, if you admit to it. You must deny it." He heeded her advice and, in doing so, apparently impressed the neighbors to such an extent that they left and never bothered him again.

Without question, failing to take responsibility is a major recurring theme in Chinese society. Once, when a typhoon devastated a particular area of this country, the government responded by not responding at all, which, you have to admit, is highly novel. When asked why no relief efforts were being mounted, officials threw up their hands and declared that that particular swath of land wasn't their responsibility. Aid workers were only sent in after it had become a national scandal, something that Taiwan has no shortage of.

Just prior to 9/11, four construction workers were building an embankment in a river in central Taiwan when they got caught in a flash flood. As the waters swiftly rose, the men latched on to each other for support as their foreman frantically called 911. After receiving the call, the local fire department passed the message on to the local police department, who in turn contacted the air force, who claimed they were only responsible for situations occurring higher than two and a half kilometers above sea level, and then suggested that the police try the airborne squad of a larger police department located in a nearby city. They did, only for the city police to inform the local police that they had better try the air force again, seeing as how they were closer to the situation. After a few more rounds of debate, it was finally decided that the city police's air squadron should indeed send a helicopter to the scene, but by the time the chopper had gotten off the ground, the men had been swept away and drowned. It was, after all, two hours after the initial request had been made. Rumors spread that the pilot on duty at the time had been drunk and that locating another one had caused the delay. The police denied this. Of course. Furthermore, although no one could seem to get a rescue helicopter into the air, at least one news helicopter was quickly on the scene, broadcasting a grainy image of the four men standing precariously in a line as the hoary river raged around them.

Units from no less than four fire departments responded, although unfortunately they ran into some equipment problems. Specifically, they forgot to bring any. What they needed was a rope gun, but the first two crews had left it behind, the third arrived with a broken one, and the fourth arrived too late. Needless to say, this was a debacle.

A month later, the government, keen to illustrate its resolve in beefing up the country's emergency services, held some training courses but these didn't go quite as planned. In one exercise, rescue workers tested flair and rope guns, but none of them worked. And then, as news crews broadcast live, a cameraman was thrown into a river when two police boats collided with one another. And one month after this, in what was to be a simulation of how the river tragedy should have been handled, and would be handled in the future, the rescue helicopter crashed next to a river, leaving the co-pilot in a coma and injuring five others.

Although one government official did resign over the initial incident and the president issued an apology and compensation package to the victims' families, none of the relevant parties would concede to even a trace of misconduct and spent the next few weeks pathetically smearing each other in the press. When the government eventually heaped blame on all of them — the police, the air force, and the fire department — they took it badly, with firefighters traveling to Taipei to protest by burning their uniforms. But hey, at least they didn't lose face.

All countries and cultures have their idiosyncrasies and certainly the case could be made that Western people are overly confrontational, not to mention argumentative, and given to excessive complaining. Cut in line in the West, and you're likely to be reminded in no uncertain terms of just where it begins and ends, but do it in this part of the world and everyone stares straight ahead pretending they didn't notice. Although I think a middle ground would be ideal, as you've doubtlessly noticed we don't live in a world of middle grounds or ideals. If I had to pick which way of doing things was preferable (and thankfully, I don't), I'd probably have to go with the Western one. It's far from perfect, and, of course, I'm biased, but at least people are aware that they may be held accountable for their actions. And besides — it's *so* much easier to get a telephone.

CHAPTER 10. LOOP DEE LU

The other day, *The Taipei Times* ran this headline on the front page: "Vice President Moved to Tears by Shuma the Singing Camel." The subsequent article described how an Egyptian camel had been trained to "sing" in what resembles an Arabic chant. Apparently, it travels the world performing concerts and even has its own CD entitled *Soul Camel to Cairo*, if you can believe that. While under quarantine at the Taipei zoo, Taiwan's vice president, whose name is Annette Lu, was given a sample of the camel's vocal skills before it was to perform at the National Concert Hall. She was so overwhelmed by the experience, evidently, that she burst into tears.

Taiwan's vice president would appear to be rather prone to fits of tears. Once, during the last election campaign in this country, she started to sob uncontrollably as she told a crowd that there was simply no hope for Taiwan unless people made the right decision and voted for her party. Although a bit theatrical, it's exactly the kind of thing you'd expect from some not-altogether-with-it developing nation, and is really only noteworthy here in light of the fact that her audience was a class of kindergarten children.

"The trouble with practical jokes is that they often get elected," or so said Will Rogers, leading me to conclude that I should never underestimate the intelligence of a cowboy. Unless, of course, that cowboy happens to be George W. Bush. That Bush is a buffoon, there is no question, but Taiwan's VP could give him a run for his money any day in a "Who Sounds Dumber?" contest.

The SARS epidemic (Severe Acute Respiratory Syndrome) was a big event in Taiwan, as it was in China and other parts of the world, accounting for over 850 deaths. Using China's mishandling and attempted cover up of the fatal illness as an excuse to smear Taiwan's arch-rival (China jailed the doctor who broke the story), Ms. Lu lambasted the communist giant, but then went on to liken SARS to World War III. She also wondered aloud if the disease weren't God's way of punishing modern day people for giving undue attention to material wealth and comfort. Indeed, commenting on who deserves to live and who doesn't is nothing new for this woman. While elucidating on AIDS during a guest appearance on a television show, Taiwan's second in command posited, "Some say the reason AIDS spreads is because God can't take it anymore. God felt that it was time to mete out punishment, or there wouldn't be any difference between men and animals." I wonder if anyone has had the heart to inform this poor, misguided soul that humans *are* animals, or that millions of children have been born with this dreadful disease. Paradoxically, when later remarking on issues of public health, Lu stated that people with health problems ought to try and heal themselves by repeating the mantra, "I'm fine. You're fine. We're all fine."

There's more.

A while back, a vicious tropical storm devastated parts of central and southern Taiwan and was especially hard on the mountainous regions, which are home to some 13 different aboriginal groups. Unfortunately, the mudslides, flooding, and destruction were exacerbated by excessive mountain farming on the part of said tribes. The vice president's solution? Move all of the storm victims (read: "natives") to Central America, thereby giving them a fresh start while helping Taiwan to expand its "territory." The problem with this, you see, is that, in addition to the rather obvious racism, Taiwan doesn't *have* any extra territory. It has instead a precarious string of Latin American diplomatic allies that it has procured through dollar diplomacy. Needless to say, all this talk of loading the country's indigenous people onto freighters and shipping them off to Guatemala caused a bit of a stir among the aboriginal community, and waves of public protest ensued. However, to demonstrate that Ms. Lu wasn't alone, a fellow female party member declared that the government had misspoken because, "it had become stupid from coddling the natives for so long." Lu then threw grease on the fire by claiming that the tribes' people were merely pretenders, and that the country's true aboriginals were a race of "black dwarves." Shortly after making this statement, Ms. Lu visited the areas ruined by the storm. The first thing she did was ask where all the local brothels were, demanding to know why something wasn't being done about them.

Interestingly, this wasn't the first time Lu had tackled the issue of mudslides. She once came up with five social ills that she deemed to be plaguing her country and creatively dubbed them "the five mudslides." But I suppose, "the five mudslides" has more of a ring to it than *Barriers Overcome: A Hen Who Crows at Dawn*, which is the title of a textbook Lu wrote on feminism. People who have purchased and read the book report that it's extremely effective in combating insomnia and propping up wobbly tables.

In addition to being a published feminist, the vice president is a novelist and a lawyer, having obtained her law degree from Harvard. She is also somewhat of a celebrity. You see, Annette Lu started out as a democracy activist back in the days when Taiwan was under martial law. As a matter of fact, she was a political prisoner who actually faced execution, and she wrote her novel *These Three Women* on toilet paper while in jail. Like her feminism book, I'm willing to bet that it's little more than attractively bound toilet paper now, but admittedly it's an interesting anecdote. Paroled after five years because she needed cancer treatment, and because Amnesty International pressured the Nationalist government into releasing her, she went on to beat her disease in the US before returning to a democratic Taiwan, where she promptly joined politics and was eventually named the running mate to the current president, no doubt to garner the female vote.

Lu is in her early sixties now and never married, and, well, she looks it. Despite this, at least two dozen male students in their late teens and early twenties have told me they think she's a catch. "Like a grandmother," they say. And it's not just students. An English teacher rented a billboard next to a highway (for nearly $30,000) to profess his feelings for the spinster *cum* vice president and claimed that he was even thinking of publishing a book to express his "unchangeable love" for her. Another suitor, a debt collector and ex-con, attempted to propose to Lu by leading a 24-sedan motorcade to the Presidential Building, only to be turned away by the police. But far from being flattered, Lu stated that the men must have been mentally disturbed, which shows that she still has moments of lucidity.

Taiwan is unique in that it's the only country in the world that isn't considered to be a country. Taiwan and China represent the outcome of a civil war which culminated in 1950 and saw the island of Taiwan become the last holdout of Chiang Kai-shek's Nationalists, who fled the Communist takeover on the mainland led by Mao Zedong. China still regards Taiwan as a "renegade province" that must eventually be recovered.

Given this, Taiwan needs to have a charismatic, intelligent, and articulate individual to champion its cause for independence and formal recognition internationally. Whom did the ruling party choose? Vice President Annette Lu, who is sent on one dollar-diplomacy mission after another to embarrass the country abroad after having perfected the art at home.

To cite an example, Taiwan ran an ad campaign in New York calling for a seat at the UN with posters that read UNFAIR. I thought the ad was quite clever, with UN written in red, FAIR in black, and a clearly stated request written below. Traveling to New York, Lu claimed that New Yorkers couldn't understand the ads, but I'm willing to bet they just didn't care. The ads were fine and it's not everyday that Taiwan produces something in English that's legible, let alone intelligent. This is a place that, until very recently, had a large sign at its international airport saying, "No Drugging" and showed a picture of a giant cockroach.

When I first set out to write about Lu, I thought it would be fun to have a go at Taiwan's clown-like vice president. Politics in Taiwan seems comical to most Westerners and to more astute locals and Annette Lu seems to personify all that is wrong with it. But then something strange happened. I actually sort of — just a wee bit mind you — grew to (*ahem*) respect her. Given that she recently prompted everybody to do things "the Tai Chi way," and has stated that Taiwan needs to adopt both "Hello Kitty diplomacy" and feminism in order to deal with the PRC, this is a very big step for me.

However, having read her biography, I was reminded that she had survived two ordeals with cancer and one assassination attempt, and was the second in command of a government that had locked her up and was about to kill her for speaking up for civil liberties. Also, China can't stand her, and has called her "the scum of a thousand years" and "the scum of the nation." She's always bashing them, and I think they deserve no less than to have to listen to her. Sure, she makes between little and no sense when she speaks, *but at least she's allowed to speak.* And in attempts at gaining formal recognition for democratic Taiwan, she's personally pestered the UN as well as Bill Clinton and Jimmy Carter. Call me soft, but I can't help but concede to having just a smidgeon of admiration.

Also, we're both a couple of fools. You see, the article about the singing camel was an April Fools' joke. (In my defense, news stories in Taiwan often read like parodies. Well, OK. I'm a little slow sometimes.) Even so, despite my newly found degree of respect, I don't think I'm going to be renting a billboard anytime soon.

Chapter 11. A Very Tall New World Order

English, in case you haven't noticed, is a monster. The medium or dominant language of science, medicine, general academia, foreign language teaching, aviation, computing, business, the media, tourism, and diplomacy, it remains unchallenged as the preferred means of international communication. Although it is problematic to pinpoint with any high degree of accuracy the number of people who speak English, it's generally acknowledged that there are something like 350 million native speakers, 350 million speakers of English as a second language, and another 100 million or so speakers of English as a foreign language, making for a grand total of approximately 800 million.

What's more, English is the official, co-official, or at least a very widely spoken language of the following countries (take a deep breath here): Antigua, Australia, the Bahamas, Barbados, Belize, Bermuda, Botswana, Brunei, Cameroon, Canada, Dominica, Fiji, Gambia, Ghana, Grenada, Guam, Guyana, India, Ireland, Jamaica, Kenya, Kiribati, Lesotho, Liberia, Malawi, Malta, Mauritius, Namibia, Nauru, New Zealand, Nigeria, Pakistan, Papua New Guinea, Palau, the Philippines, Puerto Rico, St. Christopher and Nevis, St. Lucia, St. Vincent, Senegal, Seychelles, Sierra Leone, Singapore, South Africa, Surinam, Swaziland, Tanzania, Tonga, Trinidad and Tobago, Tuvalu, Uganda, the United Kingdom, the United States, Vanuatu, Western Samoa, Zambia, and Zimbabwe.

That was 57 countries, but some linguists list additional territories where they deem English to hold a special place, making for a number of 77. This catalogue includes places like Nepal, Dubai, and Hong Kong. And even in parts of the world where English is neither an official language nor widely used, you probably wouldn't have to go very far to find someone who understands it. Take Northern Europe or East Asia, for example.

If you're like me, reading through such a list probably couldn't help but generate at least a mild twinge of pride that somehow failed to reach fruition due to a contradictory impulse to get out a map and find out just where the heck half of these places are. English, for better or worse, is even making inroads into other languages, and significantly so in some cases. German officer workers complain about *der Boss* perhaps because of *der Dresscode*, while the Italians have to adhere to *il budget* while meeting *il deadline*. Even in France, where Anglicisms are closely monitored by the Académie Française, people might finish out their day with a little *online chat* or by watching some *le foot* on the sports channel. When Koreans are hot they turn on the *air con*, whereas the Japanese might help cool off with an ice cold *biru* as they view a bit of *basi-baru*. In fact, Japanese has somewhere in the vicinity of 20,000 English loan words in its lexicon, requiring a separate alphabet and a special dictionary to deal with them.

The use of English as a global trend has led to the creation of a somewhat frenetic multi-billion-dollar industry to facilitate its learning, a vast amount of which goes on in Asia. Supposedly, there are more English learners in China than there are people in the United States. In Taiwan, English learning ranks right up there with shopping, eating, and napping (sleeping is considered a hobby here) as a passion among teens and young adults, while kids stream like ants to their booming language schools sporting brightly-colored school backpacks: little walking advertisements. At the university level, textbooks are often the very same as those used in the US and graduates can look forward to job interviews being conducted in English. Furthermore, people of all ages often study at language schools in the evenings to help them at their jobs, to enhance their careers, or just to socialize and have fun. Indeed, English is generally considered to be cool and it's difficult to find a product or shop without the language featured on it, although, that said, it is seldom correct.

Yet despite the enormous and commendable effort to learn the language, many people seem to be going through the motions while waiting for the day when they can pick up their overpriced textbooks, electronic dictionaries, and instructional CDs, and hurl them all right out the window. This isn't because someone is about to invent some sleek-looking oral translation device or a pill that facilitates language learning, but rather because any day now, English is going to come crashing down from its pedestal to be replaced by Mandarin Chinese.

China is expected to be the world's largest economy within the next 20 years. Language, as everyone knows, is intricately bound up with issues of identity, politics, and power. According to many Chinese people, children from Antigua to Zimbabwe will be placing their English studies on the back burner in order to learn Mandarin and give them that competitive edge in the world of tomorrow.

A glance at the writing system shows how daunting that task would be. Under Symbols, in Asian layout, Microsoft Word offers so many rows of Chinese characters that it takes a full 70 seconds to scroll through at a brisk clip. In fact, because of the complexity of the written word, it requires several more years of study than an alphabet-based language for children to learn to read, and for non-native adults to become competent enough to handle a newspaper it is said to entail a decade of dedicated, diligent work.

The language does not lend itself to the kind of categorization familiar to Westerners. Dictionaries are organized according to the word's radical, such as the "water radical" or the "fire radical." There are 214 of these and they are not always easy to spot, as they sometimes take various forms and a character may contain more than one of them, leaving the task of deciding on which one is "logically" the prevailing one. Once the radical is identified, count the number of strokes in the character and that's how you will find your word. Stroke numbers easily get into the teens (one word has 84 of them) and sometimes the exact number is unclear, or disputed, leading to additional complications.

Then, of course, there is the spoken aspect and the well-known fact that Chinese is a tonal language. To fully learn a character in Chinese, then, means mastering its pronunciation, its tone, its meaning, its radical, and the number of strokes it has, along with learning to recognize it in its various incarnations, i.e., computer-generated script, cursive script, seal script, calligraphic forms, and so on.

To complicate things even further, there are two main writing systems. In Taiwan and Hong Kong, people use the traditional or complex characters, while in China the government has introduced a simplified system. This means that a person from Taiwan and another from Hong Kong would become virtually illiterate upon arrival in China proper, although they could communicate with each other — in writing, but not orally, as Cantonese and Mandarin are mutually unintelligible. Indeed, perhaps before claiming the world will speak Mandarin, Chinese people had better work on getting each other to speak it.

There are an estimated 870 million speakers of Mandarin in the world, putting it in the top spot in terms of number of speakers, but also signifying that a very large number of Chinese people (over 1.3 billion in mainland China alone) don't speak it all. Beijing, Shanghai, Hong Kong, Taipei, and Singapore, the five main economic and cultural galaxies in the Chinese universe, employ spoken versions of Chinese that are divergent to the point of being incomprehensible.

By some estimates, there are as many as 8,000 dialects of Chinese, many as dissimilar as French and German. With such variation, it can easily be argued that dialects are not dialects at all. But this is rarely emphasized as it tends to ruffle Chinese sensibilities.

Beijing Mandarin, or the Beijing dialect as it's more commonly known, has been nominated as the version people are supposed to use, but in the south, largely due to the hilly terrain, there is such a degree of disparity that one village might not be able to communicate with the next. Indeed, Mao Zedong himself, who spoke what is known as the Xiang dialect, was said to be unintelligible to most Chinese even when he spoke formally. And although this hitch is often tidily dealt with by claiming that the written word is the same everywhere, this is simply a myth. In addition to the aforementioned simplified-complex schism, Cantonese utilizes another 3,000 so-called specialized characters that other Chinese can't read. What's more, many of the so-called dialects don't possess a written component at all.

The reason Chinese people believe Mandarin will soon dominate the world is two-fold. In addition to the obvious cultural and linguistic bias (which we all possess), there is a more powerful element at work. In what certainly harkens back to pre-modern days, almost any myth or legend floating in the breeze has the potential to be latched onto and made gospel. Truly, urban legends, myths, and superstitions fly unfettered in Chinese society and are deeply, deeply ingrained. Asking if they are true, or more poignantly, what the truth is, simply isn't done. Critical thinking is no match for popularly-held sentiment.

There was a time here when my students would correct me whenever I referred to residents of Taiwan as Taiwanese. That was pejorative, they said. A university professor had publicly stated as much, adding that Asian countries were given the suffix "—ese" as a racist inside joke. I pointed out that we say "Cambodian" and "Korean," along with "Viennese" and "Portuguese," and that although the suffix could be disparaging in certain cases (i.e., New Yorkese), with nationalities it wasn't negative at all, but most remained unconvinced. One student even told me that a taxi driver in Washington, DC had informed him that "Taiwaner" was preferable to "Taiwanese," which would be perfectly acceptable if it were in fact a word. But as with the misinformed professor, someone said it, so it must be so; and if the taxi driver was older than my student that would lend the notion even more credibility. Besides, it was even on the Internet.

But getting back to Mandarin's potential as a *lingua franca*, Chinese people recently had their beliefs reinforced when the acronym BRIC came into vogue in reference to the burgeoning future markets of Brazil, Russia, India, and China. This created quite a stir in Taiwan. Suddenly, I had people telling me they wanted to major in Russian and Portuguese, and that, because of BRIC, Mandarin would soon be the big man on campus.

Deciding to put just what (and how) Chinese people think to the test, I put together a survey regarding Mandarin and its future role and asked 100 university students or university graduates (many of them English majors) for their thoughts.

Asked if Mandarin would one day become the new world language, 88% responded, "yes," with 75% claiming this would occur within the next 50 years. Of the 88%, nearly 59% believed that complex characters would become the international standard, effectively implying that the masses of China would have to relearn how to read and write. The next question was, "If simplified characters were to become the international standard, would Taiwan have to adopt this system in keeping with the standard?" More than 40% responded, "no." In choosing which spoken version of Mandarin would become dominant (Beijing or Taipei), 42% chose the Taipei accent with 35% claiming that they didn't understand the Beijing accent.

When asked whether they thought it possible for "Mandarin to become the official language of international organizations such as the European Union," a resounding 85% of the respondents claimed it was. No less astonishing, 59% of those who said Chinese would not become the new global language also indicated that they thought this was possible.

For the next question: "If Taiwan can be considered a country, how many countries presently employ Mandarin as an official language?" only 36 % ticked the correct answer of "3" (China, Taiwan, and Singapore). Sixteen percent chose "6" as the correct answer, and when I politely asked them what the six were, many would reply, "China, Taiwan, Singapore, Hong Kong..." and then stop, declaring that they "couldn't remember" the other two. As mentioned, people in Hong Kong, an hour and a half away by plane and the second most popular tourist destination for tourists from Taiwan, speak Cantonese. The territory ceased to be a country when it was handed back to China in 1997 and TV in Taiwan is chock-full of obviously dubbed programs and movies from the former British colony.

When asked why they thought Mandarin would become the new world order, 4% cited the influence of Chinese culture while 47% ticked "economics." The majority, 49%, chose "The fact that China has the world's largest population." The follow up question was, "By 2050, it is estimated that the population of India will surpass that of China. At that time, do you think it possible for Hindi or another Indian language to become the new global language?" Of those who attributed the rise of Mandarin to China's population, over 88% answered, "no."

In regard to why Japanese culture and language haven't had much impact internationally, despite being the world's number-two economy, 85% chose "English and Western culture are simply too powerful," over "Japanese is too difficult," "Japan is an Asian country," "They haven't exported enough cars," and "Western people don't like sushi," although two people chose the last one. It would be nice to think they were joking, but somehow I doubt it.

One hundred percent agreed that English was currently the international language of business, medicine, diplomacy, and tourism, and the majority correctly chose "at least 40" as the number of countries that currently employ English as an official language, perhaps suggesting that they're not totally unaware of what Mandarin would be up against, although given the other responses, they don't seem to appreciate the significance. The final question was, "Foreigners will find learning Chinese easy because: a.) The grammar is easier than English. b.) There is no grammar. c.) Chinese isn't easy at all." A full 12% chose "There is no grammar." It is one thing to be a little shaky on the rules of grammar, but it is striking to think that college students might be unaware they even have (and use) grammar.

As a bit of an aside, one thing I hadn't bargained for when administering the survey was the difficulty involved in getting respondents to complete it correctly. It was written in Chinese (I had it translated and typed); those surveyed were asked to tick the most suitable response, but many wrote in their own responses, some of which looked to be straight from another dimension. One person wrote down that Chinese would spread via foreign students in Taiwan. "They'll go back and teach people in their own country," she informed me, whereas another two girls attributed the failure of Japanese abroad to the fact that it originally comes from Chinese. What's more, many of the respondents failed to notice one or more pages of the questionnaire. I had to ask about a third of them to make adjustments.

But here's the statistic that I find the most impressive. Out of the 112 people asked to complete the survey (12 were invalidated due to mistakes or their insistence on adding their own answers), 110, or 98.2%, smilingly obliged. In North America, it would have taken weeks to do a project like this, but here it took only a few visits to Starbucks. It must be said again that Taiwanese (or Taiwaners, if you are a cabbie from Washington) are an infinitely cooperative and friendly bunch, which almost makes up for their belief that Mandarin spoken in the "Taipei dialect" will soon be the working language of the EU and the entire world.

Chapter 12. But that's Not Logical, Captain

Whenever my mother (bless her) receives a copy of my former university's alumni newsletter in the mail, she promptly sends me an e-mail, assuming something urgent is afoot. "I think you'd better contact them, pronto," she tells me. "It seems like they're looking for you." Apparently, one of the alumni folks even called once, inquiring after my whereabouts and employment status. Actually, I would gladly put my skepticism aside and inform them in detail of my present location and fiscal condition except that, for one, they'd probably injure themselves laughing, and for another, I have a vivid recollection of standing outside the campus bookstore in the cold and rain in a rather long queue in order to sell used textbooks back to the school for something like 0.0006% of the cover price. Granted, I could have kept them, but let's face it: the prospect of a week's worth of instant noodles is difficult for most students to pass up.

One textbook I did keep, though, was *Attacking Faulty Reasoning — A Practical Guide to Fallacy Free Arguments* by T. Edward Damer, which was required reading for a logic class taught by a classically eccentric professor who hailed from England. Thickset and with a mop of frizzy hair, the lecturer could often be seen trundling about the corridors in a white lab coat (he was a philosophy professor) and a pair of Ray Charles sunglasses, usually in possession of a mysterious Styrofoam cup. And during class, when not commenting on how moronically dull Canadians were, he would repeatedly refer to London as "the intellectual capital of the universe." But oddities aside, he was a charismatic individual with a keen intellect and razor sharp wit, and this considerably made up for the fact that he tended to deliver the bulk of his lectures to a cluster of trees situated just outside the classroom window.

The course's section on argumentative logic, which was complemented by the Damer text, essentially trained us to construct logically sound arguments, and, more importantly, to analyze and deconstruct unsound arguments, and I found this vastly engaging. It's also been tremendously practical, as I couldn't help but notice that even if you don't seek out conflict and argument, they tend to crop up.

With argumentative logic, the idea is to be able to identify your opponent's error and recall prescribed techniques on how to refute it, but I've found that directly telling them the name of the fallacy they are committing is usually enough to render them speechless, thereby allowing you to win by default. And it's even more impressive if you can invoke the error's Latin name.

Take someone who has, for example, just told you that his and his cohort's view on something is superior to yours because "two heads are better than one" and inform him in a deadpan tone that they are engaging in an argumentative fallacy known as "improper use of a cliché," which holds that no single aphorism can wholly constitute an effective argument, and that by extension their case fails to meet the "sufficient grounds criterion" of a valid argument, and 90% of the time, you'll have won without another word. Actually, that's a "fallacy of fake precision," utilizing mathematical precision or statistical evidence that is impossible to substantiate. And although I'm sure you spotted it, I'm guessing you probably couldn't have labeled it, not that you'd need to in order to refute it; my point is that when done correctly, it can work wonders in intimidating your opponent.

But despite a bookish, albeit casual, interest in formal logic, I have to admit that I'm no Aristotle. One summer, for example, here in Taipei, I twice shut down an ATM by inserting my bus card into it. Not very logical. Nevertheless, adhering to any system of reasoned thinking, formal or otherwise, can make living in Asia rather trying at times, and this is especially so in Chinese society. Indeed, if two of the shortest books in history are *Great Italian Military Victories* and *Who's Who in Finland*, then a third would certainly be *Chinese Logic*. Unlike Korean or Japanese, which both contain thousands of English loan words, many of which deal with modern inventions and imported ideas, Chinese only possesses a handful, one of which is *loji*, or logic, implying that until the arrival of the Europeans the concept simply didn't exist.

Next month, summer vacation will begin and I'll start to teach university students English classes that include a writing component. Teaching writing, even to advanced Chinese students of English, can be a real struggle and this has a lot to do with trying to impart a sense of structure and how to utilize the logic associated within that structure. For example, most students (and remember, I'm referring to adults here), when asked to state their position on a certain issue, almost always employ this kind of reasoning: "I think X is bad because I don't like X," or "I think X is good because I can benefit from X." A common substitute for this is: "X is good because my (grand)parents told me X is good." Occasionally, Confucius takes the place of parents or grandparents.

Once, I had a part-time job here marking essays for the country's pre-eminent overseas study preparatory institute, and in the thousands of papers I looked at, not one of the aspiring foreign students ever thought to support their position or concretize their claim with specific examples or statistical evidence. But never mind that. The overwhelming majority of them couldn't even treat the topic objectively. That, you see, is a foreign notion. As a point of reference for almost any subject, people in this part of the world use themselves and judge things based almost solely on how their feelings are impacted. Instead of saying, "I think..." they say, "I feel..." and rather than gesticulating "I'm thinking," or "I've got an idea," by pointing a finger upwards or toward the head, they touch their breast. Furthermore, if people cannot conjure an emotive response to whatever is being discussed, they invariably state they have no opinion, with the upshot being that they rarely possess an opinion on anything.

There's a joke about this. A reporter is standing in downtown Seoul asking people for their thoughts on the North Korean economy. "Excuse me," he asks. "What's your opinion of the food shortage in the North?" The first person he interviews is an American who responds, "What's a shortage?" The second is a North Korean refugee who answers, "What's food?" and the third is a Chinese man who replies, "What's an opinion?" Incidentally, the fourth person is a South Korean, and he answers with, "What's 'excuse me?'"

Looking at written work is like looking directly into the thought process and all too often what you see is baffling. And in concurrence with being extraordinarily subjective and wishy-washy, assignments are littered with direct translations from Chinese, and these give you an ample understanding of how ingrained this manner of thinking is. Consider this concluding remark: "After all, if you study hard you will definitely succeed." Pointing out that you can study as hard as you like only to slip in a puddle and break your neck, and that *ergo* this is not an acceptable line of reasoning, perplexes the students at first; however, after a while, most people eventually see why they shouldn't say things like this in English.

Interestingly, the presence of poor logic in Chinese culture could be said to have been officially sanctioned by one of China's most esteemed scholars, Lao

Tzu. In writing his *Tao Te Ching*, the ancient sage left an indelible mark on Chinese thought, and both Asians and Westerners alike have been trying to figure out what the heck he was talking about ever since. Partly political, partly moral, and partly what would nowadays be called a self-help book, the thin volume is, at its core, a mystical discourse on the ethereal Tao or "Way" and is considered to be one of the all-time top Chinese classics, right up there with *The Analects* of Confucius and Sun Tzu's *The Art of War*. It is also riddled with faulty logic. Take for example this passage on how to rule a nation.

> Banish wisdom, discard knowledge
> And the people will be benefited a hundredfold
> Banish human kindness, discard morality
> And the people will be dutiful and compassionate
> Banish skill, discard profit
> And thieves and robbers will disappear

Lao Tzu also makes the recurring claim that passiveness will always defeat aggression, and that, more or less, there is no point in attempting to better oneself. Inaction is preferable to action, he says, and you should just be content with your lot. After all, "He who has once known the contentment that comes simply through being content will never again be otherwise than contented."

Although I do think it might be a good idea for over a billion people and much of a continent to at least be aware of what logic is, I'm fully aware that it is neither necessary nor feasible to continually subscribe to logic, even within the bubble of academia. To paraphrase that great twentieth-century thinker, Spock, "Logic may be the beginning of understanding, but it isn't the end." Then again, Spock also said, "Captain, I'm endeavoring to construct a mnemonic circuit using stone knives and bearskins," so there you go. But truly, logic can only take us so far.

Enough of this. I've got a load of clothes in my Taiwanese washing machine and the thing's making a bunch of funny beeping sounds, no doubt indicating imminent meltdown. It's highly temperamental at the best of times, but I suppose, with the model name FUZZY LOGIC, I should have expected no less.

CHAPTER 13. THE HITCHHIKER'S GUIDE TO THE (CHINESE) MORMONS

One morning last spring, I was contentedly reading the paper over breakfast outside a café in Taipei when a man sat down next to me and asked if I'd be interested in purchasing a package of "health socks." "Three sets for $120," he pitched. "They possess *Chi.*" For $20 a sock I thought they should have possessed a complimentary pair of shoes, but I simply informed him that I knew what they were and that I wasn't interested. "Oh, you've heard about these before?" he asked, surprised. Indeed, I had. My neighbor had made a small fortune selling them online before her husband put a stop to it, saying that she was suddenly the chief bread winner (thus causing him to lose face) and that she had become too busy to prepare his dinner. Far from being made of some *Chi*-generating fabric, the product consists of nothing more than attractively packaged sets of Italian hosiery featuring exotic markings that many Chinese people can't decipher, i.e. the Roman alphabet. Only moments later, I was accosted once more, but this time it was by a pair of Mormons, an occurrence I took to be a kind of sign. After all, it's not every breakfast that two separate parties attempt to sell you the benefits of magical undergarments.

Hardly a day goes by where I don't see or run into a pair of young, handsome, lily white, and ultra confident "elders" of The Church of Jesus Christ of Latter-Day Saints, and to be completely candid, there are few things that bother me more. But, on this one occasion I actually heard them out. The two young men informed me that in 1823 in New York, a 14-year-old boy named Joseph Smith had a vision wherein an angel named Moroni told him to seek two gold plates buried in the ground nearby. He did, finding that they were covered in the hieroglyphics of Reformed Egyptian, the language of an ancient race that had made its way to America from Jerusalem. These ancients, they explained, were the forefathers of the American Indians. Joseph Smith then dutifully transcribed the plates into what became *The Book of Mormon*, a copy of which I subsequently asked for. This loopy little spiel, along with statements to the effect that black people had cursed skin, and that the holy underpants they wear had once saved a friend of theirs from an exploding hand grenade, made me wonder if the ever jubilant members of the LDS, or Latter-Day Saints, weren't in the habit of dropping LSD.

They also gave me a schedule of service times and a brochure entitled *For the Strength of Youth*, a kind of behavior guide filled with sentences like, "Dancing can be fun... however... when dancing, avoid full body contact with your partner," and "Satan may tempt you to rationalize that sexual intimacy before marriage is acceptable when two people are in love. That's not true." In fact, the booklet offers moral guidance on everything from how to speak to what type of lighting to provide at a get-together. An apparent appendage to it can be found on the Internet explaining just what to do in order to suppress inappropriate urges because, according to the LDS, sexual sin is second in severity only to murder. Supposedly, tying your hands to the bed posts, wearing oven mitts, or asking a friend to hold your hands until you fall asleep will do the trick if the prescribed cold shower doesn't.

I'd always assumed that the Mormons were simply an austere order of Christians, but research shows that they aren't Christians at all, although they portray themselves as such in order to fit into the mainstream and to land recruits who are then taxed (or "tithed" as they like to call it) at a considerable 10% of their income. At the crux of their belief system is the notion that human beings are the spirit offspring of a god named Elohim, or Heavenly Father, along with his wife, who is simply known as Heavenly Mother. This couple reside somewhere in the vicinity of the planet Kolob, where a single day lasts a thousand years, hence bringing a whole new meaning to the phrase, "What a long day." But, despite the fact we are all the children of Elohim, we may not have all been birthed by Heavenly Mother, and this is because Elohim is a polygamous god. Among the few to have ever known the identity of their true mother was Jesus Christ, who was begotten by Mary of Nazareth after Elohim traveled to Earth for a hasty marriage followed by sexual intercourse, never mind that Mary was his daughter in addition to already being wed to Joseph. According to the Mormons, Jesus would grow up to become a polygamist himself.

If you feel distraught by any of this, you may take comfort in the knowledge that a simple conversion is all that's required to put you on the path toward becoming a god yourself. One day you will join your celestial progenitors some-where near Kolob in order to engage in space sex (it's only a sin on Earth appar-ently) and create your own spirit children, who will then inhabit other worlds throughout the universe. Godhood then, is the driving force behind Mormon ideology. Millions of earthly spirits will ultimately worship them, but they have to prepare for their future role now because the end is near. Or "nigh," as they like to say.

Deciding to take up the elders' repeated invitations to attend an English lan-guage service, I visited their opulent (or as they describe it: "imposing") new temple in downtown Taipei, taking a seat at the back just as they were about to sing a hymn. "You want hymn book?" asked a local man who took the seat next to me. "We sing together?" "No thanks," I replied. "I can't read music," and looked up to notice that the owner of the voice was wearing a white sports jacket, an emerald green tie, pink pants, and pink and white sneakers. I had been wonder-ing what brand of locals the Mormons would attract, and I got my answer more or less immediately.

For the next hour and a half I sat through 10 so-called testimonials, which consisted almost entirely of members of the church speaking to the congregation about, well, nothing in particular really, after which they would close with vari-ous mantras attesting to how they knew they were "the most righteous people on Earth," and that "the Mormon Church was the only true church," and so on and so forth. Besides being very poor speakers, 7 of the 10 spent a considerable amount of time crying, and I'm not talking about tears of joy. It started with the first fellow, a Japanese American doing business in Taiwan. He had (brace yourself) gotten angry and yelled at a few tardy employees at a company meet-ing. How could he have done such a thing? Elohim, give him strength. Another man wordlessly wept and blubbered for more than two minutes after recollect-ing how his son had narrowly missed being crushed by a falling cabinet. For all the inane smiling and upbeat image projected by their missionaries, attending a service had all the gala of a mass funeral. What made the whole thing stranger still was that most people would start off talking about something normal, like a camping trip, or their family, but then would suddenly begin bawling and declar-ing Joseph Smith to be the prophet of God, or *Gad*, as they prefer to pronounce it.

The only speaker who actually possessed the ability to string words together to form coherent English sentences (despite all of them being native speakers) was an American woman who conveyed an anecdote about how she had run into an English woman in Taipei who suggested that the Mormons stop harassing Chinese people and go home. "But we don't harass anyone, do we?" she asked an audience that collectively murmured, "No." "But, we *do* have a mission," she continued. "The end is nigh and we have a responsibility to Gad to spread the message!" She followed up by adding that she was directing her "testimony" to the elementary school students present so that they might begin to tell their friends about the Earth's imminent destruction as soon as possible.

Next, I attended a class in another part of the building where I learned more about the impending apocalypse by way of a film entitled *The Ten Virgins*. In it, Jesus returned to a village where five virgins were prepared for his coming and five weren't. Those ready were taken back by Christ to whatever quadrant Kolob is in while the others remained on Earth to perish in fiery destruction. Although a six-year-old could have understood the point, the presenter, a Canadian woman, alternated between meticulous explanation and posing the most undemanding questions imaginable. Even so, a fair amount of those in attendance didn't seem to comprehend them. One question was, "How did the prepared virgins feel when Jesus arrived?" They were ecstatic, and, of course, she was looking for this or a similar word in the way of an adjective, but instead got responses like, "He has come!", "Joy!", and "Prepared!"

She then went on to inform us that the end was nigh and that only the righteous would be saved. The rest would be incinerated. The signs were all around us, she said, and cited the 2004 tsunami, which had occurred because "people are not listening to God." She instructed us that when we see similar tragedies, such as wars, diseases such as AIDS, and any and all natural disasters, we ought to rejoice as it means the scriptures are true. Besides, she declared, *all* of the major religions had stated that the tsunami was a sign of Judgment Day. Incidentally, the scenery in *The Ten Virgins* looked more like Jerusalem than I would expect Jackson County, Missouri to resemble. I mention this because, according to the Mormons, that is the place where Jesus will return.

Miraculously, if you will, I ran into the woman who presented the film in a sandwich shop a mere three days later. After introducing myself, I politely told her I thought her ideas were, well, interesting. However, when I asked her if she really believed that more than 150,000 lives had been snuffed out by an angry god, and that I ought to feel happy about this, she insisted that I'd misunderstood her. I assured her I hadn't and went on to ask her exactly which major religions had commented on the tsunami being a foreshadowing of Armageddon. Well, she couldn't name any, eventually admitting that she'd read a newspaper article where a high-ranking Muslim cleric claimed to see "the name of their god" in satellite images of the destruction. She thought this was intriguing. When I asked her what the name of their god was, she got nervous and said she had to go.

My curiosity was piqued and the following Sunday, I decided to go back for more. Wearing my Sunday best, I sat in one of the side pews so as not to attract too much attention. Two guest speakers were slated to talk, and the first was a retired psychologist who had a bone to pick with the congregation. One in ten people in the audience today had some sort of physical or mental disability, she said. "One in ten," she repeated emphatically, and urged everyone to have a good look around so that they might see what the faces of disabled people look like. "Go on," she said. "Do it." I craned my neck to the right to see that the entire assembly was staring straight ahead. This seemed to really upset her. "Discrimination within the church has been going on for too long," she pronounced, "and it has to stop." She went on to give example after example of people she'd known who'd been ignored or ostracized by church members for displaying signs of physical or mental deficiency. She seemed bitter, but at least she was talking about something real. However, she then went on to relay an anecdote about a man with schizophrenia who had been shunned by the Mormon community for acting — as she put it — "crazy." "And he would," she said. "He would act totally crazy. So, we said to him, 'Leon, you're acting crazy again. Leon... you're ... acting... crazy... again. You need to take your medication. You know you act crazy without your medication, Leon. Now, take your medication.' And you know what? With medical guidance from two of the elders, he was usually OK."

We broke for lunch, and a girl who had sat down next to me introduced herself and asked if it was my first time there. I replied that it was my second, whereupon she beamingly asked if I needed to speak to someone. I thought this was odd, as I was speaking to someone now. "Thanks, but I'm just here to listen," I told her, and then asked her if she'd ever heard of Kolob before. She said she hadn't. "Really?" I asked. "Do you mean you've never sung this hymn?" I inquired cordially, showing her a number from their green hymn book entitled "Hie ye to Kolob". "Oh, *that* Kolob," she responded rather uneasily, and added, "I'd better go find you someone to talk to." She left hurriedly, casting a nervous glance over her shoulder as she made her way down the aisle.

Next, it was off to find the classroom where the Judgment Day lady would be giving her lecture. However, in attempting to get there, several men tried to redirect me upstairs where we could have a "private chat." Obviously, word had gotten around about the sandwich shop conversation. I was impeccably polite, and told them that I appreciated the offer, but that I was just there to listen. As a last ditch effort, one man tried to physically obstruct me from entering the class, but with a smile and a, "Pardon me," I brushed past him. During the lecture, two women came in to ask me if I wouldn't feel more comfortable elsewhere, but I just smiled again and said I was fine. There was a big sign out front saying, "VISITORS WELCOME," after all.

Today's talk was on education and what we could do to continually improve ourselves academically. In a similar vein, the speaker wanted to know what living in Taiwan offered in terms of unique educational opportunities. As for the first question, most people agreed that we should read the Bible and the works of Joseph Smith. Regarding the second question, the majority was of the opinion that Taiwan was an ideal place to learn Chinese. The woman agreed, although she admitted that despite having lived in China and Taiwan for nearly eight years, she could hardly manage a word of it. "I guess I would learn," she said lethargically, "if I just had *any* desire to do so." Then, when someone suggested that people could take up calligraphy as a way of bettering themselves, she turned to write it up on the white board under "flower arranging" and "Chinese water color painting," but stopped abruptly, obviously unsure of how to spell it.

All fired up with inspiration from the class, I was thinking I'd leave early and go catch a movie when an affable middle-aged gentleman clapped me on the back and asked me if I'd like to accompany him to the next class, which was an all male affair. "The women usually go do their thing, and we do ours," he told me. "I guess you could say it gives us a little break from each other," he added with a wink. "Sure," I replied. "Why not?" He then introduced me to his young son-in-law whose name was Gary, but whom I mentally dubbed Günter as he looked like a poster child for the Hitler Youth movement. As we sat down and waited for things to get underway, I asked Günter if he could explain to me what Kolob was.

"Kolob? What's Kolob?" he replied.

"Well, I saw it mentioned in your hymn book. I think it's the place where Elohim is said to reside."

"Oh, right. *Kolob*," he said, fixing me with a look.

"So, what is Kolob?" I prodded.

"You know something?" he asked, in a bit of B-movie histrionics. "I really don't know."

"Is it a planet?"

"Could be. Could be. Let's just say it's a place; a place where many people live."

"Is this place in outer space?"

"Well, it might be *in* space, or I guess it could be *near* space," he told me, doing his best to sound sagaciously enigmatic.

"What are you fellas talkin' 'bout?" asked Günter's father-in-law.

"Oh, our friend here was just wondering what Kolob was. Apparently he's never read the Bible before," he said, and then gave me a vicious look. But I was undeterred.

"Kolob is in the Bible, is it? Where? Could you tell me? I've been looking for it but I can't seem to find it in there." This threw him.

"Uh, well, I'm not sure. I guess..."

"It's right here," the kindly father-in-law interjected, completely oblivious to the animosity that had been brewing between me and Aryan Boy. He then read us a passage from another Joseph Smith book entitled *The Pearl of Great Price*. Yes, Kolob was a planet. Yes, Elohim lives there. Yes, it is Heaven. "Thank you," I said, when he had finished. Günter shot me a fierce look, and then the class began.

"Today's class is on coffee, tea, and alcohol, and why we should abstain from them," declared the sharply-dressed speaker, knitting his brow and assuming a purposeful expression. "But don't worry. It won't be boring. We've got a video and a whole jar of homemade chocolate chip cookies that my wife made, and I'll be passing them around momentarily. Today's video is a story told by the current president and living prophet of our church, Gordon B. Hinckley. Now, as you probably know, Mr. Hinckley will actually be coming to Taiwan in two weeks time, and he will be speaking at this temple. And of course, we are delighted to have him here because it's the very first time an LDS president has ever come to this country."

"Actually, that's not true," said a grey-haired man sitting in front of me. "Spencer W. Kimball was here back in '74."

"Is that right?" the speaker stammered. "Oh, well, right. Uh, thanks. Well, anyway. Help yourselves to those cookies everybody and let's get this video started."

The video was a 30-minute yarn spun by the aging Mr. Hinckley about the four members of a Mormon relay team who had gotten complacent the night before a major race and decided to have a glass of wine each. They lost. Couldn't see that one coming, could you? This unbelievably dull allegory, which was narrated in excruciating detail ("And then Jim Ritter put on his track shoes. The laces were blue. They had been a gift from his grandmother Edna P. Ritter, who had been a nurse...") was followed by the usual round of comprehension questions for toddlers so that they all might answer in unison and feel like they were part of their very own little track team. "Was alcohol good or bad for us?", "Was God trying to tell those athletes something?", "Was he trying to tell *us* something?"

The speaker then brought up Chinese people's fondness for drinking tea. "You know how they are," he decried. "*Every time* you sit down with one of them, they try and offer you a cup of tea. I mean, they just don't *know* any better. But

Joseph Smith knew," he went on. "Even before scientists knew, he knew that tea and coffee were bad for us. He said there is something in them, some ingredient that temporarily lifts the spirit, but then leaves it to fall."

"It's the caffeine!" someone shouted. The speaker nodded and everyone followed suit, swiveling their heads around and murmuring in agreement.

"What about the caffeine in chocolate?" I asked. You could have heard a pin drop. "I mean, we're all sitting here and eating chocolate chip cookies. Those chocolate chips are filled with caffeine."

Well, you would have thought I'd asked if anyone were interested in joining the Church of Satan. The man was quite visibly spooked by my inquiry, emitting a gasp and taking a full step back. Regaining his composure, he claimed he wasn't aware that chocolate contained caffeine. And besides, he explained, they weren't chiding caffeine. They were just talking about the hazards of tea and coffee. Oh, and alcohol. That'll cause you to lose relay races. But then when Günter's father-in-law asked if it were acceptable to drink red wine (his cardiologist had recommended a single glass per day), the speaker said he should switch to grape juice. When the man pointed out that he had already asked his doctor if he could drink grape juice, and that his doctor had told him it had to be red wine, the speaker pulled a face and asked, "And why on Earth would a doctor order you to drink wine?"

"Apparently, it's got something in it," said the man. "I don't know what it's called. Something that's supposed to be good for you."

"Anti-oxidants," Günter and I chimed in unison, but the older man had never heard of them. Neither had the speaker. Class was dismissed and I said goodbye to the older gentleman and Günter, who gave me quite a shot on the arm as a sort of special farewell. But at least he only gave me a shot on the arm.

For a time, whenever missionaries would solicit me, I would use the opportunity ask them a few questions in order to better understand their mindset. But after a while, I began to feel guilty as it soon became apparent that they were not what you might call intellectual heavyweights. Once, for example, in attempting to explain why Christianity wasn't up to snuff with Mormonism, an "elder" said something to the effect that Christianity had been chosen arbitrarily by the "leader of Rome." When I asked him if he meant "emperor," he responded by saying that he didn't know his first name. During another conversation, I was asked to make a donation. "Where will my money go?" I inquired. I had read that virtually every penny stays within the church.

"Well, if you don't want to give cash, you could give us a quilt," one of the missionaries informed me.

"A quilt?" I asked.

"Yeah, we would send it to a place like Afghanistan, and then our people there would give it to a leopard."

And it's not just the difference between a wild cat and a person suffering from a chronic disease; these people don't appear to know much about the founder of their faith, either.

Joseph Smith was born into a large impoverished family in Vermont on Christmas in 1805. As a boy, he was known by his neighbors as an "indolent teller of tall tales" and as a young man he became an occultist, eventually getting involved in something called money-digging. Money-digging was a popular fad in early 19th century America whereby people would divine for buried treasure, much in the same way people divine for underground wells. To aid him in his divination, Smith used what is known in the trade as a seer stone, a kind of crystal ball that allowed him to see things under the earth. He eventually founded a money-digging company, bilking heaps of cash from naïve investors. In his subsequent capitalist venture, i.e. his church, he made up a story of a vision of an angle named Moroni and then wrote *The Book of Mormon*, borrowing heavily from Indian folklore, tenets of Free-Masonry, and The King James Bible, which he plagiarized liberally. The Egyptian plates he was supposedly transcribing from were said to have been written more than a thousand years before The King James Bible was published. Also, because Smith was only partially literate, the book he produced was rife with errors and had to be edited again and again before he finally proclaimed it to be "the most correct book ever written."

The tiny religious circle he founded moved southwest from New York picking up converts along they way. They were essentially sent packing from every state they entered (including the promised land of Missouri), ultimately deciding it would be best to head to the then faraway state of Utah, where they could exist as a counter to Christianity, monogamy, and the US government, which is precisely what they have been doing ever since. You see, another precept of Mormonism is that before the polygamous deity Jesus Christ arrives from outer space to collect the righteous and destroy the wicked, the United States government will crumble and the Mormon Church will step in and take its place. Yet, in spite of such seditious ideology, the Mormon Tabernacle Choir, who actually have an album entitled KOLOB, performed at the inauguration of George W. Bush, along with the inaugurations of five other presidents.

The Mormons also believe in post mortem baptisms and have reportedly baptized hundreds of millions into their sect this way, including many of the Jews who died during the Holocaust and other notables from Shakespeare to Napoleon. In 1993, various Nazis were also baptized, including Adolf Hitler and his mistress Eva Braun. The couple was even "married" to each other in a Mormon temple. On top of all of this, not to mention a lengthy and well-documented history of polygamy, incest, pedophilia, corruption, counterfeiting, intolerance, espionage, violence, and murder, the members of the LDS have long promoted racism, essentially espousing that white is right. The reason for this is that our color and terrestrial situation in general are dependant on how we behaved as pre-mortal spirits in space. The lighter we are, the better we were. Although the organization has taken steps to hinder open bigotry, it's still at the heart of their philosophy.

Mormonism is now a major world religion with over 10 million members and an estimated $30 billion in assets. Indeed, they take in over $6 billion annually and have over 60,000 full time missionaries working worldwide. At present, there are nearly 43,000 Taiwanese Mormons (50 new converts are made per month) along with 94 Mormon "churches" or centers located island wide. Admittedly (for Taiwan), these are not staggering numbers but it is a significant trend nonetheless, especially when you consider how far removed Mormonism is from traditional Chinese culture. Or, at least that's how it would first appear. Upon closer inspection, there are actually quite a few connections. Both the Mormon religion and Chinese society are based upon strict hierarchies that demand obedience and don't allow for questioning. Both entail a high degree of clannishness, neither seems to have any sense of irony or much use for logic, and each possesses what you might call a persecution complex. Undeniably, a number of interesting cultural themes come into play here, but chief among them has to be critical thinking, or rather, the almost total absence thereof.

People in this part of the world seem wholly preoccupied with, and cannot get beyond, appearances. Taking things at face value seems to constitute value. *Esse quam videri*, espoused the Romans; "To be, rather than to seem." Within Chinese culture, the exact opposite is often held in regard. This, along with the fact that education doesn't allow for critical analysis, equates to an extraordinary degree of cultural naïveté, but seeing as how naïveté itself is encouraged and commonly held in esteem, this shouldn't come as any great surprise.

This year, I taught a wonderful novel called *I Am the Cheese* to five classes of senior high school students. The book's protagonist is a teenaged boy who seems to have lost his memory and is being helped to regain it by a man who appears to be a psychiatrist. The reader quickly realizes, however, that something is seriously amiss, and it soon comes to light that the man's sole purpose is to intermittently rouse the boy from his drug induced stupor long enough to extract information from him for his own gain. No matter how much I hinted or drew their attention to things the "doctor" would say or do that indicated clearly that he wasn't a doctor and that his intentions weren't at all noble, nobody seemed willing or capable of scratching below the surface long enough to see it. Students in every class insisted he was a doctor, even after I expressly and emphatically informed them that he wasn't. More than a few had trouble processing this. After all, doctors are good, and in Chinese society they are all but idolized.

It's the same with the topic of mainland China. Despite that country's enormous military buildup, habitual saber rattling, and constant meddling in Taiwan's affairs, many people here don't seem to view it as a potential threat. Indeed, if you ask a Taiwanese person directly if China is a "friend or foe," the answer you are most likely to get is, "I don't know. I never really thought about it before."

And so, against the likes of the Mormons, people here don't stand a chance. The Mormons are well-groomed, well-mannered, and well-dressed, and, consequently, locals seem to enjoy stopping to chat with them. The Mormon temple in Taipei is now featured on a Taipei City Government video as an example of the city's architecture and a photo of two Mormons talking to a little girl currently graces a primary school textbook. Nobody is even remotely aware that they are a cultic group of latent white supremacists who wear magical underwear and hold that God is a polygamous space alien, and I seriously doubt it would cross anyone's minds to, say, do a bit of research before signing on with them. Like with the evil "doctor," an authority figure shall have to tell them. It's the only way.

Chapter 14. What's In a Name?

Walk into any major bank in Hong Kong, Shanghai, Singapore, Seoul, or virtually anywhere else in metropolitan East Asia, and chances are that there'll be a staff member on hand who can assist you in English. In Taipei, however, and in spite of an ambitious tendency to refer to itself as a burgeoning "international city," this usually isn't the case, which is sort of charming in its own right, but can also make you slightly nutty, depending largely on your disposition *du jour*.

Whenever I venture into my bank, the main branch of the second largest financial institute in the country, it's always the same. The tellers spot me coming in the door and then swiftly look away pretending that they didn't. Each seems to have their own strategy for ignoring me thereafter. Some start shuffling papers, others swivel around in their chair to talk to a person behind them, one or two slink off to the water cooler, and a few — and this is my favorite — put their heads down and become incredibly still, hoping perchance that I'll just sniff and paw them a little before moving on to a more alert looking individual.

When I say, "Hello" in Chinese, the frightened-looking teller usually heaves a sigh of relief and exclaims, "You speak Chinese!" In fact, not to toot my own horn, but my bank Chinese is second only to my Subway Sandwich Chinese, which is useful because even at the foreign exchange counter they don't speak much English, and it has frequently prevented my lunch from being mangled by some clumsy teenager.

Now, don't get me wrong. I'm not of the opinion that everyone should speak English. I'm not one of those language imperialists. In fact, the only people I expect to be somewhat competent in it in this country are doctors, customs officials, foreign affairs police, my own students, and staffers at foreign exchange counters. Also, let me make it clear that there are many good things about going to a bank here. You are sometimes served tea, there are people whose job it is to fill in forms for you, and they even provide eyeglasses for seniors who may have forgotten theirs. And I think that all of those things are wonderful. Moreover, things tend to move along pretty quickly. It must be said that Chinese people are not into making you wait.

However, having said this, just about anything involving official procedure here can be enough to cause you to tear your hair out. The Chinese fixation with bureaucracy is a constant source of bafflement for Western people and I've seldom encountered an expatriate who didn't have some kind of horror story to tell. Outside, all is chaos — people and vehicles move about in a manner reminiscent of sub-atomic particles — and yet civil servants and bank tellers insist that you dot all your i's, cross all your t's, fill things out in quadruplicate, hand over a pile of photos, and occasionally even provide a set of fingerprints. But even though they expect a great deal from you, you shouldn't make the mistake of expecting very much from them.

Not long after I arrived in Taiwan, I was at my bank remitting money when the clerk asked me to dictate my account number to her so she could write it in on the pertinent form. When I got to the number four, she suddenly stopped writing. I repeated, "Three, seven, two, four... four... *four*...." But she just froze. She didn't know the word "four." Again, I don't expect people to be fluent, but I do expect them to know single digit numbers, especially when they work at the foreign exchange counter of the largest branch of the second largest bank located in the capital of a wealthy East Asian country. Call me picky. But let's forget about simple numerals for a moment.

Just in front of my apartment building is a bank where I sometimes go to in order to pay my rent. Once, when the teller asked for ID, I handed her my resident card, only for her to examine it at length and then ask me what it was. "It's a refrigerator," I responded flatly, but she just looked at me blankly. Ironic humor hasn't caught on here yet. "Actually, it's an alien resident card," I clarified in Chinese, and pointed to the bold font title at the top of the card, which says, in Chinese, "Alien Resident Card." However, that didn't seem to help matters much, and she went off to ask her coworkers if they knew what it was.

These incidents seem all the more peculiar, considering that would-be bank tellers in this country have to take a grueling test with fierce competition and a pass rate of less than one percent. The candidate must be familiar with a broad range of topics, usually including a bit on Confucianism and perhaps a little Tang Dynasty poetry thrown in for good measure. Chinese people, in the Confucian tradition, have tests for nearly everything. The government here, at one point, was even considering having tests for marriage in an attempt to deflate the embarrassingly high national divorce rate of nearly 40%. I knew a girl here, who, after finishing her law degree, wrote a test to become a federal judge. She was 24 at the time. My girlfriend's sister, who did her masters in education, had to write a test to determine which high school she would be assigned to (the higher the mark, the better the school) and one of the questions she had to answer was, "In the movie *The Lord of the Rings*, what was Frodo Baggins's uncle's name?"

Interestingly, a common problem for Westerners in this part of the world is finding a staffer at a bank or government office who can understand your name. In Chinese, the family name comes first, so that Li Xiaolong's given name is Xiaolong and his "last" name Li (Li Xiaolong is Bruce Lee's Chinese name). This, along with the fact that Western people's names are transliterated into Chinese, so that Brad Pitt is rendered phonetically as *Baladu Pitu*, with each of the five syllables being assigned a character, keeps people almost totally unfamiliar with any names other than Chinese ones. Granted, it certainly isn't imperative for everyone to understand how foreigners' names are formed, but this does cause problems when those foreigners are your customers.

In the Republic of China, the key piece of identification when doing banking is your bank book, and for years the name that appeared on mine was TRO, or the first three letters of Troy. This, as you may already have guessed, is because Chinese names almost always consist of three characters, hence their computer could only spit out three letters. If the name on your bank book doesn't match up exactly with the name on other ID, or, say, your traveler's cheques, then sorry, but it's out of their hands. Luckily, after going to my bank for such a long time, I can usually find an employee who recognizes and can vouch for me, so this little breach of regulations is overlooked. One time, though, a woman refused to help me because my signature didn't look *exactly* like the one on my identity card. In order to help debunk the mystery of non-Chinese names, I took out a piece of paper and signed my name five or six times, after which I asked her if they all looked precisely the same. She admitted that they didn't, but this only seemed to confirm her suspicion that I wasn't who I claimed to be. Again, one of the other clerks acted as guarantor, but the doubting woman warned me that next time, my signatures had better be identical.

The mystification over signatures is largely attributable to the fact that, to this day, Chinese people all carry name chops, which they use to stamp or "sign" documents. Not to say that using signatures is a more valid method, because one is just as arbitrary as the other, but you have to admit that chops are just a tad antiquated if not totally out of step with the rest of the world. And those are just the name chops. Like tests, there are stamps and chops for everything. Remit money, and your receipt will have more blue and red smears than a War of 1812 battlefield. (I have here in front of me a two-page medical checkup with no fewer than 17 different stamps on it.) The ink gets all over the place and clerks wear arm protectors all day. Sometimes, after watching a clerk hand roll the inky date counters on a series of stamps and chop away (and boy, do they chop), I'll impart to them, "You know, we used to use those things more than a hundred years ago." The reply is invariably a surprised, "Really? And what do you use now?" "Nothing," I answer, but it never seems to sink in.

Another facet of doing banking in the "international city" of Taipei (Move over Hong Kong!) is the part where bank tellers ask you if you have a Chinese name. I've been asked this question literally dozens of times. They just don't seem to realize that even if I did have a Chinese name, it wouldn't be legally binding, nor would it be printed on any identification.

Last year, after getting a tax refund in the form of a cheque, I decided to deposit it in another branch of my bank just down the street from the tax office. Both buildings — the bank and the tax bureau — are located on "Old Street," a commercial artery adjacent to the point where Taipei's Danshui River meets the sea. The clerk wouldn't let me do it, though, citing that the name on the cheque wasn't TRO. That was OK, I told her. I had all kinds of ID, and proceeded to take out my bank card, my credit card, my passport, and two local identity cards. "Sorry," she said. That wasn't good enough. Then she wanted to know why all the names on my identification were different. I explained that they weren't different, as such, but rather just in different orders. Sometimes it was first, middle, and last name, and other times it was the last name, comma, first name, middle name. Occasionally, the middle name was omitted or replaced by an initial. I even took off my school ring which has my signature engraved on the inside, and she and two other clerks scrutinized it for nearly half a minute before solemnly informing me there was nothing they could do.

Unimpressed, I pointed out that it was a government cheque from the tax bureau located right down the street, and that it would have to be cleared before being deposited. I added that I could access my bank account with their bank card, meaning that either it was mine, or I had stolen it, and if I had stolen it, I was either very stupid or very brave to be standing there and talking to them with the surveillance cameras rolling. I wrapped up my little speech by informing them that if anyone was at fault, it was them for not issuing me a bank book with my full name on it. I even illustrated how there wasn't enough space for a non-Chinese name, but alas, my arguments fell on deaf ears. Then, quite irritated, I asked them to call the branch that had issued me the bank book.

"OK," they said, "And which one is that?"

"The one on Guanqian Road," I replied.

"What number on Guanqian Road?" they wanted to know.

"I don't know the address," I responded.

"What's the branch number then?" the wanted to know.

I searched through my bank book in vain. "Wait a minute," I said. "Why do you need to know the branch number?"

"So we can find their telephone phone number," came the response. This was too much, and my face suddenly took on the hue of a Chinese lantern.

"Look. *You* should know the branch number, *and* the phone number, *and* the address, because it's the *main branch of this bank*! It's right down town. In the middle of the banking district across from the Taipei Main Railway Station. You know? In the center of *your* city? An enormous brown building on Guanqian Road? Do you even know where Guanqian Road is? Huh? Do you? Is any of this getting through?" But it wasn't, and I had to make the 12 kilometer trek by subway and deposit my cheque there. When I asked the teller there how I could find out a bank's branch number, she politely informed me that it was in the dead center of the front of my bank book. "It's right here," she said, pointing. "But because this is the main branch, it just says, 'Business Branch.'" So it did. I hadn't noticed.

But before I made the journey downtown, I let the staff at the other branch know what I thought about their service, and just to bring home to them how ridiculous they were being, I resorted to doing something extremely cruel: I asked them to tell me what my name was.

Laying out the pile of ID on the counter, with my passport in the middle, I said, "OK, I'll leave, but before I do, I want you to tell me the person's name on these pieces of identification. If I am not who I say I am, then at least tell me who I am not." But they couldn't do it. There were three of them, and none of them could read English phonetically, let alone point out which was my surname and which was my first name, despite the fact that it tells you which name is which on any passport.

But perhaps I was asking too much. Figuring out names, numbers, words in their native language, and how to get in contact with their own main branch were far beyond the scope of these people's capabilities. Maybe the next time I should just ask them to recite me a Tang poem. At least that could calm down an upset customer a little, and maybe, if I were lucky, they would read me this one.

> With money I save you from knife,
> I know yourself too love your life!
> Please live freely, live in the river,
> Don't seek the great sea to arrive!

CHAPTER 15. PUTTING THE STAIN IN SUSTAINABILITY

I live in a tiny little community just north of Taipei called Zhuwei, which is pronounced *Jooway*, and which would translate to something like "Bamboo Encirclement" in English. As neighborhoods go in Taiwan, it's not a bad one, being comprised of an assortment of modern high rises set amidst a dissonant array of older, squat, concrete houses. This architectural hodgepodge clusters around the local metro station and extends back for a kilometer or so into patch of dark green rolling hills. I live in one of the high rises and my apartment offers a rather arresting view of a river with a serrated, temple adorned mountain as a backdrop.

A couple of weeks ago, the mountain, which is more than the 600 meters tall, did something magical: it disappeared. No, David Copperfield wasn't in town, nor was it reduced to a heap of boulders by an earthquake or a handful of the 800 odd *To Taiwan with Love* missiles that China has pointed at this place. It was, rather, cloaked in that great veil of modernity and progress better known as smog. Although bad air can occur in almost any urban environment, I find this more than just a trifle unsettling as the mountain I'm referring to isn't much more than a kilometer away.

This happens every spring in Taiwan, which commences more or less in April. God, or Buddha in these parts, pulls his giant celestial lever and I put the heater away and turn on the fan. In a month, I'll turn on the air conditioner and will keep it running pretty much nonstop until November when things start to become bearable again. You'd think that an island in the Pacific Ocean would be breezy, but in Taiwan it's incredible how still and sultry the air can get. Humidity is often in the nineties and when combined with all the exhaust, the air can be absolutely horrid, causing me to ask myself just why it is I live here. In terms of air pollution, the country's only saving grace lies in its modest dimensions. After a few days of stagnant, foul air, the wind picks up, or it rains, and most of the crap gets blown away.

Taiwan, you see, is an environmental disaster. Looking at a satellite photo of the island-nation, it resembles a leaf floating on water. However, there's something very wrong with this leaf. Nearly half of it is grey. To be certain, it looks as though someone has taken a giant cement mixer and paved over half of an island. Fortuitously, the other half is comprised of formidable and largely uninhabitable hills and mountains. If this weren't the case, there probably wouldn't be a scrap of vegetation left anywhere, barring, perhaps, for the fisticuff prone plant life occupying most of the seats in the national government. Much of the problem has to do with the sheer volume of people who live here. There are nearly 23 million people in this tiny country, making for a population density of 632 per square kilometer, second only to Bangladesh. The other major problem is the casual attitude that the government, and people on the whole, take toward pollution and general waste.

For starters, Chinese people love elaborate packaging. An ideal product should have parts wrapped up individually, be placed inside a large, intricately designed, and ultimately unnecessary box, and then be put into one, if not two, plastic or paper bags. Go into a bakery here, and you will see people buying perhaps ten items and having each of them wrapped individually even if they are identical. When you tell the clerk that you don't need a bag for, say, a doughnut, they look at you as if you have three heads. "And where are you going to put it?" they ask. "In my mouth," I always reply, but this usually goes over like the proverbial lead balloon. The same thing happens when you tell them they can put more than one item into a single bag. "But this is bread, and that is a croissant," they inform you, as if you are unaware of what you purchased. I still don't know how to say, "Well, it's not like I'm asking you to put mustard on ice cream, now, is it?" in Mandarin with the desired effect, so I just respond with something like, "Oh, that's alright," and then try to pick up whatever they whisper to each other after I've turned to leave. And after an item's gone into a cellophane bag, out comes the colored plastic one with the store logo and handle. If you declare that the cellophane bag is fine, they say, "But this one's got a handle. It's more convenient." And again, if you say you don't need a bag at all, they'll often reply, "OK, you don't need a bag," and then mechanically proceed to put your purchase into the cellophane bag, because apparently it doesn't constitute a bag. Or they'll interpret your statement to mean that you would prefer to have the item put into a plastic box. These are a people who are plainly on a mission to package your cookie. Where I come from you usually have to bag things for yourself. Here, you have to plead with them to stop.

Finally realizing that people were overusing plastic bags, the government claimed they would ban them, but only ended up introducing a sturdier recy-clable one that stores charged a paltry three cents for. Consumers were asked to reuse them, but this didn't take. The program was abandoned after three years because it was discovered that it actually caused more waste owing to the fact that the recyclable bags were significantly thicker than the originals. Now, things are back to the way they were, except that some stores charge three cents for the non-recyclable bag. Taiwan's government also initiated a national recycling pro-gram (which it called a "garbage revolution"), although I seriously wonder if it works given that on several occasions, I've seen janitorial staff in Taipei's metro system mixing recyclable stuff in with regular waste. But what's more telling is that six months after the country kicked off its revolution, it was discovered that none of the waste was actually being sorted at the processing plants. Then again, consumer waste is just the tip of the trash heap.

Taiwan may be little more than a speck on the map, but it ranks as number one in a number of areas. It currently has the tallest building in the world, its Jade Mountain is the highest in North East Asia, it produces more laptops, moni-tors, scanners, and cell phones than anywhere else, people work longer hours than even in Japan (an average of 72 per week), and it's peerless in that it's the only nation on Earth not to even be considered a nation, and that takes some doing. But not wanting to hog the international spotlight in holding top spot for everything, Taiwan can finally claim to be at the bottom of one world ranking, and here I am referring to the recent global survey on environmental sustainabil-ity compiled by Yale University, where Taiwan came in dead last. Well, actually, second from last. The only country rated lower was North "Bury Yer Nuclear Waste Fer Cheap Here" Korea. Coming in 145 out of 146, Taiwan ranked lower than such countries as Iraq (currently at war) and found itself 11 places behind China, a country that boasts having 16 of the world's 20 most polluted cities and recently admitted that 10% of its arable land was completely poisoned.

Taiwan's Ministry of the Environment wasted little time in dealing with the survey, promptly dismissing it as "unfair and biased" and therefore inaccurate, which is, it must be said again, a major recurring theme in Chinese society: a denial of responsibility or wrongdoing even when presented with proof, or in this case statistical evidence from an impartial and highly regarded source. It's always everyone else's fault except for who's actually to blame. There's little regard for the truth. A more recent (and locally conducted) study found that between 1990 and 2004, Taiwan actually doubled its output of carbon dioxide emissions, hence giving it its second "world's worst record." Globally, Taiwan is ranked 22 in terms of C02 output, contributing roughly 1% of the annual world total. Rather than deny the findings this time, the government reacted by doing nothing at all.

But the results of these two reports shouldn't come as a bombshell to anyone who has visited this country. Walk down a main street in Taipei, and you may feel as if you are breathing in iron filings as an endless stream of cars, motor scooters, and buses zips by, while at night, the city does its best impression of a scene from the film *Blade Runner*. It's estimated that Taiwan has a whopping 300 cars per square kilometer, making for a number more than 15 times higher than in the US. Add another 10 million motor scooters, shake well, and it's not difficult to fathom why the place is almost perpetually enveloped in some sort of haze.

And then, of course, there is the matter of soil pollution. Outside major cities and towns, agriculture and industry casually coexist in an arrangement which is nothing short of detrimental. The water situation is also in a bad way. The reservoir that provides Taipei with its drinking water actually runs motorboat tours. Furthermore, rivers here are little more than toilets for factories and residences. I have never seen one that didn't resembles a cesspool, yet incredibly, I once saw an English tourist magazine running a feature called *Rivers of Taipei*. These are places that you want to clean up, and, in the meantime, hide. Showcasing them to people from countries like New Zealand or Canada just isn't a good idea and it made me wonder if people realize how bad they are.

The mayor of Taipei realized how bad they are, though, and ordered that they be cleaned up. Six months later, he took a boat ride on the river I live next to in order to see whether things had improved or not. He did this in the very scientific manner of dipping a cup into the river, taking a whiff, and then declaring, "It smells much better than it used to!" while giving the cameras a big smile and an exuberant thumbs up. Just then someone spotted a corpse floating by. Apparently, they find about 10 of these a year in the river. And here, I'd always thought it was just driftwood. A couple of years ago, a sewage treatment plant near the mouth of the same river, which I can see from my window, lost something to the tune of one million tons of raw sewage when one of its pipes was struck by lightning. For days, the town I live in smelled like a latrine until the river managed to flush everything out to sea, thus making it the fishes' business. Incidentally, Taipei's latest motto, in both English and Chinese, is "Taipei — Healthy City."

One of the most beautiful places I have seen in Taiwan is the very southern most tip of the island. A picturesque lighthouse greets you as you enter a maze of footpaths walled in by opaque tropical foliage and leading to a roughly hewn shoreline of volcanic rock. It's best visited in the early evening when you can sit and watch a sky streaked in ginger fade over the silvery Pacific. I was quite taken with the place, but shortly after I visited it a Greek freighter broke up just a kilometer off the coast, dumping hundreds of tons of oil into the water. Despite the fact that it's a conservation area and constitutes part of a national park, the minister of the environment didn't consider it to be a serious problem and promptly left the country for a vacation. Meanwhile, the government decided it would be best to deal with the dilemma in the traditional manner of vigorously demanding money from the ship's owner instead of mounting a clean up response, which wasn't begun for days.

To counter its own reliance on oil from the Persian Gulf, Taiwan has gone nuclear, with four plants accounting for half of the nation's energy needs. Two of these are located within 20 kilometers of Taipei on the edge of a semi-active volcano, and in an area of active geological faults, and this in a country where earthquakes and typhoons are routine. One plant is new but the three older ones have all had more than one serious accident. I read an estimate claiming that if there were ever a Chernobyl-like incident here, as many as seven million people could die and attempts to evacuate would result in little more than pandemonium.

In 1980, Taiwan's Atomic Energy Commission began the construction of a nuclear waste disposal facility on a tiny volcanic island off the southeast coast of Taiwan. A local administrator signed off on the deal, thinking he was agreeing to the construction of a fish cannery. Like the rest of the island's inhabitants, the man was an aboriginal and illiterate. Currently, there are nearly 100,000 barrels of nuclear waste on the island, something local residents remained in the dark about for nearly a decade. Partly owing to the fact that the storage trenches were poorly constructed, the contaminant has begun seeping into the ground. The government has been promising to remove the facility since 1996, but hasn't even outlined how or when this will actually occur. The plant itself, which is only about 50 meters from the Pacific Ocean, denies there is any problem.

However, when it comes to the environment and waste management, Taiwanese people may take some comfort in knowing that their garbage collectors are amongst the world's most qualified. The Taipei City Government requires that candidates for the job pass both a written and physical test. A few years back, the physical component saw 6,000 people vying for just 150 positions. It entailed a 90-meter dash which the runners had to undertake while carrying sandbags on their backs. A sort of Garbage Olympics, if you will. In addition, garbage collectors are also English-speaking, or at least in the city of Tainan, where sanitation trucks have been outfitted with speakers that blare out simple English lessons.

Also, it should be mentioned that not all people in Taiwan have an inherent disregard for their ecosystem. Take for example the recent efforts of an elementary school teacher, who, after discovering a natural spring on the grounds of her school, decided to take action. Deeming it a superb educational opportunity, the educator helped turn the wetland area into an ecological park replete with fish, frogs, butterflies, and egrets. She even constructed a pavilion featuring solar-powered lamps. As a reward for her efforts, her school was awarded a hefty quarter of a million dollars from the Ministry of Education to expand the park. But unfortunately, it was discovered that the spring was nothing more than a leaky water pipe that had lost an estimated 45,000 tons of water.

As a matter of fact, there *are* grassroots environmental organizations in this country, but they are poorly funded and therefore no match for the government. Taiwan's biggest polluters are (and always have been) state owned enterprises, and interference in even cottage industries is almost unheard of due to fear of lost revenue. One of the biggest concerns regarding the introduction of the recyclable bags was that producers of the regular bags would suffer. Authorities don't even regulate pesticide spraying here. And so, with no one to keep it in check, Taiwan's government remains solely responsible for taking concrete measures toward bettering the situation. And this is what has me so worried.

CHAPTER 16. FROM BANGKOK TO ANGKOR

To my knowledge, no one has ever written anything that could be called a modern-day travel narrative about Taiwan, and so I toyed with the idea of doing one myself before concluding in the end that it would be too depressing. Sure, when it comes to scenic spots and places of interest, there are a few diamonds in the rough, but mostly it's just rough. This is a country whose tourist slogan is "Taiwan Touch Your Heart" (the tourism bureau has denied it is incorrect English) and where tourism photos are either airbrushed until they resemble holograms or are taken from a helicopter. I figure it's just a matter of time before they start taking them with the Hubble Space Telescope.

It was in this frame of mind that I decided to go elsewhere in Asia for my vacation, eventually hitting on the notion of spending a couple of months exploring Thailand, Cambodia, and Nepal.

Thailand, quite simply, is a superb place for a holiday and the reasons for this are many. The beaches are lovely, the scenery is stunning, the food is incredible, it's moderately priced, getting around is a breeze, and the people are laid back to the point of being just about horizontal. It's little wonder, then, that the nation sees over seven million tourists annually. While there, I visited the ancient ruins of Ayuthaya, took in a kick boxing match in Bangkok, had a gander at the Grand Palace, and did the national circuit of beaches. As for details of my three-week adventure, I have very little to report. You see, as ideal as Thailand is for traveling and unwinding, it is decidedly less so for travel writing. It all seems to go so smoothly.

The only thing even remotely noteworthy occurred on the way back to Bangkok after having explored the southern portion of the country. After boarding a bus and settling in, a white-haired man with square face and a jaunty mustache struck up a conversation with me about music from the sixties and seventies. Essentially, he was an aging hippy from the Netherlands, who spoke halting English in a peculiar kind of half Dutch, half Jamaican accent. He told me he'd been living in Thailand for over a decade. He was a kindly fellow, although an alcoholic, or so I inferred after we stopped for lunch and he drank his. Back on the bus, and verbally ablaze from the local fire water, we somehow switched from speculating on which Beatle had had the best solo career to discussing politics. This was a very bad idea as he clearly had some rather serious grievances with the local government.

"I am living now in zis run down public housing complex in Bangkok, man," he complained loudly. "Und it is really za pits! Und you vant to know vhy it is zo run down? I tell you vhy. Za king! *It iz alvays za god damned king!* Ee should be shot, man! Zen, vee av no more problems, man!"

In the midst of this very vocal diatribe, I suddenly recalled the "Dos and Don'ts" section of my travel guide where it said something like, "Almost anything goes in Thailand as long as you don't poke fun at the Buddha, spill beer on a monk, or say bad things about the king. The Thais hold their monarchy in even higher esteem than their religion and disparaging the king is no-no number one. That shouldn't be too hard to remember now, should it?" I didn't think so, but apparently my guide book hadn't been translated into Dutch yet. Thai people don't speak don't speak much English, but I think they may have caught a couple of key words because several of them were turned around and coolly assessing my interlocutor. I decided to deal with the situation in the same manner I deal with many of life's problems. I took a nap.

Luckily, nothing came of this, but foreigners are not above being prosecuted for slighting the monarchy in Thailand. In fact, in 2007, a Swiss man was given a 10-year jail sentence for doing just that. Luckily for him, he was quickly pardoned by the king and only deported. Interestingly, the Swiss fellow had also lived in Thailand for a decade and had committed his crime, which involved spraying paint over pictures of the sovereign, after being denied alcohol. It was the monarch's 79th birthday, and so the sale of liquor was prohibited.

The next morning, I was on a flight to the rural town of Siem Reap in northwestern Cambodia to see the famous ruins of Angkor. On the plane, I kept thinking about how odd it was that I would soon be in Cambodia. This largely had to do with an experience I had in grade eight, the year a large contingent of Southeast Asian boat people ended up in eastern Canada, with most of them somehow finding their way into my homeroom class. The majority was Vietnamese, but there was one fellow from Cambodia whose name was David Sok. The school's 850 students acknowledged David's flight to freedom by dubbing him Dirty Sock and treating him with general disdain. I didn't mind him, though, and once, when I asked him about Cambodia, he conveyed that he was escaping civil unrest and pulled up his pant leg to reveal a rather nasty bullet wound. Coincidentally, just a few weeks later, I saw the deeply emotive film *The Killing Fields*. As early as junior high school, I had scratched Cambodia off my "places to visit" list.

From Siem Reap's airport, a rudimentary affair set amidst brilliant green rice paddies, I was escorted by motorbike to a family run guest house that a friend of mine had recommended. Sure enough, it was nice and clean and the owners were cheerful, accommodating, and English speaking. They suggested I spend the afternoon taking in some of the local sights seeing as how I'd arrived too late in the day to start the tour of Angkor. Due to security reasons, it was not permitted to drive around Siem Reap without a guide, so after arranging for a motorcycle driver for the next few days, I headed off to see what else the town had to offer besides thousand year old ruins.

"Hello. My name's Khra," said my driver in a vowel heavy, nasalized Khmer accent. "My father was killed by Pol Pot."

"My name's Troy," I responded awkwardly. I had no idea what I should say.

In light of the country's history, it's not all that surprising that a communist regime ended up running the show in Cambodia, but no one could have predicted what would follow after they came into power. After finally achieving independence from their French overlords in 1953, ending nearly a century of colonial oppression, the Cambodians wasted little time in establishing an autocracy (or rather: monocracy) that they could call their very own. Manifesting itself in a shady individual by the name of Norodom Sihanouk, who was backed as the nation's rightful leader in Geneva in 1954, this government was overthrown and replaced by an ironfisted military regime in 1970, which in turn was toppled by Pol Pot and the Khmer Rouge five years later. Then things got really bad. Subscribing to a an ultra radical form of Maoist socialism, the Khmer Rouge announced an end to traditional civilization and ominously proclaimed it to be "Year Zero," to mark the inauguration of a self-sustaining agrarian utopia. Having effectively proclaimed the nation to be a giant farm, they then instituted a massive cull. City dwellers were rounded up and forced to relocate to the countryside *en masse*, and an earnest campaign was undertaken to rid the nation of pre-Revolutionary elements, which, translated, equated to things like money, schools, and religion. Next, the peasants were to be "reformed" and this meant that virtually the entire educated class simply had to go. Doctors, teachers, students, artists, and even people who wore glasses were branded as parasites and summarily put to death in what came to be known as the killing fields. It's now estimated that as many as 1.7 million people, or something like one out of every five, perished at the hands of Pol Pot's murderous regime, and most of the perpetrators have never been brought to justice. At the risk of sounding heartless, there is now a strategy in place to remind tourists of this horrendous tragedy as often as possible in order to evoke sympathy and donations. And donations were what this day's trip was all about.

The first stop on my afternoon tour was a landmine museum, which, in actuality, was a corrugated iron hut filled with every size and shape of mine conceivable. There were also a good number of "Danger Mines!" signs and some pretty horrific photographs on display. And then there was the literature. I learned that there is anywhere between 6 and 10 million anti-personnel mines in Cambodia, or approximately one for every man, woman and child. Additionally, there are an estimated 500,000 tons of UXOs, or "unexploded ordinance," left as a sort of parting gift from Uncle Sam as a result of the Vietnam War. (Cambodia is, by some estimates, the most bombed country in history.) Each and every month, up to 300 people chance upon a mine or UXO, and around half of them survive — with amputations. Even more disheartening is the projection that it will take up to two centuries to remove them all, although the Cambodia Mine Action Center, a local organization largely dependent on foreign funding, is doing its utmost to step things up.

The mine museum was run by a soft spoken gentleman who had been a child-soldier for the Khmer Rouge and whose job it was to help lay the mines. In the early 1990s, he assisted the UN on one of its mine clearing expeditions, and in 1999, he opened his museum despite pressure and threats from the government, which claimed it would be bad for tourism. Entry to the museum was free but you were expected to make a donation, so I did and then bought a T-shirt.

Next, it was on to an orphanage sponsored by a French organization, where I bought some postcards and pencils made by the kids. Then, we visited a killing field, despite my protestations to my driver that I didn't want to go. He insisted, however, saying it was only a small one. Most people are doubtlessly familiar with the images of stacks of grinning skulls, the schools turned into "courts" and torture chambers, and the chilling mug shots of the victims that the Khmer Rouge snapped just before doing away with them. I'd once seen a documentary on the era that had caused my eyes to water and my stomach to turn, and what with it being a beautiful day on a what was supposed to be a vacation, I wasn't sure if I was up to experiencing it firsthand or not. Yet, surprisingly, I wasn't all that affected. We parked the bike in a dirt parking lot surrounded by bushes and grassy fields, and I made my way up the steps of a shabby shrine and peered through a dusty pane of glass to find a tumbling pile of brownish skulls and a few bones. I took a picture, put a couple of bills in a box, and went back to the bike. Then, it was off to the zoo.

Asian zoos are customarily sorry affairs, and in a country as poor as Cambodia, this one was certainly no exception. Still, it would have been agreeable enough (if that is the right word), if it weren't for the personal tour I got from the zookeeper, over my protestations that I'd be just fine ambling around on my own. Although a friendly fellow, I simply had no idea what he was saying. In showing me the crocodiles, he declared, for example, that, "Al Gates is a man," which I eventually realized was meant to be, "(An) alligator (can) eat a man."

This went on for a half an hour or more. He would make some sounds and I would smile and feign comprehension. Things I learned included, "Tease a parrot, have sex galore," (These parrots have six colors.) and "Dizzy Pat is not eternal," which I'm assuming was "These bats are nocturnal." And those were the ones I could actually make out. Usually, it was something like, "Monkey imda wild is banana as such is monkey do." The last exhibit on the tour, right next to the outsized bird cages, turned out to be the man's home, which he introduced to me by saying, "And diesel is mouse." At this juncture, he imparted how meager his salary was and then began begging piteously for a few dollars. It was understood all along that he'd want a tip, so the histrionics were all the more unwelcome.

The next day, I arose early and bought a pass to Angkor Wat, or, more precisely, Angkor. Angkor Wat is the principal and most impressive of the nearly 1000 temples that constitute the ruins of Angkor. The word "wat" is simply Khmer for "temple." On the way, my driver informed me in excruciating detail about what a hard life he had had. In fact, he launched into a similar song and dance whenever any Westerner came within earshot. If a foreign tourist made the mistake of getting too close, my driver would walk right up to them and announce, "Hello. My name is Khra. My father was killed by Pol Pot." He was also extremely condescending. When I saw a banana tree and casually remarked how it was the first time I'd ever seen one, he started mocking me. "You no know banana tlee? Oh, I sink you only know city — *bas* and *ka*. You no know tlee. You no know cow. What you know?"

Angkor didn't disappoint, though. In fact, it was — for lack of a better word — amazing. For one, the ruins cover an area of almost 200 square kilometers and take a full three days to see. Built between the 9th and 13th centuries, and influenced by Hindu temple design and cosmology, its symmetrical decadence, precision bas-reliefs, along with the eerie splendour of its spiral towers and never ending array of serenely smiling deities certainly qualify it as being one of the most impressive architectural undertakings in the history of mankind. At sunset, the lakes and moats would turn into bands of silver as the ancient, auburn structures cast long and imposing shadows while changing hue again, and again, and again. It possesses a splendor beyond description. Unfortunately, the experience was seriously blighted by the hordes of vendors and beggars.

"Hello" in Khmer is *joom reab sour*, although a more realistic rendering would be "HELLO! ONE DOLLAR!?" Packs of kids swarm you and will track you for minutes before giving up trying to sell you guide books, post cards, and T-shirts, which most tourists buy and then prominently display in a futile attempt at warding off future muggings. There's no question they need the money. After textiles, tourism is the biggest source of income in Cambodia, but the soliciting *really* wears you down. I've heard many people say that India is the single most stressful place for travelers, and although I'm willing to take their word for it, I would wager that Cambodia would come in a not-so-distant second. I may be uptight, but one would be after a 3-day marathon of people yelling, HELLO! ONE DOLLAR!? ONE DOLLAR, SIR! YOU BUY!? YOU BUY!? YOU BUY, SIR!? YOU BUY T-SHIRT!? YOU BUY HAT!? YOU BUY POSTCARD!? SIR, WHAT YOU BUY!? SIR! ONE DOLLAR, SIR!? PLEASE, SIR!? YOU BUY!? YOU BUY!!? YOU BUY!!!? Truly, I have never been somewhere that was so astonishingly beautiful while at the same time being so unbelievably annoying.

Once, after I'd gotten cornered in one of the decaying labyrinths by a squadron of women trying to sell me a baseball cap, I walked toward a policeman I'd spotted, thinking they'd leave me alone. "Sir, you buy police badge? Sir, you buy?" he asked me, as I drew near. "One dollar only." They even charged a dollar for using an outhouse, which I'll charitably describe as horrid. Bear in mind that this is in the middle of the jungle.

On yet another occasion, as I was riding on the back of the motorbike and listening to my driver's umpteenth sob story, I saw the most incongruous thing. Up ahead, a fish sprang out of a pond and onto the road, where it wiggled for a couple of feet or so before giving up. There was another pond on the other side of the road, hence giving the impression that it was trying to cross the road. Two other men also witnessed this and my driver stopped to talk to them. After passing around cigarettes and expressing their dismay, one of the men took off his shoe and whacked the thing over the head a couple of times before picking it up and placing it in a box on the back of his bicycle. Personally, I thought it deserved a little more for its effort, but in a way perhaps it was fortunate. After all, it would never have to hear, "HELLO! ONE DOLLAR!?" ever again.

Chapter 17. Nepal — A Trilogy in Four Parts

Part One — Reaching Nirvana

After a year of living in Korea, it occurred to me that "fat, drunk, and stupid" was no way to go through life and that I really needed to spend more time exercising and less time quaffing down cheap draught with my fellow compatriots. It was with this outlook that I decided to try something I'd never done before: mountain hiking. There is no shortage of mountains in Korea, and conveniently there was a sizeable one just a short distance from where I used to live. Indeed, I saw it daily (it was hard to miss) and when gazing upon it, it sometimes felt as if it were, well, beckoning me.

Initially my body was startled by the experience, but it got used to it. Approaching the summit, the stone steps gave way to a dirt path that wound its way through jutting crags of white and grey stone along the mountain's lengthy crest. The view was equally conspicuous, with the outskirts of Seoul spilling out of the northeast and hills stretching away to the west until they fell away into the Yellow Sea. I was hooked, and made mountain hiking an almost weekly ritual. In Taiwan, I continued with my newly found hobby, finding that it offered much in the way of balance to living in the neon and concrete confusion that is Taipei. Over time, I became mildly fixated with the notion of hiking in Nepal, and so, after my planned jaunt around Thailand and Cambodia, I scheduled a month there and was set to arrive at the end of October, the optimum season for hiking.

In Bangkok, I purchased a ticket from a travel agent who informed me that there were no economy class seats left for the day I wanted to fly out on, but that a first class ticket wasn't all that much extra. Never having flown anything but budget before, I went for it, spurred on by a whisky ad vision of myself reclining in first class while Mt. Everest loomed out the window. At Bangkok's international airport, I assuredly swaggered up to the first class counter to check in only to have the clerk point out that I was in fact holding an economy class ticket. My affair with luxury had come to an abrupt end. To be certain, it never even began.

Grumbling, I meandered over to the real person counter to discover that there were no window seats available. The best I could do was a middle seat on the right or "Everest side" of the plane. However, by the time the captain announced we'd shortly be underway, the window seat was still vacant. "We're just trying to track down one of our passengers," the voice announced. Thinking my luck had changed, I suddenly caught a glimpse of a large grey and white blob laboriously trundling down the aisle while knees, elbows, and the occasional shoulder were retracted to make way for its passing. As it came into focus, it took the form of a man — an enormous man — sporting a ten-gallon hat and a belt buckle that could have doubled as an anchor. Perplexedly attempting to match his ticket with physical place, the individual stopped beside me and bellowed, "How ya doin' partner? I thank that there's ma seat." I shuddered and got up to let him in, hardly a speedy procedure.

Finally settled, it wasn't long before we got to talking. Make that, *he* got to talking. As a matter of fact, he never stopped. "Ma name's Earl," he drawled, extending five pudgy digits in my direction. Earl was a retiree from Tennessee. He had seen a television show on Mt. Everest and had been so taken with its grandeur that he blathered on about it until both his wife and "the boys from the shop" suggested that he put a lid on it and "go see the gosh dang thang up close and personal." He had spent the last two years planning his trip, he conveyed, his first outside the US of A.

"Ya thank we goin' be able ta see it from this here plane?" he inquired fretfully. "That's what it says in my travel book," I responded, but 20 minutes later, over the jungles of Myanmar, Earl started to get fidgety.

"Is that them over there?" he asked of the window.

"Is that what?" I ventured.

"The *Himalayas*," he responded incredulously.

I politely explained to him that we had just left Thailand and still weren't far from Rangoon, as could be seen from the flight path displayed on the console a foot from his nose. Furthermore, seeing as how the flight was a little over three hours, within which time we were scheduled to fly over a considerable slice of India, it would probably be some time yet before we'd be seeing anything snow capped.

"I'll let you know when they appear," I said, but this failed to placate him, and he anxiously called to one of the flight attendants.

"Excuse me, Ma'am, but could ya'll tell a fella when we're gonna pass by Mouneveris. I came all the way from the Yewnited States ta see it, and I certainly don't wanna miss it."

Apparently, the woman's English training program hadn't included a section on the Southern twang, so I translated, and she ended up telling him the same thing I had, adding that the pilot would make an announcement when Everest became visible. "I hope ta heaven he don't forget," Earl informed her.

Earl then went on to inform me that as part of his research he had read two travel books on Nepal and that he was going to do the first leg of the Everest Base Camp trek. "Wow," I thought. "Imagine that. Two whole books." But seriously, this took me by surprise. In addition to being no spring chicken, Earl looked like the type of person who'd be lucky to make it to and from the bathroom without getting lost or injured. When I imparted that I was going to Pokhara to do part of the Annapurna Circuit, Nepal's most popular trek, he said he had never heard of it. When they served lunch he couldn't get his tray down due to his distended belly, and ended up with the butter tub stuck to his thumb. Next, he emptied his orange juice onto his lap, after which he exclaimed with a hearty chuckle, "Earl, it's just like yer wife says. You are *the biggest* jackass on Gad's green Earth." After eating, he fiddled with his camera while looking uneasily out the window for the next hour and a half until the Himalayas finally made their appearance.

"There they are," I declared.

"Where?" he replied, but try as I might to point them out, he simply couldn't see them. This didn't stop him from snapping a photo, though, with the lens cap still on. After I respectfully drew his attention to that, he yelled something like, "*Gad nammit!*" and pulled maladroitly until the piece took wing and hid itself mischievously somewhere under his chair. When Everest's signature 8488-meter-high peak eventually came into view, Earl was again at a loss. As everyone "ooh'ed, "ah'ed, and clicked away, he just kept asking me pathetically which one it was. "It's the tallest one," I answered in earnest, unsure whether I should laugh or cry. Not wanting the boys from the shop to rib him too much, I helped him snap a few photos and even retrieved his lens cap for him. A short while later, we landed and parted ways. I wonder whatever became of old Earl.

At the Kathmandu airport, it was my turn to experience travel shock. As we were descending, I noticed a building labeled Domestic Terminal, which is where I was headed as I wanted to fly to Pokhara immediately. The reason for this was that I hoped to get a hiking permit that afternoon as the country was about to embark on a five-day Hindu festival, meaning that all government offices would be closed. Nepal is a nation that takes festivals very seriously, with no fewer than 23 per year, or about one every 16 days.

As I exited the terminal, I was greeted by about 40 touts all shouting, "Taxi sir!" and, "Nice hotel!" Having lost my bearings, I didn't know exactly which way the domestic terminal was and so I made the unfortunate error of trying to ask a member of the frenetic mob how I might proceed there. "Oh, it's just a short drive, sir. You cannot walk there. Follow me, sir." "Is it that way?" I asked, but the guy wouldn't tell me, and kept insisting I had to take a cab. Meanwhile, about a dozen other people were vying for my attention. I managed to push through the crowd but a band of them followed me. I got rid of the last few by running in a zig zag pattern away from them with my travel bag slung over my shoulder and the last of the hangers on shouting, "Sir! You are *very* strange!"

Spotting the domestic terminal on the other side of a parking lot, I walked over to it but then couldn't figure out for the life of me how to get inside. It resembled a Western style house with an assortment of windows but no door. It was impossible to go around it because a galvanized fence extended away from each corner to form a large compound and other structures blocked the way to the front of it. As I stood there alone, wondering if the taxi driver had been telling the truth, a window abruptly flew open with a "*shoonk*" revealing a mustachioed Nepali man sporting a colorful cap and a pair of 1970s style sunglasses.

"Yes, sir? Can I help you, sir?" he asked.

"Uh, yeah, how do I get inside?"

"You cannot come inside unless you purchase a ticket, sir. Do you wish to purchase a ticket, sir?"

I did, I told him, and through the regular looking house window, I handed him my credit card and bought a ticket with no less than Buddha Air. Transaction completed, the clerk opened a door in the fence and I was invited into their office, where I sat on a sofa, was given tea and chatted with the staff of Buddha Air for about a half an hour before making my way to the gate.

There were only five other passengers on the twin engine that we flew to Pokhara, and, needless to say, the scenery was stunning. The pilots let us come up to the cockpit to have a better view, and this was only a couple months after 9/11. Frankly, it was nice to see that the hysteria hadn't permeated every nook and cranny of the world. I arrived in the town of Pokhara just before sunset and therefore too late to apply for a trekking permit. I would have to wait until the festival was over. However, as I soon discovered, there could have been much worse places to have been stuck. ,

The guest house I checked into was the quaintest and most homey accommodation you can imagine. Spotless and tastefully decorated, a double room with a view of a garden absolutely ablaze in color cost a mere $5 a night. Incredible. And Pokhara itself was nothing to scoff at either. In fact, it was, without question, the most charming town I have ever seen. Nestled next to a splendid lake and hemmed in by terraced hills and the creamy zeniths of the Himalayas, everywhere you looked was a postcard. Each and every day, the sky took on a clear, resonant blue, while each and every evening the sunset brought shimmering hues of pink and orange to the peaks in the distance, the view of which I took in from the top of Nirvana, the name of my guest house. All things considered, it wasn't so ambitiously named.

Part Two — The Trek

I was going on Nepal's Jomsom Trek, part of the legendary Annapurna Circuit, a circular route that winds its way around 19 Himalayan mountains that boast a very impressive average height of 7074 meters. From a bazaar on the outskirts of the serene and picturesque Pokhara, I gathered up my backpack and clambered onto a rickety old green school bus fitted with plywood seats and an interior that looked as if it had been mopped down with a bucket of soot and axle grease. Once sufficiently overloâded with vibrantly dressed Nepalis, a couple of crates of chickens, a goat, and one apprehensive-looking Canadian man, we got under way, rolling precariously over a string of undulating hills to a place called Naya Pul, the trek's starting point.

For the next nine days I would do some serious walking, passing through places with names like Ghorapani, Marpha, and Larjung. Going from an area of tropical vegetation, I would follow a river valley up into hill country and on through forests of oak and then pine before eventually reaching the sandy outer edges of the Tibetan Plateau. Each day, the flora, scenery, people, temperature, and path itself would manifest themselves in a dramatically dissimilar fashion from the day before, giving the impression of doing a series of different treks, as opposed to just one.

The way got fairly busy at times with trekkers and porters as well as large herds of sheep, goats, and mules, which often meant stopping to let them pass. This was fine with me, though. I needed the rest. In fact, the first three days of the journey nearly killed me, much to my surprise and embarrassment. At one point, a group of elderly Korean women passed me, looking curiously at this breathless, struggling Westerner, no doubt thinking, "Yup. That's what a lifetime of hamburgers will do to you." I didn't get it. Although not about to enter any triathlons, I had spent the past few years hiking quite regularly. However, that said, the air was thin and I was astonished by how heavy my backpack was. I'd done a fair amount of mountain walking, but never with 20 kilograms strapped to my back. Admittedly, I'd been warned about this by two travel books, the owner of my guest house, and an Austrian man whom I met within the first couple of hours of the hike, but alas, I am a foolishly stubborn individual at times and almost always end up paying the price, as I would on this occasion.

Somewhere into the third hour, while ascending a formidable flight of stone steps, my right knee went, and I quote, "Sproing!" Not thinking that being airlifted out of the hills on the first morning of my adventure would be something I'd want to tell the grandkids, I assessed the damage, strapped on a completely inadequate knee brace from my first aid kit, and trudged on with only a few twinges of discomfort here and there. At 5:00 or so, completely worn out, I stumbled into a village called Tikedungha and checked into a very simple lodge. Having arrived after the sun's premature disappearance behind a mountain, I had to settle for a cold shower as the rooftop water tanks were solar powered, so to speak. However, this turned out to be a very bad idea, as the outside temperature suddenly plummeted and I emerged from the shower shed shaking like a leaf. Returning to my room, I put on three layers of clothing, and stuffed myself into my sleeping bag in a vain attempt at getting warmed up. I'd gone from sweating buckets on a scorching hot day to chattering teeth and shivering, not to mention slightly injuring myself. Not exactly a roaring start. After dinner, I asked the lodge owner if he could try to find a porter to carry my backpack for the remainder of the trip. My knee felt alright, but I didn't want to aggravate it, and of course, becoming incapacitated in the Himalayas doesn't come highly recommended. The kindly gentleman said he could find someone, but that they probably wouldn't be experienced or able to speak much English. He went on to say that I should have gotten a proper porter back in Pokhara.

After a frigid and fitful sleep, I awoke at a little before eight and had breakfast alone as all the other trekkers had made an earlier start. Well, almost all of them. As I sat there eating my toast, two Israelis were energetically imparting to the waiter how they had shown the Arabs a thing or two during the Yom Kippur War. "Hrwee beat them. Hrwee shoot their tanks with our planes. Khraaboom! Like that, you know? 1976. Hrit is called Yom Khhippporrr Hwarrr. Hrit is ghreat victory!" To this, the Nepali man smiled politely and stated, "That's *very* good, sir. You're breakfast comes to 175 rupees. Thank you, sir."

Israelis had become a somewhat of a recurring theme during my travels in Thailand and Cambodia. Often straight out of the army, with a penchant for

rudeness towards locals and a fondness for eyeing everybody else with cold suspicion, I had seen other tourists actually warning each other not to go to certain
places due to high concentrations of them. While in Thailand, I had been waiting alone on a bus when two of them got in with me, and one, in a greeting I'm
not familiar with, put his feet up on my bag, crossed his legs, leaned back, folded
his arms, and, finally, gave me a look that said, "Whaddaya think of that, eh?" I
tersely asked him to take them down and he did, looking impressed, even though
I was completely bluffing. He was a big lad and would have sent me fleeing like a
school girl with a single guttural retort.

While listening to the heroic details of a war that had occurred when the
storytellers were probably still in potty training, the lodge owner brought in my
porter, who turned out to be a scrawny 16-year-old with an unpronounceable
name. He stood there grinning at me dressed in a pair of sandals, a red bandana,
and a well worn yellow mesh football shirt. Sure enough, he only knew a handful
of English words, but I figured I could find translators along the way. With the
help of the owner we settled on a price and then headed off.

One thing it didn't take long to figure out was that he hadn't traveled that
way before, or so I inferred from the conversations he had with various locals
that involved a lot of question asking and pointing. Also, communication was
more of a chore than I had bargained for. In fact, about the only thing he could
say was, "Me angry," which meant he wanted to eat. He was "angry" a lot actually, and although I had agreed to pay for all his meals, he seemed to get *hungry* at
all the wrong times. I tried to explain a breakfast, lunch, and dinner schedule by
drawing clocks in the dirt but he didn't seem to get it. Then, I noticed that just
prior to getting hungry, he would walk ahead and disappear only to come back
a few minutes later rubbing his tummy and indicating that he wanted to stop.
Once, after insisting that he just couldn't go on before having lunch at 10:40 a.m.,
I saw him taking money from a restaurant owner. Although I had to admire his
capitalist spirit, thereafter, we stuck to a pretty rigid schedule no matter how
irate he got.

Another tendency he possessed was to follow me around like a puppy dog
once we had finally gotten to a guest house. I had to bribe him to go away by
lending him my Discman, which he seemed to take for some kind of magical box.
Indeed, the first time he used it, his eyes widened and his mouth fell open as he
endeavored to fathom how the invisible needle found the equally imperceptible
grooves on the shiny, miniaturized phonograph inside. Good thing I didn't have
an i-Pod, or he might have sprained an eyeball. He also exhibited a strong partial-
ity to being photographed, one which he displayed every single time I stopped
to take a picture, which, as you might imagine, was often. He would always pose

vainly, holding his head high and crossing his arms confidently. I only took one actual shot of him. Every other time, I simply extended and retracted the lens, after which I would announce, "OK!" and give him a thumbs up.

On the third day, I had the good fortune of meeting a fellow from England who was there trekking with his father. The chance encounter was the result of asking them if I could join them for dinner. As it happened, we ended up dining together for the next four evenings as we somehow always managed to stay at the same lodge, which was almost as coincidental as the fact that the son was the spitting image of a good friend of mine back in Canada. They were nice people and we got along well. As it turned out, they had also gotten a porter in Tike-dungha, realizing, like me, that they would enjoy the experience more without the cumbersome bags. The son went on to describe to me how their porter would continually communicate that he wanted to go home, and how, essentially, he wasn't the brightest light in the harbor. "Not very bright?" his father interjected. "Now, there's an understatement. I think a village is missing its idiot." I respond-ed by asking them if they thought it possible for a village to have two idiots.

I also kept meeting up with two very pleasant Scandinavian girls. Once, as we were having lunch and exchanging stories, my porter pulled up a chair and began to gape at them lasciviously. This only ended when I told him to leave. Actually, he stopped and stared at pretty much every female he saw, apparently never having seen one outside his village or family before. By this time, I was beginning to wonder if his village and family weren't one and the same.

On day four, I passed between two 8000-meter mountains in a spot ac-credited as being the world's deepest gorge. I doubt if there are many things as humbling or as awe inspiring as sauntering between two pieces of rock that have a combined height of 16 kilometers. After reaching Jomsom, I continued for another day to a place called Muktinath, which is a pilgrimage destination for both Buddhists and Hindus as well as a popular trading post for merchants from Tibet. The community featured an exceptional and very old Buddhist temple copiously ornamented with prayer wheels and fluttering prayer flags. Vast and altogether arresting views of the sunburned Tibetan plateau were also on offer. I don't know how else to describe the place except to say that was all a bit unreal, as if I had somehow stepped back in time.

The next morning, while trekking back to Jomson, I spotted the father and son team in a café, so I stopped in to say hello and order some tea. At this point, I thought it would be a good idea to settle up with my porter, who by now was driving me absolutely bonkers. When I informed him it was the end of the line, he didn't seem to comprehend, so I asked the shop owner to translate. Well, on top of the more than fair fee we had agreed upon (not to mention meals, a dozen or so extra Cokes, and a couple of complimentary beers), he also wanted to keep "the music machine," which he'd been listening to for the past two days and was now clutching for dear life. Trying to be fair, I informed him he could either take the money or the CD player but not both, so he opted for the money, staring at it as he had first done with the mysterious spinning disc. I shook his hand and thanked him, but instead of leaving he began asking for "return money" along with the CD player again until the shop owner finally shooed him away.

"I think you were right," said the father, after he'd gone.

"About what?" I asked.

"A village *can* have two idiots."

Part Three — Asian Safari

Back in Pokhara, it was impossible not to notice that nearly every little hole in the wall travel agency was offering safari tours to a place called Royal Chitwan National Park. As it turns out, Royal Chitwan National Park, or Chitwan for short, is a 900 plus square kilometer affair located in southern Nepal on a verdant albeit narrow strip of land that hugs the Indian border and is known as the Terai. Despite the fact that the Terai is a relatively obscure sliver of world geography, it is in fact a significant band of soil and has produced one of the most influential people in all of history. And here, I'm referring to Siddhartha Guatama, or the Buddha. I suppose I could just as easily have booked a day trip to Lumbini, the birth place of the great sage, who, incidentally, was born 563 years before Jesus Christ, but I thought it would be infinitely more fun to look at endangered animals through binoculars. Also, I'm just not that big on organized religion. I know. Buddhism doesn't constitute a religion *per se*. Like many expatriates living in Asia, I've flirted with and read several books on the philosophy *cum* ethical code, with Sogyal Rinpoche's *The Tibetan Book of Living and Dying* being the most compelling one, and while I couldn't see myself subscribing to the doctrine I do think that some of its tenets and beliefs are appealing, or at least interesting. But taken as a whole, they constitute an "—ism," or system, and there is no such thing as a perfect or all encompassing system. Hence, I do my best to avoid them.

Perusing the brochures for Chitwan, I discovered that the park prided itself on possessing more than 40 different species of mammals, including rhinos, tigers, leopards, deer, sloth bears, wild boars, jackals, and various types of mongoose. Its rivers and lakes contained crocodiles and a kind of fresh water dolphin, and a respectable 400 plus varieties of local and migrant birds graced its tree tops. Adding a bit of excitement to the mix, and at no extra charge to the customer, there was evidently a healthy assortment of poisonous snakes on offer as well, and these could be found slithering within the park's high grasses. Among them were the cobra and the viper. And on a smaller but only slightly less dangerous scale, the area was rife with malaria-carrying mosquitoes and a kind of tick that could give you typhus fever. Because of this, socks, pants, long sleeved shirts, and dousing yourself with insect repellent all came highly recommended.

The ethnically and linguistically distinct people who dominate the Terai, the Tharu, are purportedly immune to malaria and allegedly this has to do with the sheer amount of alcohol that they consume. As for typhus fever, there is no immunity for that, and believe me when I say this is not something that you want to get. Spread from fleas and ticks that make an appetizer of rats and then a main course of your ankles, the symptoms consist of general pain followed by some very specific pain, including a headache, backache, chills, nausea, vomiting, abdominal discomfort, and delirium. Add to this a rash that covers pretty much your entire body and a two-week 41°C (105°F) fever (hence the delirium), and you can see how this could seriously dampen your vacationing spirit. With all of this in mind, I bought a three-day, two-night package tour for a very affordable $65 and went next door to stock up on DDT.

The next morning, I awoke at dawn, said my goodbyes to Pokhara, and caught a minivan to my so-called safari lodge, which was just inside the national park's perimeter.

The lodge was simple, but it had a little garden and yard which was good for reading and relaxing, which is what I did for most of the day. Before I left Pokhara I had purchased a copy of Douglas Adams's *The Hitchhiker's Guide to the Galaxy* at one of the town's very good, if pricey, second-hand book stores. That evening, I took a stroll along the park's perimeter and watched a stunning sunset, its size and splendor having been artificially enhanced by a heat-inspired haze that India had been so thoughtful to export. After that, I ambled around the nearby village of Sauhara, had a couple of beers in a restaurant, and laughed, uncontrollably at times, at the adventures of Arthur Dent.

The sunrise the following morning was even more dramatic than its departure the previous evening and I stood in a mist filled field snapping photo after photo of it before finally getting in the van that would take the other tourists and me to a nearby elephant compound. I was going on an elephant safari, and was pretty chuffed about it. We were going in search of rhinos.

Once at the compound, we were let out, and predictably everyone started snapping pictures. Most of the elephants were chained to large wooden posts and a few looked to be none too happy about it. One mammoth one, if you will, was putting on quite a show, rearing up on his hind legs, flailing his trunk about, and emitting ear splitting blasts of discontent to the newly arrived group of on-lookers. This had the instantaneous effect of making me feel very, very guilty.

At the time, I was aware that elephants are extremely sensitive and intel-ligent. I think that that's commonly known. However, I have since learned that they actually communicate with each other via low pitched grumbles, and it's thought that each has a distinctive "voice." Another interesting tidbit about these gregarious creatures is that they get depressed when a loved one dies. At the zoo in Taipei, I remember there was an old elephant couple, and when one passed away, the other soon followed. In a similar vein, elephants are obsessed with their deceased brethren's tusks. If they find one, they will customarily fondle and stare at it with a duration and intensity that gives you the distinct impression that they are contemplating their own mortality.

The elephants that I was looking at were of the Asian variety, which are ac-tually more closely related to the extinct mammoths than the African ones are. Indeed, Asian elephants are quite distinctive from their counterparts on the sa-vanna. They possess more bulbous heads, smaller ears, and a different number of toes on both front and back feet. However, they are nearly identical to their rela-tives in that they spend nearly 16 hours a day eating, and during that time they typically put away around 300 kilograms of grub.

An organizer put us into groups of four and assigned each group to an el-ephant. In my group there was a friendly, colorfully dressed, and very talkative woman from India, who was there with her daughter, along with an American of Indian ethnicity who was teaching English in Delhi and was in Nepal on vaca-tion. Our elephant was a female and only about half the size of the raving male who had given up on his tantrum and resigned himself to moodily pacing back and forth. She seemed to bask in the attention we gave her, and we all goofily got our pictures taken next to her before climbing a set of stairs up to a wooden plat-form from which we precariously, but quite literally, got onboard. You see, the seat, or *howdah* as it's known, was little more than a wooden plank with a railing of two by fours that went around the top. Putting your feet between the rail and the baseboard, you then were to hold on firmly and pray that the whole contriv-ance wouldn't come unfastened and swing you down below to become toe jam. Actually, it wasn't so bad. Everyone occupied their own corner while the *pahit*, or master (an instructor from India where all the elephants are trained) sat in front of us just behind the elephant's head.

As we swayed and rollicked our way along a dirt road, we passed a series of mud and thatched huts where the locals were out collecting wood for their morning bonfires. Others were already huddled around these and could be seen boiling water, eating breakfast, and trying to get warm. It was early and the sun still hadn't made its presence felt. The villagers smiled and waved as we saun-tered past and we smiled and waved back. We rambled on like this for a while until the huts disappeared, and then we veered off into the brush. Soon, the view on all sides was one of dense bush and lofty, twisting trees veiled in a layer of ethereal mist.

"Should see a rhino soon," announced the *pahit* after a while. "They are fond of this area," he added, as our beast trampled through the undergrowth, snapping branches and flattening patches of wild grass. Sure enough, within minutes, we spotted a grey blob among the foliage donning a ten gallon hat and a belt buck-le that could have doubled as an anchor. "Is this here the way to Mouneveris?" it asked. Only joking. Two more blobs then came into view, and our elephant sauntered right up to them, but they didn't so much as blink. Perhaps they were used to it, or maybe they just didn't notice us. I say this because rhinos have ex-ceptionally poor eyesight, and that of course is what makes them so dangerous. Well, that and the fact that they are rather temperamental.

A rhino, you see, will spot some blurry object moving in the near distance and then, just to play it safe, will charge the thing at a speed of up to 55 km/h. When you factor in that a rhinoceros can easily weigh more than two tons and is outfit-ted with a horn as long as two feet, it shouldn't come as any shock when you spot a line in your brochure saying, "Please exercise caution. There have been fatali-ties." Additionally, their cement colored, compartmentalized, armor-like skin is covered in warts and I find this the most horrifying factoid of all.

Eventually, the rhinos lumbered off, and so did we, taking the scenic route back to the starting point while the sun burned off the morning fog. Next, we were taken back to the lodge where I napped and had lunch. In the afternoon I was going on a jungle walk and wanted to be rested up for it.

The starting point for this was at a nearby river, which I walked to after I'd stuffed myself with chicken curry and tea. There, I met my two escorts who greeted me in the local fashion of pressing the hands together as if to pray and saying, "*Namastay*." I returned the gesture and then we shook hands, introduced ourselves, and engaged in a bit of convivial banter. Before long we were under-way and trundling along a dirt path to a canoe that was awaiting us on the edge of the river. With one guide paddling in the front and the other in the rear, I felt like some pompous British peer of the realm from yesteryear perched between them with my map, camera, and binoculars. "Oh, *do* stop here ol' chap," I felt like saying. "I should like to have a go at that Bengali tiger over there alongside the embankment. After all, I've only bagged 8 of the ghastly beasts today, and should very much like to get my daily quota of 30 before tea."

As we floated along the grassy banks, I idly dangled a hand over the side to feel the water, but was abruptly admonished by the guide behind me. "Sir!" he yelled. "Do not put your hands in the water, sir! In fact, sir, please do not put your hands outside the boat. There are crocodiles in the water, sir!" Oh, right. *The crocodiles.* I had forgotten about those. Well, he wasn't kidding. Only minutes later, we passed by a few caves along the muddy banks and when I peered inside I could occasionally glimpse a pair of primordial, yellowish eyes set in rumpled and ridged olive heads gazing back at me. Bear in mind that for a person who grew up in a country with a landmass that is half frozen year round, this was about as exotic as it gets.

After cruising along for some time, we brought the canoe up on shore and started to hike. Like in the boat, one guide went ahead of me while the other took up the rear. Each of them had brought what looked to be a rake handle, which they slung across their shoulders.

"What's with the sticks?" I asked.

"Just for your protection, sir."

"Protection from what?"

"Oh, nothing in particular, sir. Not to worry," said one of them, and we continued on uneventfully for a quarter of an hour as I craned my neck about to gape around at walls of grass and brilliant blue skies.

"Do you think we'll see a rhino?" I asked.

"No, sir. We won't see a rhino. It is the early afternoon, sir. You can only see a rhinoceros in the early morning or perhaps the late afternoon. This time of day is too hot for them, sir. They do not like the heat."

That made sense. Surely, they would know the creature's grazing habits. But then I remembered reading that there were 450 of the things roaming around within the park's grounds. "Hmm," I thought, "930 square kilometers divided by 450 was roughly one rhinoceros for every two square kilometers..."

"But what if we *do* see one?" I badgered. "What should we do?"

There was a pause and the then the guide in front of me said, "You should run, sir."

"Run?"

"Yes, sir. And then you should climb a tree."

There weren't any trees in the immediate area. There was only the river, shrubs, and a lot of absurdly high grass.

We were silent for the next five minutes, and then we came to a bend in the river, where we followed the mimicking curve of the path.

And then.

I saw it.

About 35 meters away.

On the far side of the river.

A rhino.

The guide in front of me crouched down and without turning around, motioned dramatically for us to imitate him. We promptly complied, but it was already on the move. It began trotting through the narrow bit of river and swiftly gained momentum as it loped up the bank. I looked around for a tree, but there was only one within running distance and it was half dead with rot. Before I even had a chance to think of an alternative plan, the thing shot out of the bushes alongside the path and made a bee line for the brush on the opposite side. And just like that, it was gone. It hadn't even seen us, or if it had, it wasn't interested. This was fortunate because we were less than 20 meters from the thing at the point where it crossed the path, and this was close enough to discern that a couple of sticks wouldn't have been any match for it.

After that, we continued on with none of us saying very much of anything and me wishing I had splashed out for the Jeep tour. We saw a crocodile basking in the sun as it lay on the muddy river bank, a pack of chattering langur monkeys impossibly high up in the tree tops dropping bits of foliage down on the path below, and a tiger track, which the guides said was less than 12 hours old. Still. The rhinoceros stole the show.

The next day, I woke to another frosty, mist filled morning, and after filling up on toast and coffee, I met up with another guide who was going to take me on a bird watching tour. Admittedly, I've never been much for observing birds, but I have to say that I thoroughly enjoyed myself on this occasion. The guide was a friendly sort in addition to being courteous and knowledgeable, and he didn't seem to be at all put off by my total ignorance of what we were doing. Dressed in military fatigues, the man had the eye of a hawk and was excellent at pointing out nests and birds where I certainly would have only seen trees and grass. Moreover, whenever we heard a chirp or a twitter, he would immediately inform me as to what species was responsible for the birdsong, to which I would respond with various intelligent rejoinders such as, "Oh, OK," and "Really?"

After a couple hours of trekking along and putting my binoculars to good use, we made our way back to the starting point where I spent another little while looking around a museum which I found to be wholly unimpressive, not to mention anti-climactic. Set up in a series of dusty shacks, it made me wonder if somewhere in the West there wasn't a prospective market in charging Asian tourists to view musty tool sheds. All in all, though, I was perfectly content with the experience. It wasn't Africa, but it was the next best thing. After a night spent pottering around the knick knack and postcard packed tourist shops of Sauraha, I rose at daybreak the following morning and boarded a bus to Kathmandu.

Part Four — Kathmandu

The scenery from the bus was nearly as striking as it had been from the Buddha Air flight to Pokhara. The bridge laden road ahead of us twisted and turned its way along hill and mountain sides, and the lack of guardrails and overfilled jalopies both in front of us and behind served as ample reminder of just how quickly tragedy could strike. The hilliness seemed never ending, and after a couple of hours, I started to marvel at how Nepal had ever come into existence as a nation at all. The fact that people had had the fortitude to survive in such disobliging terrain was truly a testimony to the perseverance of the human spirit. The green terraced hills and ravines of grey stone and aqua blue rivulets that were spanned periodically with silver pedestrian suspension bridges eventually faded, however, and we dropped out of the rolling panorama and entered the periphery of the plain that constitutes the beginning of the Kathmandu Valley.

Something of a geographic anomaly, the Kathmandu Valley, which is only about 20 kilometers in both length and breadth, is home to an ancient culture and civilization which flourished in the three antique capitals of Patan, Bhaktapur, and Kathmandu. On this day, civilization announced itself with dusty side streets, row upon row of dilapidated brick buildings, and every manner of horn blaring, bell ringing, fume spewing vehicle imaginable. After crawling along at a snail's pace through the rush hour traffic, the bus unexpectedly pulled over and stopped in the middle of a bazaar. As merchants packed up their wares, beggars set upon the bus to target the foreign passengers who had been sitting in the front and therefore alighted first. I slipped off to hail a cab before any of them spotted me or it got any darker.

Jumping in what must have been a 25-year-old Datsun, the driver took me to the tourist area of Thamel as he simultaneously blabbered away about local politics, laid on the horn every 0.00052 seconds, and chain smoked. Once in Thamel, I took the first place I saw, which was, shall we say, basic, not to mention lacking hot water. But no matter. Night had fallen and I didn't feel like shuffling around the streets of Kathmandu with a duffel bag in search of just the right place. After an abbreviated and animated shower, I stepped into the streets of Thamel to search for a place to eat.

Thamel is your standard developing world tourist ghetto, overflowing with guest houses, restaurants, Internet cafés, travel agencies, money exchanges, book stores, CD shops, touts, hawkers, and massage parlors. It also has its fair share of art stores and carpet shops, a couple of which I ventured into. In one such shop,

I became more or less enraptured with a set of elephants carved out of soapstone and bought them to send to my parents for Christmas. The proprietor wrapped and rewrapped them, padding the box with about six weeks worth of newspaper and a few sheets of bubble wrap. The following day, I took the box to the post office and in about four weeks (on Christmas Day), I called my parents to see if they'd gotten them. As it turns out, they had, although they didn't seem to have any idea what they were, which may have had something to do with the fact that they arrived in about a thousand pieces.

And speaking of buying things I shouldn't have, I almost picked up a Persian rug. Now, if you're ever in Nepal (or elsewhere in Central Asia, I suppose) and decide to wander into a carpet shop, be forewarned: the owners of these places have to be among the best salespeople in the world. I've never seen anything like it. An American friend of mine who visited Nepal a couple of years before I did came home with a $1000-dollar rug. Although a fine piece of carpeting to be certain, at the time, I couldn't figure out for the life of me why he would bother to buy something so large and so cumbersome in such a far flung place. However, after 15 minutes of comparing various sizes, textures, patterns, and stitch counts with the shop owner, I understood why. The guy was so friendly and spoke with such a degree of self assured eloquence and buoyancy that I was soon telling myself that I could drop at least a few hundred on "just a small one." I don't know what came over me. Usually, my BS detector is on relatively high alert, but all the incense and sitar music must have been interfering with the signal. Luckily, however, the spell was broken and I left the shop with my wallet weighing the same as when I had entered.

The next day I woke up early and strode through the streets of Thamel, evading touts and beggars as I went. Passing guest house after guest house, I noted countless tourists sporting colorful Gortex jackets and carrying various types of equipment, either having just arrived for or just returned from adventures in trekking, mountain climbing, biking, or white water rafting. I was on my way to meet my two Australian friends Janelle and Gareth for breakfast at a trendy Western style restaurant replete with a leafy courtyard. The three of us worked for the same language institute in Taipei and happened to be taking our vacations at the same time and in the same place. Having done a different trek than I had, they were now, like me, finishing up with a few days in Kathmandu. After getting caught up, we walked about a kilometer to Durbar Square where we strolled around and played tourist.

The walk was invigorating. To be sure, I don't think there are many things that could make you feel more alive than a stroll through the streets of Kathmandu on a crisp, clear, fall morning. I never thought I would be here (in fact, I used to think Kathmandu was a mythical place, like Xanadu) and no amount of living in Asia could have prepared me for it. The very archetype of culture shock, the Nepali capital is where time, Hinduism, and two schools of Buddhism collide to form an impossibly intricate historical-theological labyrinth set against a similarly complex physical one. Altars and shrines abound in a morass of featureless concrete monstrosities that jut above their crumbling, brick rivals with their wooden porches and latticed windows, while the streets below are absolutely buzzing with people, livestock, rickshaws, and taxis. Moving among the throngs, you are met by smiling people, solicitations, hillocks of fruit, blankets of bric-a-brac, and streaks and splotches of flamboyant color. Overheard, signs protrude from each and every angle, while clusters of electrical wire dangle and wind their way from one jumbled black mass to the next. The sound of flutes, clucking chickens, and the Nepali language ring in your ears, while nameless aromas and odors mingle about your nostrils. It may sound cliché — indeed, it is cliché — but it is pure sensory overload. Look anywhere and something is going on, and most of the time it's something you've never seen before, or never even imagined seeing before, and that is what makes it all the more overwhelming. And thoroughly enjoyable, I might add.

Durbar Square was like the street scene without the street, and had the added bonus of an impressive collection of temples. Although all unique, many of them had recurring themes, specifically stone terraced bases and multiple tiered roofs. And in true Nepali fashion, one might be dedicated to the Hindu god of Vishnu while featuring elements of Buddhism. Also noteworthy is the fact that although many of the dates of construction are known (typically from the seventeenth century), many are not. In fact, there are several temples that no one seems to know much about at all, including when they were built or who they were built for, and frankly, I find that fascinating. Imagine a church in Europe assumed to be somewhere between five and ten centuries old, with no one being at all certain, while at the same time being equally in the dark as to which denomination it was.

Passing between two stone lions, Janelle, Gareth, and I climbed the steps and took a seat on the top terrace of the famed Maju Deval temple. From here, we were afforded a commanding view of the city and of the square itself. Down to our right, a street drama was being performed by a large contingent of people dressed in identical costumes. Involving singing, chanting, and a good deal of synchronized body movement, the act culminated in the release of a dozen or so doves. Just off stage, as it were, flute sellers, green grocers, wandering sadhus with begging bowls in hand, and barbers with little more than a chair and a bag of utensils all busied themselves in applying their trades.

From there, we made our way to a three-storey white building known as the Kumari Bahal, home to the Kumari Devi, or Nepal's very own living goddess. The Kumari Devi is a pre-pubescent girl chosen from a particular caste of silver and goldsmiths among the Newars, one of Nepal's 12 principal ethnic groups. In order to determine if the young girl is truly the chosen one, she is placed in a darkened room filled with horrible noises and ferocious looking masks. If she is unaffected, she is deemed to be "the One," with the logic being that a true goddess would show no fear. Once chosen, the girl is then shipped off to the Kumari Bahal with her parents where she stays until she has her first period or loses any significant amount of blood (by way of a cut or otherwise), upon which time she metamorphoses back into a mere mortal, which must come as a bit of a shock. It's said that to marry an ex-goddess is bad luck, and I'm guessing that once you get a taste of omnipotence, omnipresence, omniscience, and immortality it would be more than a tad difficult to lower your standards. This must make for a whole new genre of marital spats. All the tourists, us included, milled about the building's courtyard and peered through the latticed windows in order to try and catch a glimpse of the reclusive deity, but she was nowhere to be seen, so we left and hailed a motorcycle cab.

With the three of us jammed into the sidecar, we bounced and jarred our way along the city's dusty, potholed roads through a haze of choking diesel fumes before finally stopping at the bottom of a hill. Ascending its 365 steps, we were rewarded with the outline of the Swayambhunath Stupa set against a cloud bedecked sky. Purportedly the most ancient and revered holy sight in the Kathmandu Valley, being dated to the fifth century AD, hundreds of worshippers visit the spot daily. The Swayambhunath Stupa takes the form of a golden spire emanating from an oversized white washed dome. The spire is decorated with a large eye on each of its four sides in order to symbolize the all seeing nature of the Buddha. The structure is festooned with prayer flags while prayer wheels envelope its base. The three of us embarked on a few circumambulations, wafting prayers to the heavens with each spin of the wheel, before stopping for refreshments and a gander at the mountain hemmed, haze enshrouded valley below.

On our way back down, we stopped to snap some photos of the monkeys that we had seen tree hopping on our way up. Actually, the site's unofficial name is "Monkey Temple." In the midst of our photo shoot, one of the little scamps stole my bottle of water, forced the cap off by punching both of its sides, and turned his back on me to take a long drink. "Don't even think about trying to get that back," a girl on the stairs informed me. "It's gone. People have ended up in the hospital trying to get things back. Be glad they only stole your water." "Well," I thought, "it was nice of them to put up a sign."

The owner of the voice was an American who was in Nepal in order to conduct fieldwork related to her master's thesis. She asked if we could help her do a survey in regard to our observations of and interactions with the monkeys during our climb and descent, and so we obliged. She was pleasant and informative (there was a lot inbreeding among the creatures, they were born thieves, etc.), although from her voice and manner, I estimated that she had been supplementing her studies with night classes in "advanced cannabis." This is not all that surprising when you consider Nepal's recent history. In the nineteen sixties and early seventies, Kathmandu served as a kind of hippy haven known for its peace, love, dope, good food, and mountain vistas. Indeed, it was a key stop on the so-called hippy trail, which ran through Europe, the Middle East, and India. Kathmandu's Jochne, otherwise known as Freak Street, was the East's answer to Haight-Ashbury, although nowadays it's little more than a faint reflection of its former self. Although the good old days are gone, Nepal still possesses a bit of a hippy aura. In the countryside, marijuana could be seen growing by the roadside.

The next two days saw my Australian friends and me exploring the medieval capitals of Patan and Bhaktapur, two time pieces of traditional architecture and lifestyle unmarred by modern day commercial influence. It was all very invigorating, and we took photo after photo while trying our utmost to enjoy the moment, knowing that all too soon, the moments would fade away and our trip would be over.

At the outside chance that I have managed to convey what a jaunt around Nepal is like, I don't believe that I am a gifted enough writer to express how I felt when I was there. Words like "spirited," "inspired," or "invigorated," may help communicate the sentiment, but ultimately fall short. To be certain, I felt infused with a zest for discovery and adventure that I had never experienced before and haven't managed to replicate since. Of course, the scenery doubtlessly had something to do with this. Although completely subjective, I have to question whether there is landscape anywhere that could rival that of Nepal. And yet, despite the awe-inspiring displays of nature and the sense of inner connectedness that they seemed generate, whenever I reflect upon my trip, it's always the people I met who come to mind; Earl, the staff at Buddha Air, my porter, the English father and son, the Scandinavian girls, the safari guides, the carpet salesman, Janelle and Gareth, the monkey girl and countless others who I haven't mentioned here. Even brief encounters seem to have left deep and enduring impressions. As enduring as any mountain.

CHAPTER 18. GOO MAO LING VIET NAM!

"Hello, do you speak English?" I inquired politely. I was calling the Vietnamese consulate in Taipei to inquire about the specifics of obtaining a visa. Through the static, a curiously accented variety of Mandarin came back at me. "Uh, can you speak Chinese?"

"I can try," I said. "I want to apply for a visa and was just wondering..."

"You have to come *here* to do that," answered the man gruffly, the din of background noise nearly drowning out his words.

"Yes, I know. I was just wondering..."

"It costs $40. You have to come to our office to apply," he repeated tersely. "You cannot do it by telephone."

"Right, I understand, but ... *I was just wondering...* do I need to bring anything besides my passport?"

"Yes, $40."

"And that's all? My passport and $40?"

"Yes, that is all."

"What about photos?"

"Of course you need photos! How can you apply for a visa without photos?"

"How many do I need?"

"Two."

"And do they need to be color or black and wh..."

Click.

He hung up. As I soon discovered, it was a wonder he had answered the phone at all.

Presenting myself at their office the following week, I was somewhat startled by what I saw. In a shabby looking room of absurdly modest proportions, were about 50 diminutive, darkly clad, jabbering individuals. Half of them were huddled around a table filling in forms while the other half mobbed a pair of stone faced clerks seated behind an undersized counter, assailing them with queries and requests. The clamor was unbelievable and the scene was one of pure pandemonium. People shouted at each other from across the room in Vietnamese, Taiwanese, and Mandarin while others elbowed their way toward the pair of staffers. It was obvious that if you could make it to one of their windows, you were deemed worthy of being dealt with, and so it was a free for all.

But this wasn't nearly as curious as the fact that every single person present seemed to be thoroughly enjoying themselves. People smilingly shoved each other out of the way, laughingly pushed, and gleefully jostled. Suddenly, every office I had ever been to in Asia seemed rigorously efficient, and every bad experience trivial. After about 20 minutes, I finally made it to the counter and used my size to block up the window so nobody could charge in.

"I want to apply for a visa," I said.

"Copy first page of passport," instructed the man.

"Right. And where do I do that?"

"There," he said, pointing. The edge of the photocopier was located just under my right elbow. I took a single step back so that I could raise its lid, and that was all a family of three needed. With their daughter sandwiched between them, the middle aged couple stole in past me, the mother shoulder charging me out of the way and the father fending off challengers from the opposite side. After some more jockeying, I regained my former position and managed to apply for the visa, being told to come back in two days to pick it up. I thanked the clerk, and he nodded blankly before unceremoniously tossing my passport and application form into an enormous cardboard box situated behind him. I was going to Vietnam. From Hanoi in the north to Saigon (officially Ho Chi Minh City) in the south, I had set aside 23 days to explore a country which — to be completely honest — I had never particularly wanted to visit before.

This largely had to do with a first hand account I once got from my good friend and former roommate upon his return from an extensive trip throughout Southeast Asia. "*Never* go to Vietnam," he warned. "Those people are *relentless*. There's a *reason* why they won that god damned war." Furthermore, while relaxing on another vacation, I picked up and perused a well thumbed, 15-year-old travel book on the country and could still remember encountering sentences like, "The tourist industry in Vietnam is virtually non-existent," and, "The Vietnam War helped spawn a nation of criminals," as well as, "Between Hue and Ho

Chi Minh City (a distance of roughly 1000 kilometers) don't even think about getting off the train. Organized crime and law enforcement are one and the same, and there have been numerous reports of muggings and violent attacks on foreign tourists." Recently, however, Vietnam had become something of a hot spot in terms of travel, and I figured it couldn't be overlooked in any account of Asia. Besides, it was still very cheap.

A few weeks later, I boarded a Vietnam Airlines flight and took my seat. Before long, a flight attendant was passing out moist towels and newspapers, so I took a copy of the *Vietnam News* and scanned the headlines. "Transport Sector Reviews Productive Year," "Over 81,000 Jobs Created Last Year," "Vietnam and Laos Successfully Bolster Security Ties," "Tenth Congress to Focus on Party Leadership and National Renewal." It was only the second time I had read a "communist" newspaper and I must admit that I find them to be fairly intriguing. There is less pretence of presenting objective information, but more than overtly distorted information they offer paragraph after paragraph in a stilted twaddle without ever actually saying anything at all, which is, of course, an art form in itself. Snapping the broadsheet open, I dug into the main story.

The 10th annual National Party Congress would focus on increasing the Party's leadership and fighting capacity while also boosting people power across the nation. These key focus areas, along with a need to focus on work aimed at helping Vietnam make the transition from a developing country to a developed country, were identified at the Party Central Committee's 13th plenum, which closed in Hanoi yesterday. The 13th plenum ended successfully yesterday with delegates reaching consensus on preparations for the upcoming 10th National Party Congress, said Party General Secretary Nong Duc Manh.

I just loved that: "would focus." We *would* focus on these areas (if a certain unnamed condition were to transpire), but until that time we are perfectly content in simply "identifying key focus areas," not that we are going to do anything about them, mind you, although in theory we would. For the time being, however, you may rest assured and take no small degree of comfort in knowing that we are fully aware of just what the issues we ourselves have raised actually are.

All the headlines and articles were virtually indistinguishable, weighted equally in vacuous flimflam. "Nothing Wrong Here," "Please Go About Your Business," "Why Not Ask Your Flight Attendant for a Real Newspaper?" Then, just as I was about to have a stab at the bleak looking entertainment section, I noticed a commotion at the front of the plane. Actually, I was sitting at the front of the plane, so it was pretty hard to miss.

A couple of flight attendants were trying to persuade a woman to leave the plane (we hadn't taken off yet, you'll be glad to know), but she wouldn't budge.

Instead, she backed herself into an alcove and got out her cell phone. Soon all the flight attendants were gathered around her and yelling, but she defiantly stood her ground. Eventually, the pilots emerged from the cockpit, then the police came, and finally, important looking men with expensive suits showed up. They yelled too, but the woman was unmoved. After some time, I heard one flight attendant say to another, "We'll have to clear everybody off the plane for security reasons." But we didn't move, either. Rather, we waited for an hour and a half, until a man showed up with a document which the woman signed. Then, she put her cell phone away (she had been speaking into it the entire time) and left the plane.

Once in the air, things got even more interesting. Indeed, before long, the flight was like one big party. Almost all the Vietnamese people around me ordered beers and whiskies (it was an early morning flight) and this fueled their volubility. People got up — drinks in hand — and smilingly made their rounds while talking animatedly and slapping each other on the shoulders. They couldn't all have known each other, but peering around at them, you would swear they did. As someone's toddler sat on my foot and played with a bag of garbage, the man to my left and the woman to my right decided to get acquainted, and for the first time, I got my first real dose of what Vietnamese sounds like.

In case you have never really had a good listen to it before, the Vietnamese language bears a striking resemblance to the type of crashing noises ordinarily associated with disgruntled waiters in foreign kitchens. A jumble of clanging consonants and alien vowel sounds formed in some nether region of the mouth compete with each other somewhere over the tongue, clashing violently before tumbling out past the lips and piercing the air. It is shrill and metallic and painful to listen to. I know this because the man and woman blathered away to each other for two hours, with both of them apparently mistaking each of my ears for some sort of mouthpiece. No wonder so many American soldiers had gone mad, I reflected. Every time someone spoke, they must have thought they were being fired upon.

After clearing customs at Hanoi's shiny new airport, I exchanged US dollars for Vietnamese *dong*, brushed off several touts, and then nearly got conned into purchasing a ticket for a bus that didn't exist. Finally, and in spite of a manifest lack of signage, I managed to find the shuttle bus downtown. The exchange rate was 16,000 Vietnam *dong* for every $1, and so I sat on the bus examining the bills and trying to do a couple of practice conversions. Each bill had an image of Ho Chi Minh on it, while the 20,000-*dong* note had the added bonus of a factory scene. Four fleshy workers in white lab coats could be seen cheerfully operating an assembly line of what looked to be bomb shells. In the background, a fifth worker was busily stacking them up in a poorly arranged pyramid that appeared on the verge of collapse.

Expansive rice paddies stretched away from the highway to Hanoi. In the distance, pointy topped mountains loomed in the haze. On many of the fields, houses rose up to four and five stories, done in traditional architecture and vivid colors. Most of them were yellow with intricate wooden doors and burgundy tiled roofs. What they possessed in height and depth (they must have been 30 meters long), they lacked in width. These were the famed "tunnel houses" with their distinctive narrow frontages of perhaps seven or eight meters. A nation-wide phenomenon, this has to do with an ancient feudal law whereby property tax is based solely on the breadth of a building's facade.

Communist Party billboards, with their 1950s style caricatures of chubby families grinning at the hammer and sickle competed with advertisements for scooters, soft drinks, and tampons. Vietnamese employs the Roman alphabet, albeit with an added array of tone indicators and foreign doodles and squiggles, and this seemed totally at odds with the surrounding scenery, so quintessentially Asian. Because Vietnamese is related to and once employed Chinese script, it's rendered in monosyllables, so instead of "Vietnam" or "Saigon," it's actually "Viet Nam" and "Sai Gon." I tried to pronounce the words as you would in English, but it didn't work, and after a while this became frustrating.

I had heard that traffic in Vietnam was appalling, but on the highway it didn't seem so bad. In an instant, however, this assessment got reversed. A large road abruptly intersected with the highway, but instead of an overpass or a set of traffic lights, there was only a tiny assemblage of flimsy plastic boxes arranged in a circle with white arrows painted on them. Our bus, following the curve of the boxes and direction of the arrows, turned into three lanes of oncoming traffic. Horns blared, people shouted, dozens of scooters zipped by, and my life flashed in front of my eyes. It was insane. But every subsequent intersection turned out to be identical, and after about 30 minutes, I had grown somewhat accustomed to it.

We arrived in Hanoi's historic Old Quarter, and I went to check into a place called the Prince Hotel. However, when I got there, a man standing outside reported that there were no more rooms and that I should follow him to another branch of their hotel just up the street. Ignoring him, I went inside only to be informed that they were, in fact, full. Outside, the man showed me his card, which read "the Prince Hotel," so I followed him for a couple of blocks and checked into what was a "tunnel house" building of French colonial design. A charming place with lofty ceilings, it possessed an ancient-looking and nearly vertical stairwell. The room was equally impressive, featuring a desk set of mahogany and marble and the tallest and heaviest door I have ever seen. It must have been four meters high. If it weren't for the TV and refrigerator, it could have been the 1930s. I checked in and then went back up to my room to have a nap, having only gotten a couple hours sleep the night before. The bed was damp and reeked of perfume. The architecture wasn't the only French influence, evidently.

A couple of hours later, still a bit groggy, and scented like a nineteenth century *prostituée*, I descended the precipitous stairs and handed over my key and wallet to the receptionist. A sign in the room suggested relinquishing all valuables or the management "...would not to be responsible." I watched in amused curiosity as the man took my wallet and wrapped it up in newspaper. This done, he got out a roll of scotch tape and went through about a third of it in sealing up the newspaper. Finally, he handed me a blue felt tipped marker and told me to sign my name on it. "Vietnam style," he said, and chuckled.

After only about 15 minutes on the street my senses experienced a sort of meltdown. The place was absolutely swarming with people not to mention torrents of horn blaring motorcycles and plodding cyclos, which are a kind of outsized, inverted tricycle with a passenger chair affixed between the two front wheels. Every few steps someone asked me if I needed a motorcycle or a cyclo, and every third hawker I passed solicited me, usually in Vietnamese. The first floor of each and every building was some kind of business with the merchandise often tumbling out onto the sidewalk. Wherever goods were actually kept inside, women sold their wares from blankets. More women walked around in their conical hats (the tapered straw ones) carrying two large and cumbersome looking baskets of fruit suspended from the ends of a bamboo pole. Street corners were crammed with people sitting on red, foot-high plastic stools and engaged in eating, drinking beer, sipping green tea, or passing around long wooden tobacco pipes. Shop owners could be seen burning piles of "ghost money" as offerings to their ancestors. The Chinese do this too, but they at least use canisters. Here, each city block was marked by a smoldering pile of ash heaped onto the road. Little kids tottered past them and motorbikes sped through them. Jumbled tangles of electrical wire coursed through enormous banyan trees converging in knots of 40 or 50 at the crowns of crooked poles. In fact, everything was slightly crooked not to mention caked in a layer of filth. Streets were overflowing with litter, open sewers could be seen through grates, and the exhaust fumes were literally dizzying. The smell of shit was never far off, and every time you crossed the street, you took your life in your hands. My travel guide described the area as being ideal for young children.

But this is all old hat apparently. Indeed, the Old Quarter has been humming along like this for over a millennium. More than 700 years ago, all of Hanoi's ex-

isting guilds established themselves here, naming the streets for the type of merchandise they sold and it is still like this today. My hotel was located on "Comb
Street" (although it felt more like "Flower Street"), and was adjacent to "Sugar
Street" and just up the way from "Scale Street." The latest industry to arrive was
that of tourism, and it had been transplanted right on top of the whole thing. The
upshot of this was that hotels, travel agencies, and Internet cafés flanked shops
selling pickled fish, herbal medicine, and coffins.

I strolled around for an hour or so, head swiveling wildly, and praying each
and every time my foot stepped off the sidewalk. Eventually, I stopped for dinner
at a place selling Western food. Sated, I did some more exploring and popped
into several book and music stores. What wasn't second hand was copied and
I must say the selection was impressive, although generally of poor quality and
often incorrectly labeled. I thumbed through a copy of Michael Moore's *Downsize Thia!* (The actual title is *Downsize This!*) and inspected an unofficial Rolling
Stone's compilation to find such classics as *Baint it Black* and *Sweet Fighting Man*.

Outside, it was dark and chilly, so I thought I would try and warm myself up
by going for a brisk walk around the Old Quarter's central attraction, Hoan Kien
Lake. Couples occupied every bench surrounding the body of water, while white
light bounced off the awnings of the towering green trees, illuminating the grass
and footpath below. The road enveloping the lake was itself encircled by a stylish
ring of French edifices, behind which sprawled a city comprised of short, narrow
structures. With the exception of the Old Quarter, Hanoi is still very much a
case of culture superseding commerce. There wasn't a skyscraper in sight.

The walk was pleasant enough, despite the beggars and the solicitations for
"massage" ("masa"), marijuana ("mali-lang-lang"), and motorcycles ("motobai").
A typical sales pitch went more or less like this: "PSSSSTTTTT! Hey! Hey! Hullo!
Hullo! Motobai? Hey! Whey you go? Whey you ka fra? Amelica? Hello! We go
motobai? One dolla? You wan massa? Young gull? Vey goo, vey nai (very good,
very nice). Mali-lang-lang? Hullo! Hullo! Hey! Whey go you!? Whey you go!?"
And it went like this about every three minutes or so. What was worse was that
no one seemed prepared to take no for an answer.

Making my way around the lake, I re-entered the jumble of streets and shops
of the Old Quarter, where I settled on a convivial looking place, got out a book,
and ordered a large bottle of Hanoi Beer. It was surprisingly good. Things had apparently come a long way from the days depicted in *Good Morning Vietnam!*, where
Robin Williams's character discovers that Vietnamese ale is brewed with only
the choicest formaldehyde. Later, I tried a Saigon Beer. It was good too, but I'd
have to give the edge to the Hanoi. After two large bottles, I walked back to

the hotel, took a nice hot shower, and fell onto the bed. Thankfully, they had changed the sheets.

The next morning, I was awoken by singing, if you can call it that. The three guys who worked the reception desk were having an early morning round of karaoke, bless their souls. The tuneless performance reverberated up the stairwell, bounced off the high walls of my room, and bored into my skull. After a shower and a complimentary breakfast of toast and bananas, I went outside, and took a deep breath with the thought of bellowing, "GOOOODDDDD MOOOOORNING VIETNAM!!! I thought better of it, but had the words echoed to me even though I had not spoken. "Goo mao ling!" yelled a wretched-looking figure cheerily. "Cyclo? Hey! Whey you go? My cyclo numba one. I know. I know," he exclaimed, but I ignored him and hailed a cab. The cabbie informed me that he was on his way to pick up someone else, but that he would call somebody to pick me up in a couple of minutes. Sure enough, an identical cab came along shortly and I showed him where I wanted to go on my map.

We drove west through the consular district, with its proud flags and regal looking embassies. At my destination, the meter read "19,200 VND" (Vietnam *dong*), or about $12. We had only gone two kilometers. I didn't know how much a taxi in Hanoi should cost, but I knew it shouldn't cost this much. The driver pointed to the meter and gave me a smirking look. I handed him the equivalent of $6 and reminded myself to watch the meter being activated in the future. He didn't even bother to protest. Next, I dodged about a thousand motorcycles in crossing the street, ultimately making it to the other side and to the entrance of the Ho Chi Minh Mausoleum Complex.

Admission to the area was free, although purchasing a brochure was mandatory. A sign saying, "KEEP THE LUGGAGE" indicated you had to check in any bags you might be carrying, so I hid my notebook in my sleeve, and handed over my small backpack. The so-called mausoleum complex was in fact an assortment of miniature parks featuring gardens, pagodas, memorials, and the like. The mausoleum itself was located somewhere in the middle of all this, although I couldn't pick it out from where I was currently standing.

After paying for the brochure, I passed by two tables of jovial and boisterous Vietnamese people smoking and drinking beer. It was 8:25 a.m. After walking past some attractive flora, the first *objet d'art* I encountered took the form of a fountain done in a kind of "fish and lotus" motif and was constructed from hundreds of moss green and jaundice yellow tiles. Up ahead, I noticed a throng of Vietnamese people emerging from a long, narrow building. They were being led onward by a tour guide with a megaphone. I darted into the place to have a look. With its wooden pews it resembled the interior of a church, but was in fact an audio-visual hall. At the front, there sat a standard 29-inch television set that was in the midst of rolling credits and emitting the kind of music that puts you in the mind of marching or assisting your countrymen in erecting a village. How anyone sitting further back than the fifth row could have seen the screen was anyone's guess, but there must have been 25 rows in all. Approaching a uniformed guard stationed behind a desk, I asked if the film would start again. He informed me, by way of scowling and pointing toward the way I had come, that it would be in my best interest to keep moving. I took a second to survey myself in order to make sure I hadn't metamorphosed into a filthy hippy sometime during the night, but I looked alright. Outside, another man — this one sporting a hideous olive uniform with red lapels and rows of silver stars — gave me a stern dressing down before ordering me to keep up with my tour group. There was a pattern emerging here, I noted.

Not wishing to be yelled at again, I shadowed a trickle of individuals down a quiet path until I came to a T-junction. Here, some people turned left into a large, nearly empty walkway while the majority turned right toward a spot where others were in the process of lining up outside what was obviously the mausoleum. Following along, I got in line behind a horde of prattling, elderly Germans. Shortly thereafter, a squadron of Koreans showed up and got in behind me. Presumably displeased with the arrangement, the Koreans quickly commenced jumping the queue. As there weren't many gaps, they decided to create some, and this entailed gently shoving and nudging the significantly older Europeans out of the way. Luckily, a couple of police officers observed what was happening and gave a few blasts of their whistles before ordering everyone to line up in single file and stay that way. For the next 10 minutes, Koreans throughout the line craned their necks around, sulkily searching for their friends and family. These are a people, it would appear, who are experts at becoming divided. After being berated a couple more times by the olive clad authorities for our unruly behavior, we all shuffled along into a foyer. Up ahead, I could see that people were being divested of their cameras and phones. "Camera! Cell phone!" barked a man as I neared the entrance. "I don't have one," I stammered, and he waved me straight through. Straight through the exit and back outside again, that is. I was back at the point where I couldn't decide whether to go left or right. I had followed the majority, only to end up joining tour groups arriving at a different gate. As the saying goes, "There is no stupidity like mass stupidity."

Sandwiched among the Korean and German tourists, I marched single file toward the mausoleum. Once inside, I managed to have pretty good look at "Uncle Ho," which is what the Vietnamese refer to him as. Oddly, he looked remarkably like Lenin, which really *is* odd because the granite structure in which he is housed is modeled after Lenin's and the good uncle's annual maintenance is performed in Russia along with the body of Mao Zedong, and, in all probability, that of old Vladimir Ilich himself. I wondered if there weren't a tourist in Moscow right now saying, "Hey, you know? That looks an awful lot like Ho Chi Minh, don't you think?"

Ho, of course, was the founder of the Viet Minh or Vietnamese Communist Party (better known in the West as the Viet Cong or VC) and was the figure the masses in the north rallied around in expelling first the French and then the Americans. Portrayed as a kindly, scholarly gentleman who wanted nothing more than to reunite his homeland under the banner of independence, many would argue that he was at heart a ruthless opportunist who terrorized the people of the north, waged war on the people of the south, and spawned a military apparatus that cynically suppressed both long after accomplishing his main objective. But even if a large number of Vietnamese held this view, which they almost certainly did, it was clear no one was saying much about it nowadays. And besides, here in the north at least, most people probably felt quite the opposite. With a huge propaganda machine behind him, Ho was being mass marketed as the ultimate patriot and seemed to be enjoying immense, almost rock star like popularity despite having been dead for nearly four decades. In his portraits, which hung everywhere, he always looked wise, distinguished, and determined no matter whether reading a book, frolicking with children, or posing in his combat fatigues. "UNCLE HO IS WATCHING YOU," I thought, and admittedly, seeing his image every 10 minutes or so did sort of irk me, but not because of the Orwellian-ness of it. Rather, it made me crave fried chicken.

You see, one of the more interesting facts regarding General Ho Chi Minh is that he resembled a thinner, Oriental version of Colonel Sanders. When Ho became president, he wore a white suit, had white hair and a goatee, and sported a pair of horn-rimmed glasses. And that's not where the coincidences end. Both men, you'll be interested to know, were born in the same year: 1890. Growing up, they both went by various names and each worked a host of odd jobs before going on to become famous. Whereas Sanders worked for a spell in the army, Ho did a stint as a chef. Both men were well educated, not to mention very outspoken, and whereas Colonel Sanders developed his 11 herbs and spices, Uncle Ho had been trained as a traditional herbalist. Their popularity even peaked around the same time. In 1975, the year Saigon fell to the Viet Cong, Ho's personality cult reached its zenith, while across the globe, a survey showed Colonel Sanders to be the second most recognizable person on Earth. Picking up on the likeness, an American company once proposed an idea for "Uncle Ho's Hamburgers" in Vietnam, but the notion perturbed communist officials and never got off the ground. But who knows? With the onslaught of capitalism, perhaps in the future, alongside KFC, we'll find a competing UHH. Just imagine the urban legends that would spring up. Soon, you'd be hearing about so-and-so's cousin biting into a chicken burger filled with shrapnel.

Once outside the catacomb, I sauntered through some agreeable gardens, looked at a house that the general lived in and worked out of for a while, inspected a couple of cars he used to drive, and ambled around a pleasant lake flanking the magnificent Presidential Palace, all the while accompanied by an entourage of about eight million other foreign tourists. Germans, Dutch, Scandinavians, Australians, French, Koreans, and Japanese seemed to make up the bulk of these. As I stopped to observe a group of Japanese snap photos of large mound of gardening soil I noticed two things. The first was that there were now oodles of smug-looking French people around me and the second was that there were audio speakers in the trees with a woman's voice coming out of them in droning, thickly-accented English, informing people of things they would never need to know. "In 2007," the voice mechanically announced, "the Ho Chi Minh Mausoleum Complex will be closed to the public on April 24th and November 12th. In 2008, the Ho Chi Minh Mausoleum Complex will be closed to the public on April 19th and October 30th. In 2009, ..." and on and on it went.

Next, it was on to the Ho Chi Minh Museum, which was housed in a drab grey building near the entrance. Strolling under an arched sign ordering you to, "LIVE, FIGHT, WORK AND STUDY AS THE EXAMPLE SET BY THE GREAT UNCLE HO!" I proceeded to an exhibit of plaques featuring Ho Chi Minh's poems and writings from the time he was imprisoned (by Chiang Kai-shek's Nationalists, interestingly enough), and these proved to be every bit as exciting as I guessed they would be. My personal favorite was this touching little limerick entitled "Anthology of a Thousand Poets."

> Of nature the ancients loved to sing the charms,
> Moon and flowers, snow and wind, mist, hills and streams,
> But in our days poems should contain verses of steel,
> And poets should form a front line for attack.

Then it was upstairs for an appraisal of art that was meant to symbolize various stages of the revolutionary movement. A huge model volcano jutting out of the floor was supposed to represent the people's overflowing revolutionary zeal, while an old Ford Edsel (a commercial failure) crashing through a wall was said to signify America's imperialistic designs on Vietnam (a military failure). Get it? Well, I didn't exactly, so I left, following a sign that said, "RECEIVE LUGGA-GA" and then made it to the entrance/exit where yet another one read, "TAKE

LUGGAGE OF FOREIGNER." Along the way, the woman's voice metallically rang out from the loud speakers. "There are over 1600 plant species indigenous to Vietnam... and I will now read them alphabetically..." No doubt, this was followed by a reading of open dates for the next 10,000 years.

In spite of some fine greenery, the Ho Chi Minh Mausoleum Complex was a pretty lackluster affair and this frightened me immensely as I had read that it was the most popular tourist destination in the entire country. Strolling out to the sidewalk, I peered up at a brooding sky before jumping in a cyclo and heading back to the Old Quarter.

There is nothing that will cure a case of the late morning yawns like being whisked around Hanoi in a cyclo at noon. At one point, my driver turned into three lanes of traffic and not one of the oncoming drivers even so much as blinked. On the contrary, they drove straight at us, blasting their horns, and only swerving and missing us by inches and at the last possible instant. I had been determined to give the cyclo experience a try, but now, surveying the two millimeters of aluminum separating me from an oncoming cement mixer flanked by 15 weaving motorcycles, I realized how incredibly ill-conceived this idea had been. I may as well have paid to sit on the hood of cab. And not only do Vietnamese people drive like they are in a video game, but what they drive with is truly a sight to behold. Motor scooters are Vietnam's answer to both the SUV and the family sedan and all manner of goods are transported on them. Although, occasionally, this entails the use of bungee cord, more often than not items are tied to the frame with string or tape. Refrigerators, dogs, stacks of crates, and entire families were just a sampling of the things I witnessed zooming by on these glorified lawnmowers, spewing out fumes and zigzagging in and out of cars and trucks. Probably the most commonly attached items were the cumquat trees. Everybody seemed to be buying one to take back to their home for a Lunar New Year decoration. From the rear, it looked as if dozens of shrubs had commandeered a fleet of motor scooters in order to head into town for a spot of shopping.

After lunch back in the noxious, yet colorful Old Quarter, I moseyed around the lake again, and thought it looked quite striking in the daylight. The water was so green I wondered if (and hoped) someone didn't regularly pour dye into it. It being light out, I was even more conspicuous than I had been at night and it quickly became evident that the relatively open area around the water was a prime spot for preying on tourists. I must have been accosted a dozen times on my way around. Usually, I had to stop, look them in the eye, and say, "No," or "No thank you," before they would finally give up and go away. They were doggedly determined.

On the far side of the green lake, I stepped onto a red arched bridge con-structed of wood and made my way to a minuscule island draped with leafy trees. Passing through a Chinese gate that read *Yushan Si*, or Jade Mountain Temple, in a scrawl of black glossy characters, I was assailed by a waft of thick smoke curl-ing away from the temple's burning incense. The caretakers were actually in the midst of repainting the characters, and the potent, oily smell combined with the oppressive smoke almost sent me fleeing back across the century-old overpass. Pressing on, I admired the lake's murky green waters once more and then en-tered the temple for a quick look around. Immediately, I found myself face to face with an enormous lacquered turtle. Arching its neck in an eternal pose, it had been placed inside a glass tank alongside a dehumidifier, its presence having to do with a local legend concerning the lake, which involves a sword and some turtles. In Asia, there's a legend behind almost everything that isn't man made. An old tree is never just an old tree, a mountain never just a mountain. However, having said that, to this day, tortoises are said to be spotted every now and again in the lake. Some think the body of water is occasionally stocked with them in order to keep the legend alive.

I just love old communist propaganda posters (North Korea has the best ones, in my opinion), and back in the Old Quarter, I stumbled upon an entire store of them. A large sign above the counter read, "Please Buy Propaganda Picture" and this amused me to no end. For a half an hour or so, I contentedly browsed around, dreaming of buying a few and using them to open and decorate a place I would call *The Kommie Kafé*. Countries such as Vietnam, Laos, North Korea, and China still put up these vignettes of plump looking, rosy cheeked, gleefully united peas-ants, while all around them society crumbles to the ground.

That evening, I decided to check out a water puppets performance at a near-by theater. In the lobby, there were loads of foreign tourists, an exceptionally large contingent of which were Korean. Koreans, as I pointed out earlier, are, to put it mildly, an exceptionally passionate bunch. Knowing this, like I do, I shouldn't have been surprised by their overzealousness in regard to taking in a puppet show, but alas, I was.

While ascending the theater stairs, a Korean man behind me twice — *twice*, mind you — put what I presume was his fist straight into the base of my spine. Just think for a moment about the dynamics involved. I stopped and asked him if I could be of some assistance, but he just threw up his hands in innocence. Once seated, I contentedly surveyed the architecture, secretly scanned the faces of the people sitting around me, and then had a glance through the brochure I had been given. Then, while blankly gaping straight ahead, I noticed something that made me think I'd entered a wormhole and re-emerged in another dimension. A girl with a bad leg, who was slowly hobbling up the stairs and using the wall for support, was shoulder checked into the wall by a jogging Korean woman who continued on, found her row, and took her seat. The girl crumpled to the floor and struggled to get up. Stunned, I sat there staring at the offending woman as she cheerily joined a group of squawking compatriots. Not one of the 30 or so people in the immediate area (and they couldn't have helped but notice) even so much as blinked. The girl managed to pick herself up, and I walked down the stairs, took her by the arm, and helped her to seat. And here's the thing: *she was also Korean and part of another Korean contingent sitting right next to me. Not one of her colleagues had thought to help her.* On top of all this, she was obviously mentally handicapped. My flabber was gasted. After finally getting settled, she looked over at me, smiled, and by way of a thank you, said, "Hello." My heart melted. Then the show began.

An orchestra of zithers, lutes, and other predominantly stringed instruments embarked on an eerie, meandering tune as the set brightened to reveal a miniaturized version of the lake temple that I had visited that afternoon. Two dragons emerged through a stage of emerald water where they danced and thrashed to the strings and crashing cymbals, eventually emitting sparks and smoke through their nostrils. Then, just as quickly as they had appeared, they disappeared back into the murky recesses of the green pool, leaving only plumes of smoke to waft up through the darkened theater.

Water puppets is a quirky, millennium-old art form exclusive to Vietnam. A team of puppeteers stand in hip waders behind a backdrop and operate a host of complex wooden dummies on poles, but to the audience, it appears as if the glossily painted marionettes are walking on water. In one scene, a fisherman got a nibble on his line, and then pulled and pulled only to reel in a sea snake that chased him about while fish mockingly jumped and splashed all around him. That sort of thing. It was all good fun.

After the show ended, I walked back outside into the chaos and pollution and then repaired to a pub on a street lined with pubs, where I quaffed down a couple of bottles of Hanoi Beer and absent mindedly watched a soccer game. The two guys working there smilingly tried to have a conversation with me, but their English was so bad we just ended up toasting each other and sharing a few Oo's and Ah's at the near misses in the match. Outside, at a smallish table piled high with empty beer bottles, I noticed four local guys sitting and enjoying themselves. After a bit, they all stood up, got on the same motorbike together, and drove off into the night.

I awoke to a damp, chilly morning and a world enveloped by a giant dome of pale grey. After trying the national breakfast of *pho*, a kind of beef noodle soup (it wasn't bad), I jumped in another taxi and pointed to another dot on my map. Ten minutes later, the driver let me out in front of a mustard yellow building of French design. An arched sign atop a forbidding doorway read MAISON CEN-TRALE, although to Anglophones the place is better known as the Hanoi Hilton. Formerly a prison used by the French to detain, torture, and execute "rebellious" Vietnamese, it later became famous when it served as a jail for American pilots shot down over the North. Nowadays, it's a museum, and so I purchased a ticket and made my way inside.

It was very absorbing and pulled no punches in presenting the French and Americans as wayward gangs of meddling and murderous imperialists. There was a guillotine as well as a dungeon which were employed by the French, along with a notable collection of old photographs. The mug shots of American soldiers were particularly moving. Not one of them brought their eyes up to meet the camera, but rather hung their heads in despair. And then of course, there was the propaganda. The "confessions" written by American inmates, conspicuously lacking in articles, grammar, and general fluency, were nothing if not interesting. Moreover, the prison was presented as having been a kind of home away from home, replete with ping pong tournaments, guitar playing, and even beer drinking. Yet despite their little slice of Americana, the participants' facial expressions ranged anywhere from forced to psychologically shattered, which was somewhat at odds with those of their exuberant captors.

After a good long look around, I went outside and caught another cab to the Museum of Ethnology. Upon arrival, I saw that two French women were standing outside a taxi and dramatically engaged in an argument with their driver. It must be said that nobody can gesticulate quite like the French. As soon as I got out of the car, one of the women walked over to me and asked how much my cab was. "Two dollars," I told her.

"And did you come from ze Old Quarter?" she followed up.

"Not far from there. Probably from the Old Quarter it would be about three dollars," I replied.

"Oh, well, ee is charging uz *fifteen* dollars."

"Oh, that's not right," I said, frowning, and added that the same thing had happened to me the day before and that it was a good idea to watch them turn the meter on. After passing this on to her friend she walked back to the cab, crumpled up a bill, and, through the rolled-down window, bounced it off the driver's head. And that was just the warm up. Her friend then advised the unscrupulous driver, by way of universal sign language, what he ought to do with his $3. Her visual instructions were accompanied by such a vicious string of English expletives as to give the impression the couple was in Hanoi on shore leave.

The driver, correctly assessing that he had lost the battle, popped the car into reverse and sped away.

While the vast majority of Vietnam's 83 million and growing populace is comprised of ethnically Vietnamese, a very significant 13% is made up of various so-called hill tribes, groups ranging from one hundred to one million in size. These peoples are ethnically, culturally, and linguistically distinct from each other and their counterparts in the urban and coastal areas, and that's what the museum was attempting to convey, albeit primarily through sanitized videos of people weaving conical hats and baskets. Of course, in reality these people are discriminated against and viewed as backward, but here, in this tastefully done building in Hanoi, their images and artwork were accorded full and equal status.

The place was filled with French people, most with contemplative "Where did we go wrong?" expressions on their faces. "If only we had treated them a just a fraction better," they seemed to be thinking, "they could now be weaving *our* baskets." I looked on as one group watched intently at a video of a colorfully dressed, camera shy woman pounding grain. Personally, there is only so long I could watch someone pound grain, especially when it's on a TV screen, and, at least to some extent, put on, but there you are. And there they were; eyes narrowed, brows furrowed, and hands rubbing chins, as if awaiting a national election result.

Bored by the basket-making process and happily diverse peoples, I went back outside into the late grey morning and walked around the landscaped grounds where they had built replicas of houses done in the preferred styles of various tribes. Some of them were truly impressive, but I felt that I ought to be viewing them in a genuine context and not on some museum ground. Still, they were nicely presented, and like the Ho Chi Minh Museum Complex, the area was filled with lovely trees. Having lived in a city for the past decade, I get sort of mesmerized whenever I see greenery, and so I strolled around admiring the ficus trees and clusters of bamboo more so than the quaintly rustic structures. But ultimately, I even became disillusioned with the foliage. Along the far edge of the grounds, there was a tiny ridge with around 30 trees sticking out of it and a bronze sign reading, "The Place for Worshipping the Forest." "Uh-huh," I reflected. "This is just a thought, but it might help to actually *have* a forest, don't you think?" Realizing that I was badly in need of a caffeine fix, I repaired to a charming gazebo-style coffee shop nestled under a gargantuan banyan tree strung with Chinese lanterns and ordered a cup of tea.

If you want milk with your coffee or tea in Vietnam, you're given a something called *Vinamilk*, a syrup with a consistency and taste akin to melted white chocolate. Even a couple of drops of it have trouble dissolving, yet they give you a whole tub of the stuff. When combined with the caffeine, it provides a real kick and this may partially account for the Vietnamese "enthusiastic" approach to driving. While sitting at a bamboo dining set designed for gnomes and sipping my sweet tea-and-sludge, a pony-tailed Frenchman made a bee line in my direction. Sporting a T-shirt that said *Sans Frontieres*, I wondered if he weren't a doctor. As he drew near, he looked at me and I at him and as he was about to enter, I offered a "Hello." He returned it with a frosty stare and an appreciable sniffle. And this, of course, is why no one likes the French.

For lunch, I ate at a restaurant called KOTO, which stands for "Know One, Teach One." KOTO is a foreign run establishment whose proceeds go toward providing career training and assistance to former street kids. Refueled, and feeling proudly philanthropic, I proceeded back outdoors where I fretfully traversed a faded crosswalk laid across a stretch of "Indianapolis 500" race track. Once safely across, I purchased a ticket to the Confucian themed, thousand-year-old Temple of Literature and wandered around its decaying courtyards. My travel guide described it as a tranquil spot, ideal for getting away from the hubbub of Hanoi, but plainly everybody was using the same book. After this, I made my way to the History Museum. More of a "history through art" museum, it proved to be quite charming both inside and out. Housed in a stately ochre building, it concisely communicated the extent of both Chinese and Indian cultural influence in Vietnam.

Once back in the Old Quarter, my cyclo driver began to demand more than we had agreed upon, never mind that I was already paying him nearly twice the going rate. He yelled, he stomped his feet, he pretended to cry, but in the end I just walked away. This was fast becoming a recurring theme. Almost any transaction had the potential of degenerating into a huge production. On several occasions, when told the bill was, say, eight dollars, I would reach into my pocket, fish out five, give it to them, and then say, "Just a minute," before retrieving the other three. (Remember, my wallet was doing its best imitation of a fish brought home from the market back at the Prince Hotel.) In the five seconds or so it would take me to locate the other bills, the waiter, or proprietor, or whoever, would start demanding the rest of the money in a manner that suggested I wasn't going to give it to them. They would even do this if I were the only customer there. Indeed, it seemed to be a kind of gut reaction.

"Eight dolla! Eight dolla! You give me eight dolla! You give me eight dolla *now!*"

"Yeah, I am. Just hold on. Here you go. Six, seven, eig..."

"*Eight* dolla! You give me *eight* dolla!"

There was a startling degree of desperation and tension to even the simplest of transactions.

Back at the hotel, I napped, had a refreshing shower, and then went back out to eat. After browsing around some art shops, I went to a travel agent to book a ticket for the morning. Then I hit the streets to try and find an alarm clock. I had forgotten to bring one. At a modern looking store selling pretty much everything, I found one and gestured to the clerk to kindly fetch it for me. Unlocking the glass case it was in, which, incidentally, contained other such valuable commodities as disposable razors and shaving cream, she allowed me a few seconds to examine it, after which she carried it to the cash register herself lest I make a break for it. Once at the counter, she took the item out of its package, inserted a battery, and then proudly illustrated that it was, in fact, in fine working order. Next, she took out the set of instructions, unfolded them, and held them up for my inspection. This was hardly necessary. Finally, she rang it in and pointed to the cash register which showed "15,6000 VND" in fluorescent green digits. That was $10. The price tag had read 56,000 VND, or about $4, but when I tried to explain this to her, she just gave me the same look my cyclo driver had given me earlier. I showed her the tag, which said, ^56,000, and then she showed me, by way of writing, that the upside down V was in fact a 1. I thought it was perhaps the Vietnamese symbol for *dong*. Plastic alarm clocks shouldn't cost $10 in Vietnam, so I told her I was sorry and left without purchasing it. She started screaming, "I open! You buy! You buy *now!*" but I just kept walking. She should never have opened it in the first place. I went back to the hotel and went to sleep. I had had quite enough of Hanoi.

That night, I slept thinly. My hotel didn't do wake up calls, so I kept worrying I'd oversleep. At 5:30, I roused myself, got my things together, and headed downstairs to settle the bill, having gotten my newspaper-wrapped wallet back the night before. After I put the money I owed on the counter, the clerk added that there would be an additional $10 surcharge for tax.

"Tax?" I asked. "What tax?"

"VAT," he answered, mopping at a dripping nostril with the back of his hand.

"There is no VAT in Vietnam," I said.

"State hotels have VAT. This is state hotel."

"Oh, really? This is a state hotel?"

"That's right."

"Could you show me some kind of state-issued license, then?" I asked, my blood boiling. It was too early for this.

"Oh, we don't have," he stammered. "Every hotel in Vietnam is state hotel. You pay tax."

"Nonsense," I said.

"No. Is true," he said, getting angry. "Is real."

Ten dollars wasn't a lot of money, but it was the principle, and I didn't appreciate being cheated by guys I had chatted and joked with for three days. "OK, fine," he went on. "We have your passport. You no pay, we no give you passport."

They did have my passport. Hotels kept foreigners' passports as a matter of course. I hadn't seen this one coming. I didn't have time to go to the police (and they might have asked me for $10 themselves), so I had to pay. I told him I was going to write all the travel guides and strongly suggest that they remove his hotel from their recommended list. He sniffled, and defiantly said I could go right ahead. "He wasn't afraid of anything," he declared, and "could handle all matters well." So, if you ever find yourself in Hanoi, steer clear of The Prince Hotel, No. 71 Hang Luoc, unless you enjoy being extorted.

I left the hotel in a dim frame of mind and shuffled down an ill-lit street under yet another dreary, sulking sky. Along the way, I stopped and bought a baguette and a couple of bananas. Baguettes, I might add, along with the few remaining regal, mustard colored mansions, were about the only remnants of the French colonial past that I could see in Hanoi. Yet my guide book made the city out to be a kind of *Paris de l'Orient*, marked by a beret wearing class of people who sat around cafés discussing Sartre and effortlessly shifting between Vietnamese, English, and French. My guide book was full of rubbish. But it had good maps and that was probably the only thing that saved it from spending the rest of its days in a filthy gutter, which was where I felt like flinging it as I made my way to the travel agent's office.

Right on time, a minibus pulled up and I got on, the last of 15 passengers, all foreign tourists. Well, all except for one. As we left the downtown area, a local man stood up, switched on a microphone (remember, it was a *minibus*) and introduced himself as our tour guide. I didn't know there would be a tour guide, and somehow doubted one would be necessary.

His name was Huang, which meant "King," so we could call him that if we couldn't remember Huang. He seemed like a cheerful sort, and while crossing a bridge out of the city, he explained that we were now over the Red River and that it was more than 500 kilometers long. He went on to say how it originated in Southern China and had been carved by a thrashing dragon. "So, as you can see, it has an interesting legend behind it and it's lily lily *looong*," he said, the majority of the sounds emanating from his nose. He also pointed out a bridge upriver that was bombed by the US and rebuilt 17 times during the American War, which is what the Vietnamese call it.

Parenthetically, as I would soon discover, traveling in this Tommy Tourist type manner was pretty much the only way to do it in Vietnam. Originally, I had planned to take local buses and sleep on jagged rocks in snake riddled jungles like a real travel writer, but it was just far too easy (not to mention economical, efficient, and comparatively safe) to follow the tourist flow. Most certainly, this took some of the romance out of it, but everyone did it. Still, at this point of my adventure, I hadn't succumbed to the idea of going it alone. Traveling this way also meant that you were constantly surrounded by people, namely tourists. Indeed, Vietnam is like a tourist corridor. People are either moving from Hanoi to Saigon or vice versa. Frequent human interaction was very much part of the experience.

Slums yielded to factories, which in turn deferred to rice fields, and these were vast and dotted with oxen driven ploughs and darkly clad figures in conical hats stooped over their crops. The colorful, towering "tunnel houses" houses were replaced by dull, tumbledown hovels, usually situated at the end of a dirt track. We drove for hours and I didn't see so much as a single tractor. People were toiling like animals. It was thoroughly depressing and so was the weather. I put in my earphones and fell asleep.

Despite the fact that I'm only in my thirties, I sleep like an old man. I've gone from not being able to sleep anyplace except for my own bed to being able to sleep anywhere, anytime, and in a pretty slobbery and snore-happy manner. If you find this repellent, I can sympathize because I'm a little put off by it myself. I catch myself doing it, and then suddenly snap out of it, afraid there'll be a crowd around me saying things like, "Wow. His mouth opened so wide you could just about see his feet." On the bus, I caught myself doing it again, so I jerked my head upright and looked cautiously looked around, but no one seemed to have noticed.

The guy sitting next to me wanted to talk. He was thin and in his early twenties. His name was Brian and he hailed from Vancouver. He explained that he was traveling with his father and his father's new bride, a Vietnamese woman named May who had relatives in Vancouver. His father, whose name was Rick, had gotten in contact with her via e-mail and they struck up a friendship. That was six months ago, and now here he was with his son on his honeymoon. After a jaunt around Vietnam, they were slated to return to Canada.

"That's great that you're traveling with you dad," I offered.

"Yeah, well. He told me he was gettin' married, so I said, 'Not without me, you're not.' I just figured I couldn't let him do it alone. He might get lost or somethin'."

At the halfway point, we stopped at what looked like a warehouse along the side of the highway. Inside there was a restaurant and table after table of tourist kitsch. A large banner reading, "Handicrafts Made By Handicapped Children," was draped above a prominently displayed group of women weaving conical hats, yet, besides a girl standing at the entranceway lamely shuffling back and forth in an attempt at getting people's attention, none of the workers were observably handicapped. On the contrary, they looked to be in fairly decent health. What was more, none of them were children. After perfunctorily glancing around at the virtual ocean of garish bits and baubles, I sauntered back out to the minibus where Huang was drinking a Coke.

"So, are you originally from Hanoi?" I ventured.

"No. I'm from a small village in the north. I rent an apartment in Hanoi," he said smilingly.

"And where did you learn your English?" I asked. "It's very good."

"In university. I studied tourism."

"I see. And how long have you been a tour guide?"

"Oh," he moaned, emitting a weary sigh. "*Too loong.* I been a tour guide for six years," he elaborated, and appeared to age instantly as he said this. His forehead became creased, and he raised a nervous hand and ran it through his hair. "I want to *retire*," he went on. "I don't want to work anymore. I'm getting *old*. Six years is a *loong time*. After this one, this trip, I will finished. I will home to my village."

As he spoke, tears welled up in his eyes. I certainly hadn't been expecting that. In the span of about 45 seconds, he had gone from a guy cheerily drinking a Coke to one who looked to be on the brink of a nervous breakdown. He certainly didn't look old (he was only 27), and I wondered how stressful being a tour guide could be. There certainly appeared to be much worse jobs about; hunching over your crops all day, for one, or taking bomb shells off a conveyer built and stacking them up into wobbly pyramids, for another.

"Right," I said. "Well, I'd better get on the bus, then," and left him to his retirement plans.

We were supposed to be on a major highway, but essentially it was a country road. And the further out in the countryside we got, the worse the driving became. Our driver passed every vehicle he could, often on blind corners. When there was no one to pass, he'd straddle the yellow line and play chicken with much larger oncoming trucks and buses. But, I suppose, I shouldn't single him out. Everyone else seemed to do the same thing. Looking out the front window was nerve racking, and on top of the total lack of road safety, there was the deafening sound of honking. Whenever our driver passed anyone — anyone at all mind you, including old people peddling their bicycles in straight, slow lines along the shoulder of the road — he would honk the horn, and I'm not talking about a friendly little "Comin' through!" toot.

There was also a very elaborate system for meeting oncoming vehicles, which entailed more horn blasts on behalf of both drivers and a good deal of frantic headlight flashing. At first, I assumed there was an accident ahead, or perhaps a patrol car, but then I realized that it was all part of the ritual. They drove like lunatics, and then to "play it safe" they blared their horns and flashed their lights every seven seconds or so.

Around noon, we arrived at a dock at the edge of a tiny little town where we alighted and walked toward a collection of junks that were bundled around a single concrete pier. Our junk was about four vessels away, and so we had to boat hop to get to it. Once onboard, we were fed a simple yet ample lunch in the cabin. There were only four tables, and so we were all crammed in together. At first, no one said much, but then, as the food came, the ball got rolling and I suppose the beer didn't hurt.

Among the group was a good humored Danish fellow named Jan who was a retired sailor and was now traveling around Asia. Then, there was a father and son team originally from Costa Rica, but long since immigrated to the US. The father, Don, was brimming over with charisma, insights, quips, and questions in regard to other people's travels and experiences. He had what could only be described as a genteel air about him, enhanced, I think, by his flawless command of English rendered in a superb Spanish accent. His son was more taciturn, which may have had something to do with having recently left the US Navy as a submariner. There was also an elderly couple from Quebec, who didn't speak much English but tried. After eating and getting acquainted, everyone went up to the deck to survey the scenery, which had begun to steal our attention through the cabin windows.

Halong Bay is Vietnam's panoramic crown jewel. More than 3000 rugged, tree strewn limestone islets jut radically from a jade sea where they loom and recede in myriad shades of grey into the ocean mists. They are ornamented by grottoes, flocks of birds, Chinese characters, and thin strips of golden beach. In our Chinese junk, we sailed for hours between them, everyone humbly marveling at their unique features. The dearth of human activity, unspoiled environment, and very audible silence coalesced to form the impression that this was almost certainly how ancient explorers must have found it. Like us, they must have been in a state of silent, respectful awe. Well, except for the cartographers. They must have been cursing up a storm.

For the first time since my arrival, the sun broke through, turning grey to blue and making quick work of the surrounding haze. After a couple of hours, we passed by the first in a series of floating villages; colorful huts built on to connected, anchored rafts. Women hung their laundry while dogs hopped from one "yard" to the next. In lieu of the family car, skiffs were tied outside the front door while large red trawlers equipped with booms and 1000-watt bulbs bobbed in the background. Without much in the way of an announcement, our boat approached one of the islands and docked.

"Now we go to see crystal caves," yelled Huang. "You bring bag and get off boat. Boat will pick you up on other side of the island. Don't forget your belongings."

I had a small backpack and then another regular bag weighted down with four or five books. Grabbing both of them, I disembarked to notice that no one else was carrying anything except their cameras. I turned around to put my larger bag back on the boat only for Huang to stop me.

"Where you go?" he asked.

"I want to put this bag back on the boat."

"No. No. You no go back to boat," he responded in annoyance. And then bringing a quivering hand up to his head again, he seized a patch of his hair and added, "Boat is leaving *now* to go to other side of the island. Next time you listen."

We were standing a mere 20 meters away from our junk. It was still docked. In fact, the skipper and the cook were both sitting on the deck and having a cigarette. They didn't look to be in much of a hurry. But not wanting to cause any problems, I turned around and trudged toward the caves, a bag slung over each shoulder.

The caves were remarkable. Huge cauliflower faced columns extended up and dripped down from a cream colored ceiling that must have been five stories high. Strategic lighting caused beams of purple, green, and red to flitter through the particle heavy air, causing pillars and walls to mimic immense, melted candles. It was a large, echoing affair and took some time to get through.

After emerging, we walked along a stone path along the hillside and made our way to another interesting (if slightly less dramatic) cave. Lugging my heavy bags, I struggled along in the rear and soon found myself alone. After exploring this second grotto, I descended a flight of stairs only to notice Huang walking up toward me. "Come *on*! We go *now*! Boat already *leave*! We come back for *you*!" he whined, and grabbed hold of his hair again. Feeling guilty, I apologized, but then feebly used my baggage as an excuse. He wasn't sympathetic, though, and we walked down to the pier in silence. But then, I got to wondering how they could have left. Surely, I wasn't any more than five minutes behind the second from last person. Didn't they do a head count? Onboard, I asked Don how far they had gotten. "Only a couple of feet," he said smilingly, "and then I noticed that you weren't here."

We sailed on through the stunning seascape and in the late afternoon, stopped to buy fruit from two women in tiny rowboats. They lived in one of the floating villages that were becoming more and more common. The sun disappeared into the sea, and I went back down to the cabin to chat with Jan the Dane along with the young Brian, his father Rick, and his new wife May. Just after dark, we arrived at the large Cat Ba Island. Some people were going ashore to stay at a hotel and return to Hai Phong by junk the next morning whereas others were staying on the boat. I was staying on the boat. Jan was leaving, and so I said goodbye. That night we ate a dinner that was identical to lunch, after which we sat around chatting and drinking beer.

The next day, I got up, got off the boat, and got onto a bus. We drove over a couple of hills and then entered a sleepy little town where we checked into a nice hotel. After getting cleaned up, I went out for a stroll and was propositioned for sex about 10 times in as many minutes. This was at around nine thirty. Ambling along a boardwalk, I snapped a few pictures of the quiet town with its dramatic, rock hemmed harbor, before making my way to a restaurant to get a cup of mid-morning caffeine. The restaurant turned out to be the front section of a small hotel. On the wall next to me was a sign that read, "Please realize the following obligations," and went on list 26 rules in convoluted English. Of note was Article 12 which stated, "Explosives, automatic weapons, poison or bad smell things are strictly forbid."

After lunch, I took a boat with Brian, Rick, and May to a place called Monkey Island. Landing on a narrow stretch of sand containing only a handful of structures, a few beach chairs, and the sign, "PLEASE KEEP AWAY FROM MONKEY — THEY MIGHT BITE YOU," we spent a few minutes observing the red faced, mangy things after which Brian and I decided to try our hand at kayaking. Neither of us had done it before but we found it remarkably smooth going and paddled a fair distance, doing a pretty large arc around a pretty large bay. Two hours later, we returned and boarded the boat to go back.

Back at the hotel, I saw Huang in the lobby chatting to a bored looking receptionist. The following day, we were slated to return to Hanoi, but seeing as how I had had quite enough of that city, I thought I'd ask about leaving the tour back on the mainland at Hai Phong in order to travel south under my own steam to a place called Ninh Binh. Huang, in his way, misunderstood me and thought I was asking him to make a 200 kilometer detour.

"No!" he cried. "Tomorrow we *don't go* to Ninh Binh. We go to *Hanoi.*"

"Look would you calm down?" I pleaded. "I am just asking you a question. Tomorrow, when we arrive in Hai Phong, can I get off the bus and go to Ninh B..."

"I told you. *We don't go to Ninh Binh. We go to Hanoi.*"

"No. Not *you.* Me. *I* want to go to Ninh Binh. Can *I* go to Ninh Binh by myself?"

"No. You no go to Ninh Binh," he replied shaking his head, his voice soaring and sharpening to a high, whiny pitch. "*You go to Hanoi! You no get off bus!*"

Once again, good old Huang looked to be on the verge of collapse. This conversation caused him to bring *both* hands up to his scalp, whereupon he grabbed onto two patches of hair and began to pull.

After dinner, I headed to the hotel bar where I found Rick and young Brian teaching May how to play darts. I joined them, and we spent a few contented hours chatting and drinking large, refreshing, and absurdly cheap bottles of beer.

"So, Rick," I asked, at one point. "Did you have any trouble with the paperwork re getting married? I mean, was it complicated?"

"No, it was a breeze," he responded.

"Really?" I replied. "I would've thought there'd have been a lot of red tape. Maybe even a few bribes here and there to make things go better."

"Oh, you mean *here.* I thought you meant in Canada. Oh, here it was a nightmare! May's family's from Saigon, eh? Ho Chi Minh City. So, I had to take all the documents I got in Canada and everything else and go there and do all the paperwork. After I got everything paid for and signed, they said I needed to get a mental health certificate. I had a health certificate, but they wanted a *mental* health certificate. So, I get in a van and go with a couple of other Western guys also gettin' married, and they drive us to some mountain somewhere outside Saigon. There was no air conditioning in the thing and it was *really* hot. I mean, we were literally pouring buckets. Anyway, they finally let us out at this rundown hospital up in the hills and *it* didn't have any air conditioning either. We all sat in this hall, sweatin' and waitin' to talk to a doctor. When it was my turn, I go in, sit down, and they say, 'What's your mother's name?' So, I tell them and they write it down. Then, they ask, 'What's your father's name?' so, I tell them that and they write that down. 'Do you smoke?' they ask. 'Yes,' I said. 'Why?' they ask, so I said, 'I don't know. Bad habit?' 'OK,' they said. 'Have you ever been hit in the head?' 'Umm...no,' I said. And that was it. They stamped the certificate and called in the next guy. Then we had to drive all the way *back* to Saigon. The whole thing took one day."

The next morning, we got to see the slideshow of Halong Bay in reverse. In the morning it looked even more splendid and surreal than it had in the afternoon. On our right, sunbeams angled through the treetops while their golden source climbed and forced the craggy formations to throw long dark shadows of themselves. On our left, the karst islets sat atop their perfect reflections, while flocks of birds and a convoy of junks vied unsuccessfully for our attention.

Once back on land, we had what was in essence a farewell luncheon, and then hopped on a bus operated by a man whose disdain for road rules made our previous driver look like Papa Smurf. After a half hour of weaving, overtaking, and honking, he finally managed to thwack a guy on a motorcycle, causing him to fall off into a ditch. Then, in a display of comradeship, he then accelerated and drove away, barreling along like nobody's business. Only a short while after this, we bypassed a recently-overturned transport truck. But the most frightening moment came when we climbed a very large and very long arched suspension bridge. Our driver must have passed five vehicles in his rush to reach the apex, over which, of course, he could not see. There was nowhere to maneuver and so if anything larger than a Go-Kart had come over the crest, that would have been it. Luckily, however, the convoy of transport trucks making their way up the other side still had some way to go. After coming off the bridge, we found ourselves on the main street of a dilapidated little town, and lo and behold, there was another accident. Slivers of plastic and chunks of metal lay scattered about the road, a baseball cap and shoe clearly visible among the wreckage. A motorcycle had been pulverized by a two-ton truck. Make no mistake. Vietnam is one dangerous place.

Later we stopped for a leg stretch and a snack at another designated roadside dive. I strolled around with Brian, and we noticed that in addition to the usual offerings of fried noodles, soft drinks, and ice cream, you could buy various sized bottles of local snake wine. Rattle snakes, looking every bit alive in death, were stuffed into bottles of rice wine, their tails facetiously wound through their open jaws and usually a scorpion thrown in for good measure. A sticker on the bottle read, "SNAKE WINE — as Cure for Lumbago and Rheumatism — One Sip Before Each Meal." I suppose. Between the intoxication and stomachache, you would soon forget about something as trifling as lumbago.

"Cool!" Brian exclaimed, inspecting a bottle. "I know someone who'd love this." Eventually settling on one, he took it to the counter and had it wrapped as a gift for a Vietnamese friend back in Vancouver. Back on the bus, a white-haired woman dressed in a lively, tight shirt and pair of electric blue pants turned around and fixed him with a reproachful look. She had joined us in Hai Phong and had spent the past two hours boasting about her grandchildren.

"Yawl didn't bah one o' them snakes, did ya?" she drawled.

"I did," rejoindered Brian, proudly.

"Oh, I don't *lak* snakes. They're the most *appallin'* things. Wah, once, I remember, I was at this snake farm in *Yewtaww* — I'm from *Yewtaww* — an' anyway, they had all these snakes, ya know, in glass tanks and such, kinda like fish? I just kept walkin' around, an' lookin' at them, an' thinkin,' 'Naw, what if there's an earthquake right naw and all these tanks come crashin' down and break and the snakes all get out and attack me?' I mean, it was *real* scary."

That sounded "real scary." It was almost as scary as the prospect of someone lighting a match anywhere near the polyester safari suit she had on. Don't think me shallow. I don't usually concern myself a whole lot with people's attire or appearance, but I just have to know what possesses elderly women to don ultra tight sweaters and form fitting slacks.

We drove on, making pretty good time, but then hit a bottleneck and spent a full 30 minutes on the bridge spanning Hanoi's Red River. Don and his son Joshua were occupying the seats in front of me and conversing in Spanish when Grandma spun around to pose a question that was steeped in suspicion.

"You two from Mexico?" she asked.

"Costa Rica," Don replied smilingly in his pleasant sounding accent.

"Uh-huh. Well, anyway, so you're not Mexican, then?"

"No, we are not."

"Oh, that's good. In *Yewtaww* — I'm from *Yewtaww* — we got all these seasonal workers comin' in from Mexico and they don't speak English, and they don't take baths, and they steal. And, oh lord, do they smell awful."

"Well, of course," replied Don. "They are just poor farmhands." He was ever so gracious about it. I, on the other hand, was struggling not to get out Brian's rattler and wave it in her face.

Finally, we got across the bridge, and Huang stood up and gleefully announced that we would all be dropped off where we had been picked up. When a couple from France asked to be let out at another spot only a few blocks away, Huang had one last conniption.

"No. No. You go to *hotel*. Hotel where we pick you *up*. Not another *hotel*."

"But..."

"No. No but. You *listen*. You go to *hotel*."

After a little more verbal jousting, Huang was seething and a collective hush came over the bus. Even Grandma shut up. But then, abruptly, he stopped staring down the offending duo, who were by now cowering in their seats, and launched into a bubbly two minute sales pitch about Vietnam. "Never forget Vietnam people. Tell your friends about Vietnam people. Ask them to come visit my country because I love my country very much and I love all Vietnam people. Thank you." I said my goodbyes to the nice folks I had met on the tour, flashed Huang a fake smile, and emerged into the chaos to find a place to stay.

It felt strange to be back in Hanoi. It was sort of like bumping into an old acquaintance you always secretly disliked. By chance, I spotted the Prince Hotel and popped into the lobby, although not to book a room.

"Hello, sir. May I help you?"

"Do you have VAT?" I demanded.

"VAT? What is VAT?"

"Tax," I said. "Do you have it?"

"No, sir. No, tax. Would you like a room? We have some very nice ones still available."

I informed him snappishly that I did not want a room, but instead my $10 back. I then explained what had happened at their partner hotel down the street, only for him to reply that that hotel had simply copied their name and that they weren't associated whatsoever. "In fact," he explained politely, "there are several Prince Hotels in the Old Quarter, but this is the only genuine one." He went on to inform me that I should have called the police, and that I still could. He then picked up the telephone and offered to call them for me. Feeling like an idiot, I thanked him and said that wouldn't be necessary. I accepted his offer to see a room and took the first one he showed me. He wasn't kidding. It really was very nice.

After a steamy shower and a refreshing nap, I went downstairs and ran into Jan in the lobby. "Ah," he said, "My Canadian friend. Here we meet again in the Cairo of the East." We got to chatting and I disclosed why I had originally chosen this place. He confided that the exact same thing had happened to him, although at a different hotel. We talked for a half hour or so, and then he left to catch a train out toward Sapa, an area in the mountainous northwest, which is home to a large share of the nation's ethnic minorities. It was supposed to be beautiful, but I had heard from travelers who had just recently returned that the fog was as thick as pea soup and that it even had snowed.

The hotel arranged tickets, so I promptly booked one for the night train to Hue (pronounced *Hway*), which is Vietnam's former capital and 400 kilometers to the south of Hanoi. In addition to the train ticket, I bought an open bus ticket from Hue to Saigon for an absurdly low price. The hotel obtained it through a company called Camel Travel. On the ticket jacket there was a logo depicting a man in a conical hat riding a camel in front of the Pyramids. You can't say the Vietnamese don't have a sense of humor.

At ten o'clock, I caught a cab to the grungy and dimly lit central train station, which reeked of smoke and human waste. Slipping through the touts and beggars, I quickly managed to find the car I was on. The train, which runs from Hanoi to Saigon (a distance of more than 1600 kilometers), is called the Reunification Express, although I can assure you that the name is the only thing dignified about it. I ended up sharing a Spartan compartment with a German couple and a man from France, who just happened to speak fluent German, and the three of them chortled away while I retired to the top bunk to continue reading a very involved book I had brought with me by Henry Kissinger entitled *Ending the Vietnam War*.

Somewhere between Kissinger's intelligently written and detail filled passages and the Leninist goodnight speech, which was being broadcast through a tiny speaker in our cubicle (in English, no less, and by the same female voice I had heard at Uncle Ho's mausoleum), I soon fell sleep. It wasn't what you would call a sound sleep. In fact, the train lunged and lurched so often that I was certain it derailed at least seven times during the night.

In the morning, I woke up and went to the bathroom, as one does. A sign on the wall read, "Don't Put Any Strange Stuffs into the Toilet." In the corridor, I stood and stared out the window. Vietnam looked exactly as expected. The train rattled past field after field of grazing cows and toiling farmers while shacks, crooked trees, melancholy hills, and an oppressive fog helped complete the image. Every so often, we would cross a bridge spanning some muddy, twisting rivulet draped with fishing net, but for mile after mile there was hardly an item or anomaly worth mentioning. Except for the garbage. A chain of pink plastic bags and general debris had amassed along the track and was searching out the corners and edges of the fields. It was all very uninspiring.

I went back to my bunk and ate a baguette and a Styrofoam bowl of instant noodles. When I had finished, I looked around for a waste basket, but couldn't find one anywhere. Confused, as I often am, I was in the corridor again holding a small pile of packaging when a service member, in not so many words, asked me what I wanted. After some miming, he nodded and said, "Ah, I know." Then, he threw open the window and grinningly indicated that I should pitch everything outside. "No, no, no," I protested, and he frowned and gave me a curious look, one that said, "But sir, that *is* the waste basket." From his expression, and from all the rubbish out there in the middle of the countryside, I wondered if all 83 million inhabitants of Vietnam hadn't been born with a litter gene.

After nearly 14 hours, we finally arrived in Hue's old imperial station. It was a damp and miserable grey day and so I opened up my umbrella and made my way past a line of vendors selling an identical and unidentifiable array of foodstuffs. Passing through the arched exit, I was virtually mugged by a group of elderly touts before finally making a run for it to a cab that gladly took me into town for five times what it should have cost. Jan had given me a card for a hotel he had stayed at, saying that the staff had been very polite and helpful, so I showed it to the driver and away we went.

The two young female receptionists couldn't seem to make up their minds whether they had a single room or not. They did, then they didn't, then only had a basement dorm. Then they proposed that I first check into the dorm, and then two hours later switch to a double on the third floor. Two hours after this, and I could check into a single on the fourth floor. "No thanks," I replied, and turned to leave. "Oh, wait!" one shouted. "OK. We have a single," she declared, and, largely because I didn't feel like walking around in the rain, I took it. After getting cleaned up, I went back downstairs and handed over my key before going out.

"Sir, our fax machine is broken," one of the girls stated.

"Oh, that's OK," I answered. "I don't need to use it."

"Oh, I mean, uh.... Could you fix it?" she asked, pointing to a large white contraption that brought to mind a snow blower. I apologized and said I'd never seen a fax machine anything like that before.

"Oh," she exclaimed dejectedly. "We *really* hoped you could help us." She then fixed me with a pleading look. Outside, the rain was drumming steadily.

"Right," I said. "Well, goodbye." I left quickly, and because it was pouring down, went to a restaurant directly across the street and ordered lunch and a cup of tea.

"Where ya from?" asked the proprietor bouncily. She was probably around 50 and still quite attractive. She had a gruff voice and a bandage across her throat. A kid clung to her leg.

"Canada," I replied.

"Oh, a *Canadian*. You look. This was written by a Canadian," she said, and pointed to the wall where it read, in blue marker, "Hey Canucks — Thu's motorbike tours are Thu good to pass up, so book one now! Go Leafs!" Everywhere, there were endorsements and testimonials scrawled on the wall. Things like, "One Thu, buckle your shoe. Three, four, book a tour," and "Thu much is never enough," were scribbled from floor to ceiling in marker. I then noticed that the name of the place was Café on Thu Wheels. The second I had finished surveying the décor, the woman, Thu, tossed a large notebook at me that was filled with glowing reviews of her bike tours around Hue.

"Say, do you know where I could book a motorcycle tour around here?" I quipped after glancing through it, but she didn't catch it.

"Yes, we do," she said. "You book."

"Maybe," I said.

"No. No maybe. You book. You here for good time not long time."

"Well, I'll need some time to think about it. I just got here."

"OK, you think, but you never go, you never know."

"*Goodness*," I thought. Where did she learn to talk like that? Probably just off base, I figured. Sensing that she had been a bit too pushy, she handed me another notebook opened to a page saying, "I'm not trying to pressure guests. I'm simply trying to entice you into having a once in a lifetime experience." "Is lunch also a once in a lifetime experience here?" I wanted to ask, but held my tongue. She had personality, I had to admit. After I ate, she launched into her shtick again, and after a few more minutes, I waved my napkin in defeat. I would book a tour, I promised her, but I wanted to book one to the DMZ first. This made her happy. I paid and left.

"Come back for happy hour!" she hoarsely called after me.

"When's that?" I asked, getting pelted by the rain.

"Anytime!"

Donning a rain coat and hoisting an umbrella, I walked down a long boulevard and across a bridge extending over the Perfume River. The Perfume River is a pearl tinted, meandering affair animated with barges and fishing boats chugging atop their own smudgy reflections. Once across, I traversed a zigzag moat before passing through a crumbling gate flanked by thick walls of ruddy brick. This was the Citadel, a two-century old French venture that had been erected with the blood, sweat, and tears of tens of thousands of imperial laborers. There wasn't much left of it now, though. What hadn't decayed was destroyed during some of the war's fiercest fighting, but there were still enough remnants to render it somewhat interesting, if not a bit gloomy. Indeed, the ominous weather and lack of people lent it a decidedly medieval feel. I explored some very old and very interesting Chinese themed temples along with Ho Chi Minh's modest boyhood home before having a gander at the old fortress's most prominent point which could be seen for miles around. The flag tower, imaginatively named "the Flag Tower," was nearly 40 meters high and flying, as you might expect, a very large national flag. Red with a single golden star in the middle, it was faded and tattered. I couldn't think of a more fitting symbol.

At a little after five, I was beginning to think it was the murkiest, dreariest day I had ever seen when it began to get even murkier and drearier. I left and walked back to the other side of the silvery river, dodging vendors and cyclo drivers as I went. Suddenly feeling hungry, I stopped into L'Hotel Indochine for some dinner. The food was good and I went on to sample a couple of bottles of Hue Beer. These went down almost too smoothly and I sat there happily, and I must say, more than a little absentmindedly, while I scanned the hotel's architecture and the activity outside on the street, and waited for the rain to let up. When it finally did, I attempted a stroll around town but soon realized this was pointless, not to mention extremely dangerous. Virtually every sidewalk was mangled beyond belief; full of holes, protruding rebar, and electrical wire. The people of Hue must twist their ankles, skin their shins, and suffer electrical shocks every time they venture outside. Ignoring cyclo drivers offering to arrange massage, I booked a tour to the DMZ, and then headed back to my hotel only to be blocked at the door, literally hauled off the street, and forcibly plunked into a chair by Thu. "You drink," she commanded. "Now is happy hour," "OK. Just don't hurt me," I replied feebly, and I meant it.

The next morning, I awoke early and boarded a bus. Before long, we were on the road and headed north on Highway 1A for the hundred-kilometer haul to the former DMZ, or Demilitarized Zone. From the window, the view was dominated by villages, national flags, orchards, and vegetable farms. As I drowsily stared at the scene outside, my occipital lobe spastically attempted to make sense of the recurring bits of visual stimuli it kept receiving. Strewn here and there on lawns and under trees was — and I hesitate to say this — snow. In point of fact, I knew that it couldn't possibly be snow, because, well, this was *Vietnam* and it was at least 12°C out, but the likeness was uncanny. And it's not as if I've never seen the stuff before. Certainly, you can imagine my reluctance in asking the question my brain kept asking, lest everyone take me for a fool. But then, as luck would have it, someone else asked it for me.

"Is that snow?"

"Yeah, I was just wonderin' that," a voice responded.

"Sure does look like it," another person said.

"No, no, no. It's not snow," piped up a Vietnamese man across from me. "It's sand. We're near the coast and there are a lot of white sandy beaches. The sand you are seeing here is just a kind of geological anomaly. But you're right," he added. "It looks just like it."

We stopped in a small town for lunch and picked up a tour guide. A diminutive man with a baseball cap, he introduced himself to us as Tam and quickly commenced outlining some of the area's history. "During the war, this place we are now passing through was known as 'No Man's Land,'" he began. "And of course, this was because it was once a total war zone. Everything you see here now — these trees, those houses — are all new. This entire region was stripped bare of greenery. Bare. B-a-r-e. It looked like the surface of the moon."

Tam proved be an excellent tour guide and was everything Huang was not. That is to say: engaging, professional, and mentally balanced. He relayed a harrowing account of how his village, which had been on the southern side of the divide, was evacuated one day to prevent infiltration from the Viet Cong. While his neighbors hastily packed up and left, Tam panicked and hid in a tree, only to nearly be taken for "Charlie" and shot dead. "You had to walk slowly and in a straight line *away* from the village as instructed by the helicopters," he said. "If you stopped, or ran suddenly, or did anything out of the ordinary, you would be shot on sight. The Americans weren't taking any chances. They knew there were VC in the area. When I was in that tree, I saw a helicopter take off in the distance and fly very low across a field and straight toward me. It stopped moving forward and just hovered there. It was so loud and I was so scared. I was just a boy. I could see the pilots' faces, and I remember thinking, 'This is it. They are going to kill me.' But then, I noticed that they were talking on the radio and looking at a map. After about a minute, they flew away. Everyday, I think about that and I thank God that I am still alive."

The first stop on the tour was at the Ben Hai River, the point where the country had been divided by a Geneva Proclamation following the ousting of the French in the North. We crossed a non-descript bridge that had been painted yellow on the South's side and red on the North's. That is, until the Americans bombed it into oblivion. But I'm getting ahead of myself. I think at this point a brief historical overview is in order.

You see, after World War II, Vietnam was arbitrarily partitioned in order to better deal with the surrender of the Japanese. Whereas the transition in the South was to be overseen by both the British and the Americans, the one in the North was to be handled by Chiang Kai-shek's Nationalists. It's difficult to restore social order when your primary aims are extortion and plunder; the Nationalists, in a kind of trial run for their subsequent expulsion from China, were sent packing by the Vietnamese Communists. Meanwhile, in the South, the baton was passed to the French principally because the Americans felt they would be able to keep the communists in check. The French, however, in their way, declared that they were returning to Vietnam in order to "recover their inheritance," which they received eight years later in the form of a humiliating defeat at the legendary Battle of Dien Bien Phu, the closing act of the eight-year Franco-Viet Minh War. The upshot of this, as has been touched upon, was that Hanoi was accorded official status in Geneva and the nation was divided with the aim of holding national elections. However, lest the communists achieve victory through democracy, the Americans made sure these elections never happened, and so two camps were set up with angry Uncle Ho in the North facing off against the nefarious and US backed Ngo Dinh Diem in the South.

After consolidating grassroots support, i.e., terrorizing and murdering tens of thousands of their own people in order to cow the rest into submission, Ho's regime then embarked on a campaign to liberate the South from the throes of foreign subjugation, starting out with notable success. Countries may not have been falling like dominoes, but villages were, and soon Diem's forces were proving themselves to be not only inept but hopelessly corrupt.

Needing a pretext to go from advisor and arms supplier to participant, the United States found one with the Gulf of Tonkin Incident, a classic piece of public deception made possible in part by prominent members of the media doing their best impression of trained seals. It all began on August 5, 1964, when a Washington Post headline declared, "American Planes Hit North Vietnam after Second Attack on Our Destroyers." Other major newspapers quickly followed suit. Shortly thereafter, President Lyndon Johnson appeared on national television to announce a massive escalation in the war with North Vietnam due to the "unprovoked attack" of an American destroyer while on a "routine patrol." He also made reference to "renewed attacks" on another destroyer that purportedly occurred earlier that day. As would eventually become known, the president's words were almost totally at odds with the truth.

The first attack actually occurred while the US destroyer was in North Vietnam waters, and, more significantly, while it was coordinating an attack on the North with the South Vietnamese navy. The "renewed" or second attack simply never occurred. It is thought that the destroyer's jittery sonar man took his ship's propellers to be those of the enemy's and that the crew responded to this false alarm by firing a few thousand rounds into the night. As President Johnson himself admitted a mere year later, "For all I know, our navy was shooting at whales out there." But the lie stuck, and soon the Gulf of Tonkin Resolution was passed allowing for the president to take whatever steps he deemed suitable in order to curtail any "further aggression" without the hassle of having to go through Congress. The powers that were simply wrote themselves a blank cheque.

Three years later, there were nearly 500,000 American troops stationed in Vietnam waging a war characterized by massive bombing runs along with so-called search and destroy missions. Ultimately, the Americans would drop 1000 tons of bombs for each man, woman, and child on Vietnamese soil, or three and a half times the total tonnage it had expended during the Second World War. As for the Demilitarized Zone, it became the most militarized zone on the planet.

Things took a turn for the absurd when Richard Nixon got elected largely on the promise to end the war. While talking extrication, the effort was in fact intensified. Nearly 70,000 more troops were shipped out and there began a massive bombing campaign on Cambodia which was concealed from the public. Under intense pressure from an irate citizenry over staggering casualties and reports of atrocities, Nixon finally made good on his pledge and the Paris Peace Accords saw the promise of a ceasefire and total withdrawal of US forces by 1973. Left to fend for itself, the South simply wasn't up to the task, and on April 30, 1975, Saigon fell to Ho Chi Minh's forces.

In total, the ordeal resulted in the deaths of three million people and saw another one million wounded. The cost to the Americans alone was 58,193 dead; 153,303 wounded; 1948 missing. The financial toll amounted to $200 billion. During their 25-year involvement, the United States never went so far as to declare war.

If you happened to be a little sketchy on Vietnam War particulars before reading this overview, not to worry. It was, after all, a long drawn out and relatively complex affair. Besides, you wouldn't be the only one. Henry Kissinger has dubbed Vietnam "the black hole of American historical memory," whereas Richard Nixon himself, speaking in 1985, stated, "(n)o event in American history is more misunderstood than the Vietnam War. It was misreported then, and it is misremembered now."

We clambered out to have a gander at the National Reunification Monument located just on the northern side of the river. You would think that all the stops would have been pulled out in constructing the thing, perhaps with the aid of a couple of Soviet planners and a fleet of cement mixers, but that clearly wasn't the case. While I hadn't been expecting anything too extravagant, I had been expecting something. All there was to commemorate the hard-earned reunion was a shabby arch, a building that looked to have been abandoned in the second week of construction, and a smallish, lackluster statue of a soldier jutting out of a dreadful little pond. Everyone just sort of mutely milled about, not knowing what to say or take pictures of. I watched a couple of young Australians climb in and out of a battered old bunker.

"This is grite. Hey. Looka thet. There's still beer cans in 'ere, mite."

"Yea. Too bad *we* dun av some beer. This tour is bloody boring."

"Yea. I giss you're right. Lit's git back on the bus. It's freezin' out 'ere."

As I stood there, observing them, an American man and his pretty Asian girl-friend moseyed up beside me and asked uncertainly, "What's that? A bunker?" I wasn't about to judge them. After all, I had mistaken sand for snow only a couple of hours earlier; however, when I politely affirmed that it certainly did appear to be a bunker, he rejoindered with an unlikely, "Sure is old."

Back on the bus, we continued north along the highway before turning east toward the coast, whereupon we cruised through a stretch of handsomely forested countryside and rubber tree plantations before bumping shoulders with the sea. Winding our way along the sandy shoreline, we silently peered out the window at the steel grey ocean as it crashed and pounded the land while undercover of a layer of fog that hung thick in the air and blotted out the horizon. A few minutes later, we arrived at our destination, the Vinh Moc Tunnels.

In accordance with President Johnson's wish to bomb North Vietnam "back into the stone age," the US commenced a massive aerial and artillery attack at Vinh Moc in 1966. The inhabitants of the littoral village woke up one day to discover a sky raining down fire. Although many of them fled, others began to excavate by hand into the only land they had ever known. What began purely as a means to survive soon became a massive underground Viet Cong base. Constructed within a bluff, the tunnels wound through the dense red clay in three levels and as many kilometers. Used for six years, the network housed between 100 and 200 people on average and bore witness to 18 births. Despite persistent bombing and sporadic, yet intense, shelling from gunships off the coast, the integrity of the structure remained completely intact with the exception of a drilling bomb which pierced the "roof" but failed to go off. The hole it left was quickly camouflaged and transformed into an airshaft.

All this was conveyed to us by Tam with the aid of a pointer and some diagrams inside a miniature, single room museum that featured a large and ponderous sign in English reading, "TO BE OR NOT TO BE." In addition to a collection of maps and original articles used in the tunnels, there were some very impressive pictures on display, namely of the "before and after" variety. One was of a nearby fishing village before US air raids, while another depicted what it resembled afterward. "From Charming to Charred," would have made a good caption. Even more arresting was an enlarged aerial shot of the narrow Ben Hai River snaking through a landscape of complete and utter crater-riddled devastation.

After the overview, we walked down a path toward the beach where we stood atop a levee while Tam quoted some more interesting facts and figures. "You cannot see it today because of the fog," he said, "but out there is Con Co Island, a very important strategic island during the war. Using the tunnels, the Viet Cong transported over 12,000 tons of military supplies to troops on the island. So, as you can see, these tunnels were very important and a real problem for Uncle Sam."

We entered the tunnels via one of the six entrances built into the bluff facing the sea. It was an extremely uncomfortable and claustrophobic experience. Not surprisingly, it was also very dark and this was in spite of a fair number of lights rigged up at various junctions. In order to help paint a clearer picture of what life under the earth had been like, dummies were set up in different rooms, such as the kitchen and the sleeping quarters, and this was quite effective. As you walked, you had to stoop, and going up and down the steep steps while folded over in the pitch black lost its charm more or less immediately. It was thoroughly interesting, though, and 15 minutes later, I emerged looking like Quasimodo smeared in red mud and dripping in sweat. I stood there for a while with the other tourists, catching my breath.

"Those sure weren't made for Americans!" bellowed the man who had asked me if the bunker was a bunker. Unfortunately, he wasn't being ironic. Having thus raised the flag, so to speak, two other Americans then began engaging him in a bit of casual chitchat while everyone else eavesdropped as they swatted at smears of dirt and pretended to inspect the surrounding plants and flowers. He was from Georgia, he was a soldier, and he was on holiday. A Georgian soldier on holiday who didn't know what a bunker was, apparently.

"Where ya stationed?" asked one of his newly found conversation partners.

"Norfolk, but I just got back from a tour of duty in Iraq."

"Oh, yeah? An' how was Iraq?" the man followed up, much how you would as if inquiring about a visit to Paris.

"Oh, man it *stank*. I mean, the money was good 'an all, but hell — there was *nothin'* to do. No nightlife, no nothin'. Just do yer shift an' drink beer on base. That's all. I mean, you go *off* base and you git killed."

"Yeah," offered the other two sympathetically.

"I ain't goin' back," he went on. "Thought about it, but nah. It's better in the States," he concluded, taking a final drag off his cigarette and then extinguishing it in a potted plant.

As the silent, mostly Northern European crowd peered at the man out of the corner of its collective eye, I felt as though I could hear all of their thoughts being transmitted telepathically in an assortment of Germanic and Scandinavian dialects. "Americans," they seemed to be thinking. "You wreck everything."

After lunch, we drove south on Highway 1A and then turned west onto Highway 9, which runs more or less parallel to, and about 15 kilometers south of, the DMZ. Between the DMZ and Highway 9 is a hilly region where a tentacle of the Ho Chi Minh Trail extended. This was the area where the Americans established their juggernaut, and, not surprisingly, where the majority of the fighting occurred. We drove along the meandering highway and soon passed Camp Carroll.

According to Tam, there was very little to see of it now, as it had been pretty much picked clean by scavengers. He gave us a bit of background on the base, mentioning that in 1972 the South Vietnamese commander of the camp surrendered and joined the North, which had to have hurt morale. Then, he moved on to a much more ominous topic.

"This whole area was defoliated by Agent Orange," he explained. "You know, one day villagers here were just going about their business when suddenly helicopters flew over and said something like this: 'Your attention please. We are now going to drop something on the trees to help remove the leaves. This is so we can better see the movement of the enemy. Do not be alarmed. It will only strip the leaves. It is otherwise harmless.' But, of course," he went on, "within a few months, people started to get sick." To be sure, the rate of cancer and birth defects skyrocketed. Not only did the leaves fall off, but the trees withered and died. Then everything else started to die. The ground and the wells were poisoned. Meanwhile, in a room on a US base where airmen responsible for spraying the chemical worked, there hung a sign saying, "Only You Can Prevent Forests."

Rolling along, we quickly came upon the Rock Pile, a 230-meter high former lookout point and long range artillery base that did indeed resemble an enormous pile of rock. The further we drove west, the hillier it got and Tam pointed out a summit where an American helicopter had crashed after being gunned down. "That one over there," he said, pointing to a steep, craggy looking mass of stone and leaf. "The chopper somehow managed to crash right on the top." He then conveyed to us how the daughter of the dead pilot had been put in contact with him and how she had requested that he take her there. "At the time, I didn't know there was wreckage on that mountain, and that's what I told her," he said. "But she told me she knew the exact point where her father had crashed and that she had it on her GPS." He eventually helped arrange for her to go there, taking her part of the way before a local boy led her up the nearly vertical peak. "The helicopter is still there," Tam added, going on to say that because the point is virtually inaccessible, it was probably the only piece of scrap metal in the entire country not to be claimed by foragers.

The next stop was Dakrong Bridge. The road on the other side of the conduit led to Laos and once served as part of Uncle Ho's trail, the 60,000-kilometer jungle supply route that provided communist soldiers with reinforcements and an estimated 60 tons of goods per day. We got out to take a look and were received by a greeting party of three filthy and foul-smelling boys who wanted to shake hands and say hello to everyone. They were from the local Paco Tribe, the only ethnic group in the country that had supported and fought for the North. Indeed, the Pacos were so enraptured with the Vietnamese communists that the entire clan had their surname changed to Ho. There used to be tours of their villages, but this idea was abandoned as the tribe's people weren't nearly so fond of pounding grain and weaving baskets for the cameras as they were of apathetically lounging around on hammocks half naked and scratching themselves. When the tours ended, the French must have been devastated.

The river valley was quite beautiful and lined with houses identical to those I'd seen at the ethnology museum in Hanoi. The river itself had once contained giant blocks of cement that were used to facilitate the transportation of equipment. The rushing waters concealed them for the duration of the war. Waving goodbye to the grubby, bare assed children, we continued on, traveling west to within about 20 kilometers of the Laotian border before turning right and laboring up a steep hill known in the West as Khe San.

If ever there was a symbol for America's misguided preoccupation and failure in Vietnam, it is Khe San. A Green Beret established combat base, the hill received intense international media scrutiny in 1967 when a succession of battles began with regiments of communist militia established in the hills just to the north. Within only a few weeks, the violent clashes had led to the deaths of thousands of Vietnamese and over 150 Americans. The cycle of skirmishes was broken, however, when US intelligence spotted tens of thousands of heavily armed North Vietnamese troops advancing on the area. The Americans, thinking the North was embarking on a Dien Bien Phu-like final showdown, assembled 5000 aircraft and augmented the contingent of fighting men to 6000. In Washington, President Johnson had a model of the area built into the White House situation room and even went so far as to demand a written guarantee from his top brass effectively stating that the fortification would be held no matter what. And held it was.

What ensued was a 75-day siege of the base, to which the Americans responded in kind by bombing the tar out of the entire area north of their position, ultimately unloading somewhere in the vicinity of 100,000 tons of explosives. For Uncle Sam, it was an overwhelming victory while for Uncle Ho it was a bloodbath. Indeed, the communist forces lost anywhere from 10,000 to 15,000 troops, although in the end that hardly mattered.

As it turns out the entire enterprise had been nothing more than a large-scale and extremely elaborate diversion for an assault on Saigon a week later in what would become known as the Tet Offensive. Yet, at the time, it was assumed by the top general on the scene (General Westmorland), that the Tet Offensive was a large-scale diversion for an assault on Khe San. Looking at a topographical map of central Vietnam, it isn't very difficult to see that Khe San is one of just dozens of hills. How it was ever chosen among the others as a crucial strategic foothold aptly reflects the level of paranoia and convoluted thinking that the Americans were employing at the time. That said, a scant few months after the diversionary attack, policy was reassessed and the base was abandoned. What wasn't trucked away was buried or blown up.

Not surprisingly then, there wasn't much waiting for me when I got to the place on this day. In fact, surveying the area, it was hard to imagine there was ever a war at all. It all looked untouched. The scarred hills and withered forests were fertile again, having been foliated in a massive post-war tree planting expedition. Khe San proper was now being used to grow coffee. There was a museum of sorts, but it was hardly attention-grabbing and the surrounding area featured nothing more than some rusty old equipment. Like with most of the other sites, it was obviously more about what it used to be as opposed to what it was now. The best part was the view. The grey skies had thankfully receded, having been replaced by a hazy dome of pale blue. The hills to the west retreated into Laos, a country I had never been to. Just a few kilometers north stood Hill 881 North and 881 South, home to some of the worst fighting during the war, while far off to the southeast was the legendary Hamburger Hill.

As the bus rolled back down the hill and past the coffee plantations, Tam wrapped up the days' commentary by relaying how a group of former Green Berets had once requested that he arrange a meeting with retired VC soldiers who had fought in this area. "First, we drove around Khe San and then later we met the old Viet Cong soldiers. The Americans said how strange it was to be back. They said that seeing how peaceful it was with all the trees grown back made them wonder if the war had even happened. They said they realized what a terrible waste it all was. It was just like a bad dream." Tam then explained how he acted as translator when the two groups met. "The Americans asked, 'Weren't you scared? We dropped *so many* bombs on you. Why didn't you give up or retreat?' The VC veterans answered that at first they were scared, but then, gradually, they got used to it. They learned that whenever they heard a bomb falling, they had to look up to see what shape it was. If it was long, like a pencil, it was OK. They could keep walking. But when the bomb was only a point, like a pencil tip, then they had to lie down flat to avoid shrapnel. Also, they *believed* in what they were doing. If they were transporting a shipment of 100 crates and only 1 got through, they would consider that a great success. They reminded the Americans that Vietnam had been controlled by the Chinese and the French. They weren't going to let it be controlled by another foreign power."

Tam concluded by thanking us and by saying how he sincerely wished we could all just get along, adding that he prayed our countries would never have to suffer what his country had. I suppose that he said that everyday. But I was quite certain that he meant it.

The next morning I got up early, ate breakfast, and then started my Café on Thu Wheels tour of greater Hue. My driver was another tiny fellow named Duong. He looked like a 12-year-old with a man's face. He was a friendly sort and spoke broken but understandable English. We zipped across the hazy Perfume River with its barges and blurry tree line reflections, before turning east and following the waterway's grassy banks, stopping in due course at the bottom of a hillock and a flight of stone steps. I began the short but steep climb and was rewarded at the top by the appearance of a seven-tier octagonal tower. This was Vietnam's Thien Mu Pagoda, the likeness of which I had seen on a hundred articles of tourist kitsch since I had arrived. Nevertheless, it was impressive, and so was the view of the river, both of which I had entirely to myself.

Continuing on the stone footpath, I passed through a gate flanked on the left by a giant bell while on the right there stood its geomantic countermeasure in the form a large stele. Both objects were housed in smallish pagodas. A stele, by the way, is a slab of stone resembling a tombstone and used for funerary or commemorative purposes. This particular one was perched atop an enormous tortoise, a symbol of longevity. The landscaped courtyard beyond the gate was absolutely splendid, walled by pines and wooden halls. A single walkway divided the complex, leading toward an urn of smoldering incense behind which sat a golden Reclining Buddha. Behind this was an aesthetically pleasing wooden temple, through the open door of which I glimpsed a grey robed monk lighting candles atop a flower laden alter.

After strolling around the perimeter and basking in the sunlight and solitude, I was about to head back out to the road when I suddenly heard an explosion of violent language coming from one of the wooden halls. I crept up to the low building for a better look, taking cover behind a tree. From there, I peered into the opened door to see a brown clad, hairless man screaming at a brown clad, hairless boy, who couldn't have been more than eight. As the other children sat silently at long tables writing with calligraphy brushes, the senior cleric commanded the offending novice to lie down on his stomach atop a bench. He then went to the wall and took down a long, thin bough. Another monk stepped outside to act as guard, no doubt concerned about intruding tourists. I tucked in closer behind the tree. Noting that the coast was clear, the lookout then gave the go ahead to his colleague who commenced whipping the boy's back, bottom, and head with the stick. The monk yelled, the bough fell, the boy screamed, and the process was repeated. It was horrible and I wondered what the kid had done to deserve it. But I suppose, I shouldn't have been so surprised. After all, violence, or, more precisely, violent self-expression, was what the monks at Thien Mu were renowned for.

In 1963, a high-ranking monk by the name of Thich Quang Duc drove to Saigon in a light blue Austin Mini to protest against the US backed President Diem and his policy of suppressing Buddhism (Diem was a tyrannical Catholic). Parking his car at a busy intersection, the man sat down in a meditative position on the street, doused himself with gasoline, and lit himself on fire. During this self-immolation, he was surrounded by a large ring of onlookers who shrieked and sobbed as he burned to death with an eerily serene expression etched into his face. When fellow ascetics attempted to cremate his remains, or so the story goes, his heart wouldn't burn. Interestingly, the public wasn't shocked by the protest so much as by the response made by President Diem's wife, who face-tiously labeled it a "barbecue party" and added that everyone ought to clap their hands and rejoice. As it turned out, the first lady's husband and brother-in-law were later assassinated by their own military. Fortunately for her, she was over-seas at the time. The first time I saw the picture of the burning monk, it was in a political science textbook I had in high school. Next to him was an empty gas canister, while in the background there sat the Austin Mini with its trunk open. The car was now on display behind the pagoda.

My guide and I then drove to the countryside outside of Hue. Thus far on my journey, I hadn't seen a single residential area that I wouldn't have labeled "run down," but along these back roads each and every home I passed looked like an advertisement for UNICEF. A hodgepodge of potholed tracks of dirt wound its way through a world of naked children, adults urinating by the roadside, women selling their battered vegetables from mats, darting chickens, plumes of smoke, and clusters of men drinking beer and gambling. In Vietnam, I think it can be safely said that while the women break their backs, the men are out breaking the bank. Even on these dusty back roads the traffic was bad. Everybody honked as they drove every which way but straight, and teenaged boys on motorcycles whipped around blind corners as if there was no tomorrow, which, for some, there probably wasn't. Past the villages, and far beyond a lengthy row of rice fields, we stopped at an old Japanese covered bridge that was situated across from a local market. I got off the bike and took a look around.

Unlike at the pagoda, there were about a dozen or so tourists present, and they were milling about in the center of the cob webbed, colonial structure. As I drew near, I realized they were having their fortunes told. "Thet's not right," ex-claimed an Australian woman shrilly. "I am *not* the chief bridwinna in my family. My 'usband is. She doesn't know whet she's talking about." Through the circle, I could see an elderly woman in colorful garb and a conical hat flashing a three-tooth grin at the crowd of onlookers. As she read the next person's palm, a thin man next to her translated. "She say you have long life. One day you become rich. You have big family and vey happy."

"She is a con-artist," Duong informed me quietly. He had accompanied me to give me some background on the bridge. "She is from the village we just passed. Nobody likes her there. She only does fortune telling for foreigners, not local people. She always says the same thing. 'You will be rich and have a long happy life.' Or something like that. And then you give her one dollar."

More interesting than the bridge itself was the small brook next to it along with a water marker. Duong showed me how in 1999, the water level reached a level of more than two meters in a massive, devastating flood. It was hard to believe, peering around now at the tranquil surroundings. The rice stalks swayed casually in the mid-morning breeze, while cotton ball clouds bustled overhead, mirroring themselves perfectly in the lily strewn rivulets.

Next, we drove even further out into the country, passing bundles of drying incense laid out on the roadside. We were headed to an old forested pagoda. Walking down a tree lined path and through a decaying Chinese style gate, I made my way around a couple of lotus ponds and past a stretch of mossy tombs and dancing butterflies, reaching the temple precisely at prayer time. Ten monks dressed in yellow (the color reserved for worship and funerals) were gathering themselves into a horseshoe and facing a banner draped altar. For nearly 20 minutes, I stood there alone as they hypnotically chanted in rising and falling tones, while one kept rhythm on an ancient looking drum and another by striking an instrument of brass. Next, it was on to the tombs of the Nguyen Dynasty emperors, who ruled Vietnam from 1802 — 1945. The area amounted to a repetitive layout of stele pavilions, temples, sepulchers, courtyards, and lotus ponds.

Later, we drove through more back roads and made our way up a leafy, imposing hill. At its crest stood a blackened, crumbling bunker. Some kids were playing cards on it. This place had once been a US lookout point and artillery position that was eventually overrun by the Viet Cong (prior to 1975). In fact, the Viet Cong briefly overran all of Hue and the immediate surrounding area. Having done so, they raised their flag over the Citadel and swiftly meted out punish to the locals for their perceived compliance with the enemy. Around 3000 people were rounded up and driven out to these very hills where they were buried, many of them while still alive. This massacre constituted the war's largest, being 10 times that of the one perpetrated by the Americans at Mai Lai. The US managed to retake Hue and even defended it successfully during the Tet Offensive. However, ten thousand people, most of whom were civilians, were killed during the fighting.

Back in Hue on this day, I was met with a surprise. As it was New Year's Eve, my hotel had laid out a huge spread in the lobby and was inviting foreign tourists right off the street to join in. I was escorted by the arm to a table, given a seat, and poured a glass of warm, frothy Hue Beer. For the next hour, I sat munching delicious food and sipping ale with three dozen cheerful and boisterous strangers. People I'd never seen before shook my hand, topped up my glass, toasted my health, took my photo, and informed me that Canada was not only very big but also very cold. The man to my right put away half a bottle of rice wine, and beaming at me, kept repeating, "Happy New Year! Nice to meet you! Welcome to Vietnam! Cheers!" A local news crew even showed up to film the scene and conduct some interviews. It was good fun, but noticing the time, I stood up on uncertain legs, said my goodbyes, thanked the owner and staff, apologized for not knowing anything about Soviet-era fax machines, and finally walked out the door and over to Camel Travel.

To be truthful, I hadn't thought very much of Hue. It was dull and drab and what little remained of its historical and cultural sites had been seriously neglected. Until the 1990s, the city and its so-called feudal structures had been labeled politically incorrect and left to rot, and rot they did. Then, dully realizing that someone might actually find the place interesting enough to pay money to see, the government reversed its policy and dubbed the relics "national treasures." However, it seemed a case of too little, too late. I must say, though, I feel a bit guilty in my assessment given the friendliness and hospitality I'd seen displayed by the Hue people, especially at the party. Undeniably, I boarded the bus to Hoi An in a much improved frame of mind.

We arrived in Hoi An shortly after sunset and I checked into the first hotel I saw. I certainly could have done much worse, getting a pleasant double for $10. Reinvigorated after a short nap and a hot shower, I went out to explore, but not before getting something to eat. As a rule of thumb, I try to avoid restaurants that aren't busy, the idea being that the more patrons there are, the less time things have to sit around the kitchen attracting critters and turning green. Even so, the virtually empty café I found just down the street appealed to me because, for one, it looked fine, and for another, I couldn't spot another one along the lengthy street I was on — and given that I was famished, this weighed significantly into my decision. I sat down and ordered a sandwich and a bowl of New England clam chowder.

There was only one other patron there, and he turned out to be Australian. I knew he was Australian because of the tongue lashing he gave the waiter when he finally appeared with his food. "Yea, thanks a lot mite. Thet was 45 minutes ago when I ordered thet. It's only beef on rise. I reckon it couldn't be much *easia*."

The waiter just stared at him mutely. The place was a family run affair. Precisely, it was the converted front of someone's home, but it was clean and they had an impressive menu. The Australian fellow ate quickly and then asked for more rice, but again the waiter didn't understand him. "Rise! Rise! *R-i-c-e*! Rise! You know? It's white? It's a grine? It comes from a field? Do you understand me?" But he didn't, so the angry Aussie thumbed to the language section of his guide book and pointed. "OK," said the local man, and disappeared into the kitchen. "Chroist!" the guy bellowed. "Ya'd think they'd bloody well speak English in a restaurant with English bloody menus!" "Sure, you would," I mentally responded. "Just where did they think we were? In some provincial town in Vietnam? The *nerve*." I tucked into my Kissinger book.

Coincidentally, I was reading about a major invasion of Laos and the Ho Chi Minh Trail conceived of by planners in Washington. This was late in the war when the Americans were nearing the point of total withdrawal. The massive assault was intended to serve as a large-scale training exercise for the South Vietnamese troops while at the same time disrupting the North's supply routes to the extent where it would take them a full two years to recover. In the end, however, the invasion proved to be a large-scale failure. Instead of seizing the trail, establishing strategic strongholds, and then setting about to destroy the thing, the South's forces turned up, fired a few shots, and then, ostensibly satisfied that they'd actually been able to find the place, abandoned it completely and returned home. In attempting to ascertain just why several top divisions had forsaken ground that was captured, and, more to the point, abandoned the mission, the Americans concluded that it largely revolved around the fact that hardly a soul in the entire South Vietnamese Army seemed capable of comprehending even rudimentary English, and hence, hadn't quite understood what they had been asked to do. Kissinger also notes the difficulty they had in finding air traffic controllers who could understand English, which must have made for some truly interesting tower-to-cockpit conversations.

After 20 minutes, the Australian tourist still hadn't received his rice, and predictably, he had another eruption. At one point, he actually went into the kitchen to yell at the proprietors. Incidentally, I waited for 40 minutes for my own meal to make an appearance, but it didn't matter. The clam chowder was spot on; straight from the can, just like Mom used to open it. As I sat there, contentedly slurping my soup, I thought I heard the Thien Mu monk again. Across the street at an electronics shop, the owner was smacking around a child of perhaps four while yelling so loudly that people in the next hamlet could have heard him. He stopped when two tourists, who had just strolled past, turned around and stuck their noses in his front door.

Full of preserved clams, potatoes, and cheap French beer, I strolled down the street in the dark and drizzle to see what Hoi An was offering in the way of New Year's festivities. At my hotel, the rather pretty receptionist had given me a perfectly legible itinerary for the evening's events and after impressing her by thanking her for it in tone perfect Vietnamese, I turned around and walked straight into a cumquat tree.

I had read that Hoi An "oozed culture at every turn," but I was more impressed by what it didn't ooze. To be sure, it had the cleanest streets I'd seen so far. Everything looked comparatively well scrubbed and the sidewalks were wide and flat in addition to being conspicuously free of trash and debris. The local authorities had curtailed the use of vehicles on certain streets and buildings had to be maintained in a manner that was considered "tasteful." By and large, this equated almost exclusively to painting one's residence or business yellow, but at least they had done something. I wandered along several of the main arteries until I got my bearings and concluded that the entire town was comprised of hotels, restaurants, travel agencies, tailor shops, and art boutiques. Then, feeling that sense of exhilaration you get when exploring a new place, I took a seat outside a tiny café and ordered a beer. And then I ordered another beer. And then I struck up a conversation with the female owner.

"Don't say, 'You come in,' or 'You buy something,' to people walking by," I advised. "That will only scare people away."

"But everyone say," she protested.

"Yes, everyone in *Vietnam* says it, but *we* don't say it. If you say that, people won't want to come in. It's not polite."

"So, what you say?"

I wrote down "Would you care for a cold beer?" and "Would you like something to eat or drink?" on a piece of paper and got her to practice saying it a few times. If she used it, I bet it would have given her an advantage. Every shop owner and clerk in the nation seemed to think that shrilly commanding you to either "come in" or "buy something" was a good way to drum up business. How they didn't notice the look of annoyance if not horror on tourists' faces was anyone's guess, but they clearly didn't.

Later, I made my way down to the center of town toward the riverfront, where I shuffled past a long row of yellow facades illuminated by red Chinese lanterns. The river itself was onyx black, but it shimmered in patches of color reflected from the lights of large model boats that had been anchored at various points as part of the festivities. They were replicas of Viking ships complete with sails and oars. Made with sections and bits of translucent colored plastic, the lights within them caused them to glow brilliantly on the still, tarry water.

Amid the boats, there floated a skiff full of people lighting candles and setting them adrift. Set into lotus shaped tin holders, more than 200 of them leisurely drifted this way and that in tiny twinkling congregations. As it grew closer to midnight, couples with flowers, families with balloons, and tourists with cameras streamed towards the stage that had been set up along the riverside. Joining them, I managed to endure a performance of singing and dancing that brought to mind a Wham! video. After this, some smartly dressed members of the local people's committee took to the stage to thank everybody for coming and outlined the evening's events. This was done in English and Vietnamese, which was fitting because the majority of the 300 or so individuals on hand were foreign tourists.

"Only 15 seconds to midnight!" a man announced shortly, and the crowd cheered. "Let's ring in together... the year... of ... the lovely... dog! Ready? Five, four, three, two, one!!! Happy New Year!!! *Chuc Mung Nam Moi*!!! Canisters of silver confetti were popped open and rained down from the treetops surrounding us, while strings of balloons were pulled roughly over their branches causing them to pop in imitation of fireworks. Apparently, fireworks were forbidden. "Now, everybody," bellowed the MC, "let's take a minute to salute our national flag!" As the tinny sounding national anthem began to play over a record player, the organizers and performers obediently saluted while standing ramrod straight. The reaction in the audience, however, was decidedly less enthusiastic. Indeed, something akin to a collective sniffle was offered up, and the Vietnamese turned to each other to chat. Once the song was over, they held a lottery and people resumed paying attention. "Wow," I thought. "A lottery." Who says Marxist-Leninists don't know how to let their hair down every now and again? Actually, it was a good time, with several prizes going to both locals and tourists. The organizers did their best to liven things up and even attempted a couple of impromptu jokes in English.

The next morning, I woke up in a damp room, ate a luxurious breakfast of processed cheese and crackers, and watched a couple of hours of BBC World News, a rare indulgence. Except for when I travel, I don't watch TV. I had been told repeatedly that everything would be shut down for New Year's Day and most likely the day after, but I guess everyone had underestimated the power of the tourist buck as nearly everything was open. Eventually realizing this, I went out to explore Hoi An by daylight. Too bad there wasn't very much of it. The sky was a blanket of grey with streaks and smudges of charcoal. It was currently in the process of darkening moods and dampening spirits by emitting an eerily consistent drizzle. I spent the afternoon walking around with a raincoat and umbrella, but still managed to get soaking wet.

Although Hoi An was charming, it was a repetitive charm. Wooden doors, sometimes elaborately carved, along with moss covered, darkly tiled roofs supplied the contrast to the omnipresent yellow veneers. The national flag angled out from virtually every structure, and besides the assortment of things that could be seen stuck on roofs — a shuttlecock here, a sneaker there — that was about it. Multiple this description by two or three hundred, and you had Hoi An.

I went on a sort of walking tour, which consisted of a leisurely appraisal of a few Chinese temples and pagodas along with a browse around four or five art shops before looking at my watch and wondering if 11:37 in the morning wasn't too early to start drinking. In a dispassionate frame of mind, I started walking away from the town in the hopes of finding something a little more authentic. Along the sidewalk, I passed a group of extremely inebriated men who giddily tried to recruit me into singing karaoke with them. Faces red as beets, half of them were dancing with each other while the other half sat around a table overflowing with empty beer bottles. All of them were crooning along to some sentimental old tune.

I continued on until the yellow houses faded, eventually being replaced by grey and brown ones. Typical of older homes in Asia, people's front doors were thrown open making it possible to see what they were up to inside. I can tell you from my snooping that the thing to do in Vietnam on the Lunar New Year holiday is eat heaps of fried food, drink rice wine until you are blind drunk, and wail tunelessly into the microphone hooked up to your home karaoke unit. After this bit of important cultural investigation, I returned to the rows of yellow structures and red flags and took a walk along the riverfront.

After dinner that evening, I set off in search of the Hoi An branch of Camel Travel only to discover that it was closed. Remembering that my hotel arranged tickets, I sauntered back through the drizzle to see if I couldn't book one there. Once inside, I found myself face to face with a man whom I took to be the owner. A short, round faced, kindly-looking gentleman, he managed a, "Can I help you?" after I had traipsed through the foyer and up to the desk.

"Chuc Mung Nam Moi," I said.

"Chung Mung Nam Moi," he replied, much more accurately.

"I'd like to book a ticket to My Son."

"I lie to beluga tickle my saw," he attempted to mimic.

"No, no. I want to book a ticket to My Son."

"No, no, I one two picket to my song."

"No, ehmm. Ticket. I want ticket. You know ticket?" I asked patiently.

"Ah, ticket. Yes, I know, I know," he answered, his face bursting into a smile. "Uh, just a moment," he added, and picked up the telephone to make a call. After talking for a bit, he hung up and said, "You waiting. Gull come back. Ticket gull."

"Oh, good," I said.

"Oh, good," he echoed, and then, still grinning, walked over to the fridge where he retrieved some ice cubes and a couple of glasses. Next, he produced a large bottle of whisky, filled up both glasses and handed me one. Motioning for me to have a seat, we parked ourselves in the lobby and toasted each other decorously during a protracted spell of otherwise awkward silence. After a few minutes, I felt a warm tingling in my extremities and my tongue turned completely numb.

The pretty girl returned, dressed in her *ao dai*, the agreeable national dress. She promptly arranged a couple of tickets and proceeded to write me out a receipt. I chatted with her for a half an hour, animated by the drink. She told me that she had worked as a hotel receptionist for three years and, not surprisingly, liked it much better than her job at a state factory.

"Working at the factory was hard?" I asked.

"No. No hard. Is vey boring. Everybody only talking and gossip. So much gossip. 'He do this... what what, she do that... what what. People is terrible.'"

"Yeah, well, people can be terrible everywhere," I offered.

"I also like this job because I can to sleep in the morning. I don't like to wake up early. I working only is in the afternoon and night."

"But doesn't the music wake you up?" I asked. I was alluding to the marching tunes boomed out at dawn and dusk from loudspeakers on the telephone poles, but she didn't have any idea what I was talking about.

"Oh, that!" she exclaimed after some clarifying. "Oh, that's just 'good morning music.' Nobody listen to that now. I even don't hear it anymore. I'm get used to it."

The next morning, I was picked up by a bus in front of my hotel and was soon chatting with two good humored Canadians named Jacques and Donny. Before long, our tour guide stood up and introduced himself. "Goo mao ling!" he bellowed. "I am your tour guide for today. My name is Nut. N-h-u-d. Nut. But Nut is very hard to pronounce for you, so you can just call me by my English name, Funny." There was laughter. "That's right. My name is Funny," he went on. "Because I like to make joke. OK, today we are visiting the Cham Ruins located in My Son. It is located in the belly of my son. It is not in my daughter. Ha! You see? I like to make joke!" There was more laughter, although this time it was out of courtesy. He then gave us a brief overview.

The Cham Ruins are virtually all that remain of an ancient civilization based on the Indian model of ancient civilizations and known as the Kingdom of

Champa. Dating from the second century, this empire dominated Indochina for more than a millennium, even managing to subvert the mighty Khmers before being assimilated into Vietnamese culture proper. The Chams' existence was unknown to the West until French explorers "discovered" the ruins in the nineteenth century. The interesting thing about these particular ruins was that they were dated from the seventh century, meaning they pre-dated their counterparts in Angkor by more than 200 years. However, as far as I was concerned, that was about the only thing interesting about them.

Although described in my guide book as both "stunning" and "magnificent" (in keeping with the "always a glowing review" motif), there simply wasn't enough left of the place to warrant such terms. Time, neglect, and several B-52 sorties had left just a handful of disintegrating brick structures wrapped in a thin layer of vegetation. Moreover, the majority of the site's statues, friezes, and altars had long ago been carted off to various museums. I do appreciate looking at Shiva figures and Sanskrit script carved into 1400-year-old buildings, when there is enough left to see, but after having seen Cambodia's Angkor and Thailand's Ayuthaya, the Cham Ruins were a bit disappointing, in fact boring. By way of comparison, it takes three days to experience the ruins of Angkor, whereas this place required not much more than three minutes. There was a well-preserved bomb crater nearby that I almost found as interesting as the ruins themselves. Luckily, Funny provided some comic relief. "At one point," he said, "it is thought that all the males left Champa. The women could not find them. They looked everywhere, but the men were gone. Even today, we are not sure where they went. Perhaps on holiday to Europe?"

That evening back in Hoi An, I attended a cooking class. The chef was even funnier than Funny, with a virtual stand up routine of jokes, many of them lewd. He wasn't afraid of having a go at people in the audience, either. It was sort of like a cooking show minus the camera crew. We learned how to sauté and bake cod wrapped in a banana leaf, what to put into a calamari salad (lots of calamari, as it turns out), and tips and tricks for making our very own spring rolls. The comedian chef called on various people to assist, and I was put in charge of frying the spring rolls. I had to turn them over with a pair of chopsticks while trying not to maim myself with the bubbling oil. I learned how to puncture them in order to let the grease drip out, and when I did, it resembled the hull of an oil tanker being breached by torpedo. After we helped cook, we ate, and the staff brought us a few supplementary dishes that had been prepared beforehand. They also brought us quite a few beers and the small crowd of apprentice chefs hung around chatting for some while.

At 6:00 the next morning, I boarded yet another bus and continued my journey south to the beach resort town of Nha Trang. It wasn't long before we were driving through some stunning scenery. Expansive rice fields of lush, swaying green extended for great distances; so great, in fact, that in places you could hardly discern where they concluded and where the towering mountains of dark, tangled green began.

As there were only five other tourists on the bus, we stopped here and there to pick up and drop off locals. Our first pick up consisted of two teenaged boys who chose the seat directly in front of me. The air conditioning was on, but they wanted to open the window. Then they wanted to throw things out the window. Then they wanted to take their socks off. Ultimately, they wanted to cuddle with each other and sing, which they went right ahead and did, never mind that it was 7:30 a.m.

At lunch, we stopped at a restaurant situated next to a strip of beach and the small troupe of tourists alighted and stretched. Forced to sit at the same table, we were then forced to think of something to say. Luckily, there was a young American backpacker type who wasn't afraid of breaking the ice. "Dude, that was like *the* bumpiest ride ever," he exclaimed. "Anybody else's behind sore?" With long matted hair and tattered clothes, I figured that if he weren't stoned now, he'd been stoned within the past 24 hours. Not having caught his name, I mentally dubbed him 'Marijuana.' Marijuana was from California, and was now "doin' Southeast Asia" owing to the fact that he had recently "graduated college."

I still haven't figured out just why it is Americans are fond of employing this phrase. Is it just me, or is there a preposition missing there? You never hear them say, "I just got back supermarket," or "I'm originally Seattle," so why is it that when they want to refer to having completed four years of higher learning they do so by utilizing bad grammar? Call me pedantic, but it seems a little odd.

It was 400 kilometers from Hoi An to Nha Trang, a trip that was supposed to take twelve hours, but which ended up taking thirteen. This had to do with the meandering quote-unquote highway, the poor condition of our bus, and the formidable mountain passes to be negotiated. In the late afternoon, we began the first in a series of these with a laborious, rattling ascent that seemed to go on forever. It was all very harrowing. Instead of guardrails, there were only some very low concrete blocks placed at various bends. I doubted they could have prevented a bus from plunging over the edge. Upon closer inspection, I doubted they could have prevented a tricycle from plunging over the edge. The views were breath-taking, though, and it was best to take them in as this would force you to ignore the road ahead. However, it was impossible not to notice the spindly line of highway carved into the upcoming mountain sides along with the red scars of mud indicating where there had only recently been landslides. Here and there, road crews could be seen bulldozing hillocks of ruddy muck back off the road.

After traversing two enormous mountains, we began a long, methodical descent. Rounding a bend, a vast bay of aqua blue was revealed, upon which was anchored a virtual navy of fishing boats — hundreds of them — all painted blue with red and green trim and many decorated with searching eyes on their bows. During our final arduous climb, the bus suddenly came to a stop in the middle of a long, straight incline. The driver took out a notepad and, gazing out toward the sea, jotted something down. Then, opening the door, he flung a tiny pile of trash into the ditch. This done, he stepped off the bus, squatted down on his haunches, and began washing his hands in the ditch. After this, he splashed water on his face. Refreshed, he stood up, stretched, and lit up a smoke. Next, he unzipped his fly and urinated — into the ditch — and in full view of the passengers. Everyone had been intently watching him, but now we were all sort of swiveling around and exchanging glances. Finished relieving himself, he walked around the back of the bus and crossed the road. Gazing down at the sheer drop, you could tell he was thinking, "*Whoa.* That's a *long* way down." He stretched some more, finished his smoke, combed his hair, and finally got back on the bus, driving for the next 10 minutes with the door open. I thought he did this on purpose, but suddenly, he made a startled "How'd it get like that?" grunt before pulling the lever to shut it. I took this as a bad sign as we were behind schedule and losing light.

An hour later, in the twilight, we passed by an accident. A motorcycle driver was lying supine next to his machine, a group of people having made a circle around him. I wondered how many people were killed or injured in traffic accidents in this country every day, but knew that that kind of information would never be revealed even if it were recorded. At a little after 7:00, we rounded another bend which disclosed five or six kilometers of lit-up shoreline. The roadside concrete huts and rice plots were replaced by hotels and manicured lawns, some of them quite striking. Romanesque revival architecture competed for space with trendy looking cafés and black-windowed barber shops emblazoned with shimmering Japanese characters. We'd honked, rattled, twisted, turned, climbed, and descended all day only to wind up at a seedy and tacky-looking beach resort.

The bus driver, who had stopped at the edge of town for gas, oil, air for the tires, and ice cream (he just couldn't have let us out first), turned off the main boulevard, made a left, and came to stop. But then he kept going, driving aimlessly all over town, making several U-turns at busy intersections, and doing a very poor job of concealing the fact that he was totally lost. The other passengers kept telling him that they had reservations at The Golden Hotel, but they were ignored. Along some vaguely lit back street, he finally pulled over at a dingy corner filled with expectant cyclo drivers and touts. I got off and evaded them long enough to dart into a Korean restaurant where I could order something to eat and figure out where I was.

The place was huge and, not surprisingly, filled with Koreans. It's amusing to sit and listen to Korean people talk. Korean doesn't sound anything like Chinese and it doesn't sound much like Japanese, either. Actually, what it resembles, when spoken *en masse*, is 50 people in a swimming pool all trying to see what it sounds like to talk under water.

"*Bul mul lu ru pulul nul dul kulgul ul mullup tul imnika?*"

"*Yeh, mu pul ul pu rul lulmul sulnul lu hul imnida.*"

In case you have no idea what I'm talking about, and I'm guessing that that's probably the case, then I urge you visit your nearest Korean restaurant and just imagine everyone wearing diving masks and snorkels.

The owner, a kindly woman who complimented me on my poor Korean, gave me a map of Nha Trang and pointed out my present location. Thanking her profusely, I studied the map and ate a delicious meal. Refueled and oriented, I stepped out into the sultry night and was immediately set upon by another crowd of touts. Since it was the Lunar New Year and I was at the country's premier resort, it took me a long and frustrating time to find a place to stay.

The next day, I groggily shook the cobwebs off and went out in search of breakfast and a better lodging. The bottle-green corridors of my hotel were crawling with kids, and the three rooms between mine and the stairwell had their doors wide open, revealing entire extended families yakking, cooking, and playing cards. I quickly found a simple yet clean guesthouse called The Orchid in a nearby lane. The Orchid was run by a polite, elderly couple whose surname was Trang. Both Mr. and Mrs. Trang spoke hesitant English in a kind of half Vietnamese, half French accent. After checking in, I headed for the beach.

Something strange happened when I got there. The grey clouds made an abrupt exit, giving way to skies of pure blue. Suddenly, the temperature soared. I sat under a palm tree and applied a quarter of a bottle of sunscreen. I strolled along a palm-lined path to the end of the beach, which turned out to be a fair walk. Outdoor cafés were packed with Vietnamese holiday makers and were clearly doing a brisk business. On the stretch of shaded grass between the beach and the main boulevard, hundreds more were picnicking, with each picnic scene looking identical to the last. Families squatted on blankets (the record for a single blanket was 14) as they sipped beer, munched pumpkin seeds, and boiled large pots of crabs. Everybody was silent and everybody was staring, as if transfixed, at the turquoise sea. Everybody, that is, except the vendors. They were out in full force and I was harassed all the way up the beach and all the way back.

Having explored the northern half of the beach in the morning, I decided to meander along the southern half in the afternoon. I took my time, stopping at a couple of fine resort restaurants along the way for a tropical shake and a bit of reading. I was still hammering away at the Kissinger book. It is an extremely detailed account of America's quarter-century-long involvement in and disentanglement from the Vietnam War, although it primarily deals with the Nixon years. It is so involved that, at times, it reads like a real-time report. Kissinger is a masterly writer, however. His style is fluid and his ideas are well assembled and lucid. Moreover, he employs a tone that is intellectual and yet never supercilious. Above all, he's superbly adept at making you see the American point of view. The US had made a promise to the people of the South. They felt they had a moral commitment to keep that promise. What would it say to the Cold War world if they broke it? Yes, the regime there was seriously flawed, but the one in the north was arguably much worse. At the time, the Iron Curtain was something very real, and they felt it necessary to let Moscow (and to a lesser extent, Beijing) know that they wouldn't be pushed around. They believed in the Domino Theory, and above all, they believed that what they were doing was right.

What is perhaps most interesting about the book is that Kissinger still does not admit that it didn't matter if what they were doing was "right" or not, given that the war was not winnable, which it clearly was not. The North would never surrender, and in a guerilla war victory is attained so long as the guerillas don't concede defeat. Mr. Kissinger reasons that if only public opinion hadn't forced their hand to withdraw, they could have won. But, short of using nuclear weapons, cold, hard facts suggest otherwise. At the point when they were about to completely pull out, the Americans had won every single battle hands down, and they were still losing the war.

People often lament that if only John F. Kennedy hadn't been assassinated, then the whole ordeal may have been avoided. It is true that Kennedy talked about de-escalation, and it is nice to think that he wouldn't have had anything to do with the malicious Gulf of Tonkin Resolution. However, as I see it, a far more interesting "what if" scenario is: what if the Americans had listened to Winston Churchill? After all, although he was consulted, he was more or less ignored. And not for the first time.

Here was a man who realized just what the rise of Nazism meant for Europe and the rest of the world and yet, incredibly, no one listened to him then, either. On top of this, he quickly grasped that Stalin was a wolf in sheep's clothing, and cautioned Roosevelt against getting involved in China. The president went right ahead and did so anyway, wasting $3 billion on the hapless and hopelessly corrupt Nationalists, who, as you know, were sent fleeing from that country.

In commenting on Vietnam on the eve of US intervention, Mr. Churchill stated that he didn't accept the Domino Theory, denying that "one colonial setback would automatically lead to global catastrophe." (I quote here from Kissinger.) He also advised against serious intervention, i.e. bombing, citing that the conflict would be "too peripheral and too dangerous to be sustainable for very long in Western public opinion." (Ibid.) Clearly, the old boy was on the sauce again.

I strolled along to the edge of the bay, where the sand fizzled out and the boulders and debris began. Then I turned around and headed back. There were a few luxuriant looking islands offshore, and the setting sun sharpened their edges and emboldened their contours. Two whitish orange brushstrokes stretched across a fading sky, while a crescent moon hung low. A star glistened here and another shimmered there. I walked back to the town.

The owner of the The Orchid, Mrs. Trang, was a dear old lady, but it was plain that at some point the cheese had slid off her cracker.

"You go out tonight?" she asked me. It was a little after seven.

"Yes, I'm going out now."

"You go to bar?"

"Maybe," I replied, wondering where this was going.

"You be careful of girl. Nha Trang girl very bad. You meet girl in bar, and then you drinking, you happy, and then..." She simulated fainting. "You understand what I mean? They put medicine in your drink!"

"OK, thank you Mrs. Trang. I won't go to that kind of bar." I didn't know how to explain to her that I had a Chinese girlfriend who would tie me down and nail shards of bamboo under my fingernails if it ever became known that I went to that kind of bar.

Dropping off some laundry at a hotel in the next lane, I continued on to a bustling restaurant where I dined well on seafood. Next, I ambled around the town, ignoring cyclo drivers and solicitations for "massage," before finally hitting on the place I had been looking for: Crazy Kim's Bar.

Crazy Kim's founder was a woman by the name of Kim Le. She and her family fled Nha Trang in the early 1980s, ultimately becoming residents of Ottawa. On her first return visit in 1996, she was so struck by the problem of foreign pedophiles preying on penniless street children that she decided to do something about it. Purchasing a house that she converted into a large Western style "bar and grill," she then began a campaign which she christened "Hands Off the Kids!" complete with T-shirts and an attention grabbing logo. In addition to raising public awareness, Ms. Le took in a group of homeless children, helped feed and educate them, petitioned local authorities to get off their backsides and do something, and then began tracking down offenders herself based on descriptions provided by the kids. The locals said she was "crazy." I was hoping to interview Ms. Le, but was told she was on vacation in Thailand. However, I discovered that her efforts have yielded at least some positive results. For example, information she provided to Interpol has led to two convictions in Germany, and she has certainly made it more difficult for pedophiles to maneuver in Nha Trang. Presently, she was in the midst of erecting a school adjacent to her bar where kids could come in and receive free lessons in English, Vietnamese, and computer science. For a mere $6.25, it was possible to purchase 100 bricks to be used in its construction, so I slapped down my money and was instantly rewarded. The staff wrote my name on a chalkboard, they rang a bell, people clapped and cheered, the bartenders thanked me one by one, and one of them slapped a "Hands Off!" sticker onto the front of my notebook. Girls smiled at me and guys gave me the thumbs up. All in all, it was a good deal.

Interestingly, at the same time I was in Crazy Kim's, British pop star Gary Glitter was in a Vietnamese prison awaiting trial. He had been charged with committing "obscene acts" with two girls, one 10 and the other 11. He ended up getting about a year's worth of jail time to be followed by immediate deportation. To my way of thinking, they missed a golden opportunity by not making an example out of him. Lest you think me severe, by law, he could have received death by firing squad.

At a little after 10:30, I left Kim's and stepped out onto the street to make my way back to the hotel when I heard a vaguely familiar voice calling to me from across the street.

"Hey, man! I know you, man! I know you from the bus, man!" It was Marijuana.

"Oh, hi. How's it going?" I asked. "Enjoying Nha Trang?"

"Yeah, man. It's OK. But *dude*. I'm like *totally freaked* after what I saw tonight at the beach. I like *gotta* tell somebody about it."

Marijuana took out his digital camera and played me two minutes of footage. He said he had been walking along the beach at dusk when two girls asked him if he wanted to join them at a food stand for a beer. He said yes, sat down, someone put a beer in his hand, he introduced himself, and then — out of the blue, and having nothing whatsoever to do with him — a fight broke out. A man who had clearly had too much to drink went berserk, brutally assaulting anyone he could get his hands on. The film showed a wiry looking individual running around punching and drop kicking people who were just standing by, eating ice cream. He punched a woman in the face, splintered a plastic chair over another woman's shoulder, and smashed a full beer bottle over a man's head. The man went down like a sack of potatoes. Some people tried to stop him and a huge *mêlée* ensued. Marijuana swore that it lasted for 30 minutes. "Ya know the craziest thing?" he asked rhetorically. "No one came. No police, no ambulance, no nothin'."

I hadn't been there, but for me, the craziest thing was that he had stood there and filmed it all. At one point, the man was doing laps around him decking people as he went. "Weren't you scared?" I asked. "Yeah, man," he replied. "But I figured *someone* had to film it." After the brawl was over, he went around collecting footage of people's injuries. It wasn't pretty. The woman who had gotten the chair broken over her arm was in a bad way, and the man who took the beer bottle looked as though he might be dead. A group of sobbing women could be seen dragging his limp body to an awaiting taxi. "What are you going to do with the video?" I probed. "I think I'm gonna send it to the police anonymously," he replied. "Yeah, I'll do that tomorrow." After he said that, I felt guilty for having judged him. He was, after all, young, and his heart seemed to be in the right place. I thanked him for sharing, wished him luck, and walked back to my hotel.

The next morning, I awoke early to the second sunny day in a row. After breakfast, I was picked up by a minivan at my hotel that drove me and a group of Vietnamese people south past the end of the beach to a tiny port that was humming with activity. Walking through a dusty and frenzied parking lot *cum* market, we descended a flight of concrete steps and stepped onto an unattractive wooden boat. Then, we sat and waited for all the other boats around us to fill up. Families, porters, travel agents, cooks, drivers, and a handful of foreign tourists hopped from the steps to our boat to the next boat and finally to their boat. There were eight boats in all, and they were all jammed around the one miniature pier like piglets at a sow's teat. In a country where everything was made of concrete (including guardrails and the odd spring roll) they apparently didn't have enough of the stuff to spare for an extra jetty or two.

All the boats left at the same time, and by that I mean at *precisely* the same time. It was like an aquatic version of Smash Up Derby. Our boat started the process by ramming the boat behind us. That boat rammed the boat behind it and so on and so forth, until all the vessels were finally dislodged. Next, everybody got turned around towards various points on the horizon whereupon they throttled it, cutting across each other's bows in a frenzied series of near misses. In order to maximize safety, drivers blasted their air horns while deckhands shouted angrily and gestured wildly at each other. Yet despite these precautions, a tire acting as a bumper affixed to the side of our boat got tangled up with one on the adjacent boat and the two vessels engaged in a brief yet intense nautical dance before crew members stopped yelling at each other long enough to unhook us. I sat there observing all this and wondered if the Vietnamese had a word in common circulation to mean "cooperation."

It was a beautiful, though windy, day and we bounced along from one white cap to the next for the better part of an hour before reaching a tiny, tranquil bay where we anchored and went snorkeling. We spent the rest of the day island hopping. It was a bit forced, but pleasurable enough. I had only been looking for a leisurely excursion and that's what I got.

On the way back to my guesthouse, I stopped to pick up my laundry at the place I had dropped it off at the day before. It was a small hotel named The Sunflower. The man had said it would be ready at 4:00 and it was after 4:00 now. Behind the desk, I found a different man from the one I'd spoken to the day before. He was in the midst of cleaning his fingernails.

"Hello. Laundry?" I asked, having learned to dumb things down a little.

"Laundry?" he replied.

"Yes, laundry. My laundry. From yesterday."

"Uh...no," he said, and continued grooming himself.

"No? Not finished? No? You don't have it?" I pressed, but he just gazed up at me vacantly.

"No," he said.

"No what?"

"Room?"

"No room. *Laundry*."

"Room number."

"No. No room number."

He thought for a moment and then slowly exclaimed, "No room, no laundry." 'Wow,' I thought. 'An entire sentence.' Well, nearly. We went on like this for quite some time. I would explain that I was there to pick up my laundry and he would respond by saying 'no.' I pointed to the sign on the counter which said "Laundry" in Vietnamese and English, but this yielded nothing. I then used his calendar to establish the date, after which I established yesterday's date. On the calendar I drew a picture of me carrying a bundle of laundry in yesterday's block. Then, in today's block, I drew one of me with question marks over my head. The upshot of my handiwork was for him to gape at me in slack jawed, bovine incomprehension.

For lack of a better idea, I slowly repeated simple sentences like, "Where is my laundry?" and "I want my laundry," but he was still flat lining. As a last resort, before I went off in search of a translator, I wrote down on a piece of paper, "Where is my laundry?" and handed it to him, knowing that sometimes people cannot understand a spoken language but may have had enough exposure to it to be able to recognize the written word. He squinted, and held it only a few centimeters from his face. Scrutinizing it, he murmured to himself, "Whey iss mai laundry? Whey iss mai laundry?" and then, without taking his eye off the note, he walked around to the front of the counter and examined the "Laundry" sign on top of it. He looked at the note and then he looked at the sign. Then he did this again. And finally, bringing his eyes up to meet mine, he said, "Laundry?"

I left to go find Mrs. Trang.

Having located her, I calmly explained the situation and asked if she could kindly render me some assistance. This took quite a while as poor Mrs. Trang's English wasn't the best. Armed with my five-foot-nothing, only partially in-the-know, pajama-wearing French translator, I marched back to The Sunflower to demand my socks and underwear. While we were walking, I showed Mrs. Trang the hotel's business card. "Oh," she said. "I know that place. Is very bad. One time, two America girls staying there. When they going out a woman come to clean they room. She clean bed, she clean toilet, she clean suitcase. You understand what I mean? She clean all they money! Many money! $500! Gone!"

By the time I arrived back at The Sunflower, the receptionist was helping three Korean backpackers to check in. Moreover, there were now two thuggish looking men in the lobby drinking and playing cards.

"Passport," said the man, and the Koreans handed them over to him. He studied them for an unusually long time.

"Is everything OK?" asked one of the Koreans politely.

"No."

"Oh? What's wrong?"

"No," he repeated, giving them the same hostile yet uncomprehending look he'd given me. This was unbelievable. Here he was working in a hotel that dealt exclusively with foreign tourists and he didn't know the word "OK." *Everybody* knows the word "OK." And instead of studying a bit of English so as to help facilitate his job, he'd obviously come to the conclusion at some point that a reasonable substitute was to say "no" rather than "yes" whenever anyone asked him a question. That way, he probably reckoned, if somebody were to ask him for a gazillion dollars, he wouldn't be obliged to pay them.

"Room?" he asked, as if he'd never seen me before.

"No room. Laundry," I said and asked Mrs. Trang to help me translate. She did, and he replied by saying that I must have had the wrong hotel. When I said I didn't (why would I have their card?), he claimed they didn't have a laundry service. By now, the two ruffians had stopped their card game and were observing me keenly. When I picked up the laundry sign and showed it to everybody, he just shrugged his shoulders and defiantly lit up a cigarette. "Mrs. Trang," I said, "please ask him where the other man is. Ask him to call him. The man who was here yesterday." Having gotten the translation, he picked up the telephone, and without dialing — wait for it — handed it to me. Dully comprehending, through the aid of my dear translator, that *he* had to call the man who was on duty yesterday, he dialed and then sat back and glared at me. He suddenly looked nervous and brought his hand up to his hair in a manner remarkably similar to that of Huang, the nerve shot tour guide. His friends were glaring, too. The tension was palpable. Someone picked up on the other end and the receptionist asked them a question. When he got the answer, he slapped himself on the forehead and slumped down in his chair defeated. Yes, a foreign man had brought laundry in yesterday, but it wouldn't be ready until seven, if that was OK. It was, I said, and Mrs. Trang and I made our exit. As we did so, his two red-faced pals gave him a stern dressing down presumably for having caused Vietnamese people everywhere to lose face.

The next day, I went on another day trip, this time to a hot spring resort specializing in mineral mud baths. I found out about this from an ad that Mr. and Mrs. Trang had hanging next to the reception desk. "*Va Phuc hoi Suc Khoe!*" it announced. "Soaking in Mineral Mud is Very Interesting!" Under this banner there was a picture of a couple sitting in a tub and the line, "More happily and exciting as soaking special mineral mud doubly." Actually, from the photos it looked alright, so I asked Mrs. Trang if she could help me book a ticket.

Located in the hills north of Nha Trang, the bus rambled through a couple of tumbledown villages before pulling into a newly built parking lot. I gave the woman behind the glass window $10 and she gave me a towel with Tweety Bird on it and pointed to some nearby changing rooms. Admittedly, I had a mild hangover, but it vanished completely after soaking in a tub of mud. Made of wood and with a large patio umbrella affixed to it to shield from the sun, the tub was filled with a creamy brown buoyant soup that smelled of sulfur. Although that may not sound particularly enticing, it felt great and the views of the nearby garden and lush rolling hills were nothing short of perfection. After stewing in the bucket of primordial glop, it was on to a mineral hot water tub and then a hot spring bath. The last stop was the massage room, probably the only one in Nha Trang that was on the up and up. My masseuse, whose name was Feng, asked me in very broken English to marry her and take her to Saigon so that she might be reunited with her family. I wish I were joking.

The following morning, the wake up call I had asked Mrs. Trang for several times failed to materialize. Luckily, I had been expecting as much and managed to get up on my own. Downstairs, Mrs. Trang was cooking me a banana pancake and preparing me a cup of tea.

"What bus company you use?" she asked.

"Camel."

"What time them say to come there?"

"7:00."

"Oh, no. You go there is 7:30. They are always late." She then called them for me, and sure enough, they were running behind schedule. As a parting gift, she pressed a rotten banana into my hand, grinned, and asked me to come back. I promised her I would, and stepped out into the early morning sunlight.

The scene at the bus station was one of chaos, as usual. Bleary-eyed tourists stumbled around attempting to figure out which vehicle was theirs, while inside, drivers could be seen playfully wrestling with each other or arguing with management over pay. One of the perennial problems with bus travel in Vietnam was that the company would inform the customers that they would be picked up at their hotel, but then, because the company was invariably late, the customer would become impatient or worried and head off to the bus company. And of course, five minutes later, the bus would arrive at their hotel. A variation of this was that the company would call all the customers at their respective hotels and ask that they come to the company after all, seeing as how they were running late. But, not surprisingly, not everyone could be reached. The result of this was a lot of frenzied driving around interposed with prolonged periods of waiting. The drama was then set to the soundtrack of arguing organizers and tense sounding cell phone calls with annoyed hotel receptionists. Overbooking was another issue. After the seats were filled, the driver or his assistant would plunk a couple of foot stools in the aisle and see if a pair of foreigners was dumb enough to sit on them. If they weren't, fine. A minute or two of verbal abuse could be endured for trying to pull a fast one. But if they were, then that was another few bucks in their pocket. The company need never know. The following morning, the whole asinine routine would start all over again. By the time we got on the road on this day, it was nearly 8:40.

The driver was the worst yet, honking when he overtook someone, when someone overtook him, when he met someone, when he saw something move, when he didn't, if he drove past water, or a tree, or grass, and at all other times. At one point, we were barreling along a lengthy and perfectly flat stretch of highway that was devoid of any form of traffic or signs of life and he tooted the horn twice. He just couldn't help himself.

In the early afternoon, we struggled up a winding mountain path where rice paddies and palm trees yielded to vegetable plots and pines. At about 1000 meters, the road leveled out and we drove past fields of potatoes and corn and a series of undulating terraced hills. People had Western style homes here, complete with lawns, garages, and driveways filled with cars, kids, and toys. It wasn't what you think of when you think of Vietnam. We arrived in the elevated city of Dalat at 2:30, pulling into a hotel driveway. A representative from the establishment was suddenly standing in the aisle and politely asking that we at least have a look at a room there before going elsewhere, unless of course, we already had a reservation. He then smilingly wished us a pleasant stay in Dalat before disappearing. This, I noted, was wholly dissimilar from the imperative approach preferred by the lowlanders. The place looked alright, so I ventured into the lobby where I encountered only the second group of Israelis I had seen thus far. They were doing what they seem to do best, which is making a bad impression.

"You want six dollars for hroom?" one of them was shouting, hands flailing all over the place. "But zer is hronly two beds! Hree want *zree* beds! Hree are five people! You count! One, two, zree, four, five! We need zree beds!"

"Yes, I see," replied the clerk. "Five people. Maybe you can rent two rooms."

"No, no. Hree don't rent two rooms. Hree go to zer ozer hotel."

Taking this as an auspicious sign, I booked for two nights. After a brief nap, I got cleaned up and went out to look around. It was a clear, sunny day, with just a few wisps of cloud shuffling across a pale blue sky. The air was crisp and cool, and there was the most comfortable breeze. Then, of course, there was Dalat itself. To be completely candid, I had assumed that Dalat would be some half bedraggled mountain hamlet, noteworthy only for its breezy and distinctive climate, but that wasn't the case at all. It was a charming, albeit sprawling, place consisting of rolling hills, tasteful houses, and smiling people who had been made prosperous by vegetable farming, wine production, and tourism. It was short on places to eat, though, and I walked around for a half an hour before finally finding a restaurant that didn't look as though it served each dish with a complimentary case of hepatitis.

In the fading light, I continued walking down a large hill past an assortment of chalets and hotels. Halfway down, things took a bit of a dip with a slew of karaokes and massage parlors, but even these were nicely built. The lake at the bottom of the hill was an admirably serene, elongated body of water seven kilometers in circumference. When I got to it, the thinning blue sky was ever so slowly blackening its rippled surface. Fringed by groves of pines, a footpath wound its way along a band of manicured lawns, sculpted trees, and colorful flowers. At various points on its large periphery there stood brightly lit hotels, a handful of cafés, and a 40-meter high replica of the Eiffel Tower. I ambled around at a leisurely pace, enjoying the fresh air and soaking up the views and lakeside scenes. There were couples pedaling boats resembling overgrown swans, vendors selling balloons, and women barbecuing shish kebabs. I walked the circumference of the lake in a contentedly unfocused frame of mind and watched the sky go from powder blue to ivory to navy and finally to black, while legions of silvery clouds marched swiftly overhead.

Tired and hungry after my trek, I stopped at a restaurant on the waterfront that looked like the place to be and ordered dinner. It was only just too cool to sit outside, so I opted for a place by the window with a fine view of the Eiffel Tower. Soon, a nervous looking waitress in a purple uniform appeared in front of me with a pad and pen.

"Hallo," she managed.

"Hi. I want a chicken sandwich," I said, pointing at the picture.

"One?"

"Yes, one."

"And this. The garden salad." I pointed again.

"One?"

"Yes, one."

"And a bottle of Coke."

"One?"

After eating, I sat for some time reading, sipping tea, and taking in the view, having reached a point in my life where this is about as fun as it gets. At around 9:00, I left and began the hour-long trek up the hill. Once at the top, I got disoriented and couldn't remember which street to turn down. I had my hotel's card, which featured a miniature map, and I showed it to three shop owners, but none of them could point me in the right direction. Indeed, each person pointed in a different direction. Stumped, I resorted to taking a taxi. The driver, who knew a smattering of English, kindly gave me a tour of the entire hillside, which included his brother's shop and his wife's hair salon before letting me out somewhere near the lake. Locating a taxi stand, I then presented myself to a collection of drivers who examined my card and deliberated for a full minute before shaking their heads and waving me away. Finally, I found a motorcycle driver who glanced at the card and said, "Minh Xuan Hotel? OK. No problem," and drove me straight to the door in about five minutes. When I approached the counter, the receptionist was far away in a world of soap opera romance, but tore herself away from the flickering box long enough to give me the key. When I asked her nicely if I could have a wake up call for 7:00, she scrunched up her face and said, "No." I went to bed exasperated and had a fitful, dream filled sleep.

I managed to crawl out of bed and after breakfast in the attached diner, I was picked up by yet another minivan for yet another day trip. My travel companions on this day were a young Vietnamese couple and an extended family of nine. Among the latter was a married couple named James and Teresa who lived in

San Diego and were back visiting relatives. They were absurdly friendly and we chatted frequently throughout the day. Before long, we were driving through an impressive pine forest. Following the curves of the hills, we steadily gained altitude, eventually stopping at a smallish parking lot in front of log cabin. Perched on a hill, the structure was attached to a fine viewing deck. The building and the timbered views beyond could well have passed for Bavaria. Outside, I walked down a set of steps through a patch of towering pines that cast long, spastic shadows in the morning sunlight and manifest breeze. At the bottom, I was rewarded with the sight of a gushing waterfall and a host of divergent foliage, as if the area couldn't decide on whether to be temperate or tropical. Marigolds, violets, roses, and chrysanthemums littered the valley floor like piles of confetti. I stood there in a state of silent veneration, listening to the steady, soothing thrum of the white rushing water before climbing back up to the crest and ordering a tea on the veranda, the view from which I could have looked at all day.

"Well that was nice," I said to James and Teresa back in the minibus.

"Yeah, it's nice," Teresa replied, "but it's kind of disappointing for us."

"Why's that?"

"Well," said James, "when we came here more than 30 years ago, the forest was so much ... how do you say that?"

"Thicker," his wife offered.

"Yeah, thicker. Actually, this whole area was like that. They cut down a lot of it for wood. It should be protected for real, but they only protect it on paper. Did you know that next year that waterfall will be gone? They're going to build a dam. Really, they should build a national park. But, people here, they just don't know anything about that sort of thing. They don't understand nature."

This was interesting. During the course of the day, they confided that they had very little in common with "real" Vietnamese people, including their relatives. The shook their heads whenever they saw piles of trash dumped along the roadside, or when the driver went on a horn rampage. "And people here," they went on, taking turns to complete each other's thoughts, "they cannot drive." "It's the same in San Diego. Immigrants, you know? They litter, they speed, they don't follow the traffic rules.... They just don't know any better."

This was the kind of thing I usually heard from people from places like Bruges or Amsterdam. It wasn't everyday you got to witness Asian people knocking other Asian people. But of course, they weren't knocking them because they were Asian, but rather because of their culture, and what they perceived as the backwardness of it. And that is the key. Race has nothing to do with anything. It's purely incidental. Groups of people are different not because of their ethnicity but rather because they share a culture, and culture is everything. It defines who we are, determines much of what we do, and provides us with our all important worldview. It is truly the force that binds. But even if you understand that notionally, unless you are properly exposed to another one, you might live your whole life without ever truly realizing this or without seeing your own culture for what it is. Quite simply, you need at least one comparative model.

After a short drive through the rolling wooded hills, we arrived at a place called Paradise Lake, and Paradise it almost was. Strolling along the edge of a bluff, we were treated to a sweeping view of golden bamboo trees, a variety I hadn't known existed. Clusters of vibrant yellow stalks poked out of the earth, supporting droopy awnings of fluttery green. In the distance could be seen an evergreen valley enveloping a blue jewel of a lake. On its surface, a single white boat inched along, while in the middle distance knolls of rolling pines receded into yet another cloudless sky.

After strolling down to the lake I made my way up a flight of stone steps and through an archway adorned with neat Chinese characters that read *Zhulin Chanyuan*, or Bamboo Forest Zen Monastery. At the top of the pine needle strewn stairway was an immaculate cobblestone courtyard dominated by the most splendid temple I have ever seen. A study in Chinese architecture, it was nevertheless decidedly un-Chinese, lacking in any of the usual garishness. Capped by a timber ceiling and brown tiled roof, its butter-yellow walls were outfitted with dark carved doors and latticed windows. Through a window depicting a phoenix delivering a scroll with its talons, I spied several monks worshiping among enormous wooden pillars and plumes of incense.

We drove back to Dalat where we had lunch. This done we then headed to a tourist hotel known as the Crazy House. The Crazy House was an avant garde inn that looked like the sort of thing hobbits might have built if they had been under the influence of magic mushrooms. I had read it described as *Alice in Wonderland* or "Salvador Dali come to life," but to me it just looked like a psychedelic nightmare, and an unfinished psychedelic nightmare at that. Only partially completed and devoid of guests, my guide book included a large touched-up photo of the place that made it appear fully constructed. The illusion was then made complete by suggesting to book well in advance.

Seeing as how it was vacant, we were allowed to inspect all its rooms. The first one I examined was called the Termite Room, which turned out to be a tiny, mirrored affair with walls and ornaments resembling a mixture of Swiss cheese and melted wax. Then it was on to the Eagle Room, where a giant eagle stood perched atop a meter high egg. The theme in this chamber was supposed to be "back to nature," but there was nothing natural about it. Back outside, I passed through a garden featuring concrete animals and wrought iron spider webs before moving on to the lobby *cum* art gallery. There, I asked to see the owner. As luck would have it, she was in.

Her name was Dang Viet Nga and she was the daughter of Ho Chi Minh's successor and former national president throughout the better part of the 1980s. Lying to her assistants by telling them I was a reporter with a "big Canadian newspaper," I was led into her office, where I found her dressed in a beret, scarf, and full length fur coat. It was shorts and T-shirt weather. She had been staring out the window, but turned to fix me with a blank gaze. Motioning for me to take a seat, she then rummaged through a drawer and silently handed me a business card. Next, she asked for mine. "Oh, I, uh... I forgot it at my hotel," I fibbed, and luckily she didn't follow up. The interview was brief, and went verbatim like this:

"You have a very interesting place here. When did you start?"

"1990."

"I see. And how much does it cost to stay here?"

"Between $30 and $60."

"Right. And has it been difficult? I ask this because, well, it's, umm, not quite finished."

"Yes."

"What's been the main problem?"

"Vietnamese people."

"What about them?"

"They don't understand me. People don't understand me. Only Hanoi."

"Hanoi? What about Hanoi?"

"Only Hanoi understands me."

"Right. I see. So, when do you think you'll be finished?"

"In four years."

"Well, I hope I get a chance to see it then."

That was it. I thanked her and left. I couldn't imagine how she ever arrived at the projection of four more years. I reckoned it could have been completed in four months, but there was no construction currently underway. She was obviously an eccentric and her eyes indicated that there was another factor involved. My guess was that she either had a substance abuse problem or was suffering from some sort of disorder. Quite simply, she wasn't all there. In the West, she could have been successful, perhaps even have thrived, but here she appeared to be eking out a living from tour groups that were willing to have a quick glance around but not willing to pay for the privilege of sleeping inside a surrealist painting. Still, it was highly original.

Late in the afternoon, we visited another temple before making our way to Love Valley, the honeymooner Mecca of Vietnam. With more pined hills, and this time a teal-blue lake, it would have been agreeable if it weren't totally overdone. The pathways were lined with tables and booths selling oodles of junk, and the vendors were extremely aggressive. Once inside the main gate, the young couple from the bus, who had kept to themselves all day, surprised me by addressing me in perfect English.

"Where ya from?" he asked.

"Canada."

"Hey, me too!" he cried, and gave me a light jab on the shoulder. "Edmonton originally. Just back visitin' some family. Whereabouts in Canada?"

"New Brunswick."

"Oh, you're a Newfie! Cool!"

In case it should ever come up at a dinner party, a person from New Brunswick is a New Brunswicker. A Newfie is semi-pejorative term for a Newfoundlander, a person from the province of Newfoundland. Although it is perfectly acceptable for non-Canadians to be unfamiliar with the finer points of Canadian geography and culture, whenever I hear fellow Canucks getting the nation's rather large territorial zones mixed up, I can't help but wonder if their parents didn't bribe their way through elementary school. But the Newfie slip wasn't so bad. I once worked with a woman from British Columbia who assumed that the nation's capital city was Ontario (a province a third the size of India) and supposed the prime minister to be Pierre Trudeau, a man who had been out of politics for two decades, and was, more significantly, dead.

This is, of course, is highly ironic given how identity-conscious Canadians are, which is to say that they are more than just a little insecure. And this can be evidenced by the mandatory sewing of the national flag onto one's backpack before heading off for a spot of foreign travel. The reason Canadians cite for doing this is that people will treat them better and won't kidnap them because, well, they aren't American, eh? Of course, the fact of the matter is that nobody cares. Most people that I have encountered are more concerned with who you are than where you happen to be from, and the majority seems quite capable of differentiating between a person's government or culture and the person himself. As for kidnappings, these happen to Canadians too, and I have never heard of an account where a Canadian was abducted only to be released upon the discovery that he wasn't an American. However, if this ever were to occur, the Canadian Broadcasting Corporation would doubtlessly produce a five-part mini-series about it.

That night, I dined well at a quaint little place on the hillside. Ordering a garden salad, cream of broccoli soup, steak and potatoes, and a glass perfectly acceptable Dalat Wine, I tucked into a little book I had bought on the history of Dalat. Here's something interesting I learned. During the war, both sides agreed not to fight there. The reason for this was that the top brass wanted to continue using the city as a holiday spot. While the war raged on the land below, its planners were sipping whisky and being entertained in their airy mountain villas just down the road from one another. I wondered if they had ever run into each other on the golf course I had seen earlier.

The next morning, I awoke early and boarded a bus to Mui Ne (pronounced *Moo Nay*). I had read Mui Ne described as a "serene, tree adorned beach resort off the beaten track" and to me, that sounded perfect. For two hours, the needle on the speedometer swayed between 30 and 35 kilometers per hour, and consequently we were passed by every single vehicle in southern Vietnam. But then, as we got closer to the coast, and the grassy meadows thinned to reveal sandy hills that were sparsely decorated with stubborn looking shrubs and contorted, leafless trees, the driver gunned it, nearly taking everyone's face off. Along one particularly sharp decline dominated by a series of abrupt turns, he would throttle it and then brake at the last second, clearly startled each and every time a poorly barricaded bend in the road manifested itself. The turns came like clockwork, yet incredibly, he never saw the pattern

After a dramatic and oscillating coastline drive, we emerged into a littoral plain and stopped just inside Mui Ne proper. In keeping with precedent, I checked into the first resort I saw. There were 10 kilometers of beach and the next hotel was nowhere to be seen. As it turned out, the place I chose was quite nice, and I splurged a little for a cute little cabin surrounded by towering palms and blazing bougainvillea. After lunch, I retired to my hut for a much needed shower and nap. My head hit the pillow and things went very black. Unfortunately, I was soon woken up by a knocking at the door. When I opened it, there was a man standing there holding what looked to be a vacuum cleaner.

"*Phong tam o dau? Ah, con rep,*" he said.

"What?"

"*Con rep. Con rep. Giet con rep.*"

"No, thank you. Not today," I replied politely, and then closed the door in his face. Refreshed from the sleep, I grabbed my camera and headed out in the late afternoon sun to find a motorcycle driver. Speeding past a few seamy looking discos and failed resorts, we wound our way through a tiny village or two before coming upon a large harbor filled with fishing boats, although "filled" isn't an entirely adequate word. I've never seen so many vessels assembled in one place. The view was reminiscent of an invasion scene in a Hollywood movie where a few genuine ships in the forefront are augmented by a computer generated flotilla in the background. In one half of the harbor, boats quite literally stretched away as far as the eye could see, being reduced to tiny specks along the edge of the distant shoreline. There must have been 300 of them; all blue, all nearly identical, and all resting up for their night's work. Shortly, the driver parked in front of a drab, concrete convenience store adorned with a giant Coca-Cola sign. Getting off, I followed the trail of yellow powder across the road and strode up a high hill.

It was a sand dune. A very large sand dune. In just a few hours, I had gone from a scaled down model of Bavaria to one of Arabia. Trundling through the golden dust, I reached a peak and had a look around. The views of the sea and the coast were quite captivating and it quickly became apparent why the rock here had been reduced to its current state. The wind whipped at the dunes' contours, sending S-shaped shrouds of dust zipping along its grooved surfaces like thousands of lost spirits. As the sun arced lower, the sky and sands altered their hues, becoming darker and crisper. I walked around for an hour or so taking pictures, and then, not long before sunset, a group of monks appeared and started walking slowly and methodically along the wind-swept fringe of the largest dune, hands clasped in prayer. It was a photo shoot, and judging by the seriousness of the photographers and their equipment, it was an important one. Although contrived, the robed silhouettes set against the sand and setting sun looked spectacular and I joined in the clicking throng, ultimately managing to get some superb shots.

The next day, I again woke early to join my day trip only to find it had been postponed to the late afternoon. Nobody had thought to inform me. I read by the pool before retiring to my room for another couple hours of rest. I was woken up by knocking again. This time it was a very insistent maid. Incidentally, the man who had come the day before had wanted to do a bit of pest control. Just before dinner, I saw him pumping huge clouds of chemicals into the bushes in what looked like a reenactment of the Battle of the Somme. Tourists fled the pool area, while diners gasped and hastily covered their noses and mouths with their napkins. Of course, this could have been done late at night or early in the morning, but then no one would have seen what a fine job they were doing.

The minivan drove up the coast for a half an hour before pulling off the main road and down a potholed dirt trail. I got out and walked through a narrow grove of dark pines, emerging to find myself on the edge of a grass fringed pond of rippling blue. A woman with a conical hat was struggling against the wind to get her wooden skiff back to the shore. Her brood of dark skinned children stood by in the tall grass shouting instructions or words of encouragement. It was an oasis, for all around it were cream colored sand dunes, and unlike the golden ones I had seen the day before, these extended clear out of sight. Having spotted a fresh batch of walking wallets, the kids ran up to us holding cans of 7-UP and rolled up sheets of plastic. One girl began pitching, and she didn't stop for the next 20 minutes.

"Hello, you sliding?"

"No, me no sliding."

"Why no sliding?"

"Me no money."

"Yes, you money. You very *much* money. You airplane Vietnam.You watch I sliding?"

"No, I no watch you sliding."

"Why? Sliding very happy."

She persevered for so long that I gave her a dollar to slide over a dune and out of sight with the promise not to bother me anymore. The instant she took the bill, the smile vanished from her face. Capitalism. It's so cold. Her work done, she shuffled through the sands back to the pond to await the next people to materialize from the grove. Having reported to her two brown skinned brothers that she had earned a buck, the two scamps ran all the way to where I was to try their luck. Poking me in the stomach, one exclaimed, "baby." "No," his brother corrected him, "Ten baby." In between snapping photos of buttery drifts propping up a powder blue sky, we did a little language exchange. I traded "sand," "sky," "cloud," and "grass" for *bo bien, bau troi, may,* and *co.* What a harsh and peculiar sounding language Vietnamese is.

Mui Ne offered three varieties of dunes: yellow, white, and red, and the red ones were perhaps the most spectacular even if they weren't exactly dunes. Instead, what they were was a tiny range of jagged hills of brittle, crimson stone. The wind had pulverized them in places, although the virtually incandescent green shrubs and trees which sprang from the rich red soil offered them at least some degree of protection. The sky above had turned to an enormous smear of greyish white and was completely at odds with the jade plants and serrated ruby knolls. After taking in this scene, we returned to the hotel, where I lounged next to the pool again and through the swaying palm tree tops observed the sky change shades until it drained itself of color.

The next afternoon, I jumped on another bus to make the final leg of my journey. We had barely left town when I spotted a similar vehicle pulled over on the opposite side of the road with a group of foreign tourists standing next to it and staring at something. "Was someone car sick?" I wondered. Our bus slowed, and suddenly all the passengers on the left side emitted a collective groan.

"An accident. A girl on a motorbike."

"Is she dead?"

"It doesn't look good...there is a lot of blood."

Everywhere you went you saw painted billboards depicting the correct and incorrect ways to do things, including how to dress. Low cut shirts and shorts were a no-no. People should be more or less fully covered. Unfortunately, they had forgotten to mention helmets.

For hours we drove through row upon row of neatly planted trees interrupted every so often by a grey smudge of a town. These came thicker and faster until we were surrounded by slums and slow moving traffic in a dingy segment of the hoary ring that encircles Saigon proper. At a little after five, we traversed the Saigon River and the city revealed itself to be a sprawling array of squat buildings, glass towers, and blinking neon. It was sliced up into sections by broad boulevards crammed with motorcycles and flanked by throngs of pedestrians, uniformed students, and gnarled trees.

The bus turned down this street and then that, and before long we were stopped in front of a colorful row of hotels and travel agencies. I checked into a family run affair and got cleaned up. Showered and with a fresh change of clothes, I ventured outside, evaded about a dozen touts, and settled on an agreeable looking restaurant where I ordered enough food for an entire village. After this, it was on to a stroll downtown.

There was no sea breeze here. It was stiflingly hot and sticky outside. I walked through a park of cuddling couples, on to a large outdoor market, and finally in the direction of the Rex Hotel, a famous landmark that was said to offer arresting views of the city from its rooftop veranda bar. Pushing a door open, an elderly woman dressed as a bell hop greeted me with a, "Good afternoon, sir." It was 7:45 p.m. "Hello," I said, and noticed a sign next to the elevator saying, "Rooftop Garden — One of the best bars in Southeast Asia as voted by Newsweek Magazine, 1993." On the sixth floor, I discovered nothing but an empty terrace and a couple of locked doors, so I took the elevator back downstairs. Back on the street, I continued on toward the floodlit and immaculately white Hotel de Ville, a classically ornate piece of French architecture now serving as the city's people committee headquarters. From here, I noticed the face of the Rex and realized I must have entered through an obscure, anterior door. Walking through the front door, I approached a woman behind the counter and politely inquired about the bar.

"There is no outdoor bar," she informed me. "But there's a restaurant on the fifth floor."

"Is it outside?"

"No, it's inside."

Thanking her, I decided to see what sort of views the restaurant offered. The elevator opened to reveal a sign saying, "Rooftop Restaurant & Bar 6th Floor." Passing another restaurant on the fifth floor, I continued on to the sixth. The rooftop bar was open and doing a brisk business. It has to be said that this is a major recurring theme in East Asia. Service people seem to be almost purely ornamental.

The views from the rooftop were indeed grand and the bar had a decidedly Western feel to it. I had a couple of drinks and then retraced my steps back to the tourist ghetto my hotel was located in. Taking a perfunctory stroll around the tourist area, I decided to stop, into a couple of stores to shop for gifts. The tourist ghetto was a sordid place, filled with massage parlors and questionable looking drinking establishments. It was all quite repulsive, with everything encrusted in a layer of grime.

Inside a used bookstore I took down a Vietnamese phrasebook and had a glance through it. Every guesthouse and bookstand from here to Hanoi must have possessed at least one of these, no doubt discarded by some naïve traveler who had thought it would be noble or culturally correct to learn a smattering of the local language. I say "naïve" because this could never be achieved through the use of a phrasebook. For starters, even if you did manage to utter a word or phrase correctly, which you never would with Vietnamese given that it is tonal and in no way connected to a European language, it would hardly matter even if you did as you would never be able to understand the response.

Moreover, phrasebooks in general tend to be tragically out of touch with both language and the real world. Take this one, for example. In the very first paragraph, it stated that despite Vietnam's disastrous past, people nowadays were optimistic about the future, something they would most likely impart provided that "you possess(ed) a minimum of language skills." I dare say that it would be hard to do otherwise. It went on to claim that the book would not be dealing with cultural values, after which dozens are listed. The reader is advised, for example, not to be frightened of people's smiles as this is a sign of something called "friendliness," adding that "(w)hat you may have to worry about, if anything, is when people keep away from you."

Regarding the language itself, the author seems to be equally in the dark. In introducing its characteristics, it's stated that Vietnamese is the same everywhere and has no dialects. "Everyone can understand each other, even though there are three distinguishable accents: northern, central, and southern." But on the very next page, you find this: "(t)here are two distinguishable accents in Vietnam — the northern and the southern." Twelve pages later: "There are many accents in Vietnam...." Finally, it makes the claim that people who speak with a southern accent should "generally" be understood by people in the north, although they may not be understood by people in rural areas.

It gets better.

After a couple pages of idioms that you would never hear, use, understand, or be able to say, they recommend that you learn the following phrases: "Sorry, I'm a terrible dancer," "Is there a (predominantly) gay street/district?" (not strictly gay, mind you), "Where can I buy some gay/lesbian magazines?", and finally "Is there a gay telephone hotline?" As I see it, if you are gay, that's your business. But, if you are gay and traveling through communist Vietnam and feel the need to call a gay hotline so badly that you memorize how to ask for one in Vietnamese, then you are in urgent need of psychological counseling. But, of course, no one in their right mind would ever think to ask that, and that is precisely my point. I returned the $12 paperback to its place on the shelf and walked back to my hotel.

The next day, I continued on with the walking tour I had begun the night before. Making my way due northwest, I stopped to look at the Reunification Palace. I had planned on going in for a look but decided against it seeing as how it mirrored a giant cinder block. It was reminiscent of the Reunification Bridge. The country had finally broken the shackles forged by centuries of foreign subjugation only to have its moment of glory commemorated with a building that, in another Asian metropolis, would have been taken for the city jail.

The War Remnants Museum opened at 1:30 p.m. and I bought a ticket and went inside. The displays were comprised almost solely of pictures and there were some very impressive ones. Of note, was one of two corpses being dragged behind an American vehicle and another of a grinning American soldier picking up the remnants of an exploded communist soldier. In addition, there was a plethora of post Agent Orange themed photos, and these were very effective at causing the viewer to cringe and look away. Many of the photos I had seen before, but it was interesting and shocking nonetheless.

There was also a list of participating nations along with the number of troops they sent. Besides the United States, these included Australia, New Zealand, the Philippines, South Korea, and Thailand. Interestingly, of these so-called Free World Military Forces, the South Koreans were considered to be the most savage. When civilians caught wind that the Koreans were in the area, whole villages would up and evacuate. A country that perhaps deserved an honorable mention was the Republic of China. The Nationalists would have liked nothing better than to have supported the US in a military capacity as they hoped this would yield nuclear weapons that could then be used "defensively" against the

PRC. The Americans informed "the other China" that their services would not be required.

Absent from the list on Hanoi's side were the Soviet Union, China, and North Korea, countries that all sent troops and all suffered casualties. Absent on Saigon's side was Canada, a country that supplied 10,000 mercenaries to fight alongside the Americans, although, to be sure, that wasn't all it supplied. It has been calculated that Canadian companies sold a whopping $2.47 billion worth of *matériel* to the United States fully knowing that it would be used in Indochina. Everything from ammunition to explosives to aircraft engines to napalm was manufactured and shipped to Uncle Sam from his peace loving neighbor to the north. Canada did an additional $10 billion in sales in (other) war related goods, including things like boots, berets, shell casings, plate armor, and military vehicles. In fact, the war was so good for Canada that unemployment plunged to a record low 3.7%. What is more, Canada-US relations have seldom been better. In fact, the Canadian government was so smitten by the United States and its foreign policy at the time that it allowed American planes to practice carpet bombing in the province of Alberta, while Agent Orange was tested on a tract of land within a military base only an hour's drive from where I grew up in New Brunswick. Due to the wind on one particular breezy day, the chemical killed crops in another township and before long, both military personnel and local residents were becoming seriously ill. One expert believes that residue dioxin still exists in the soil today. After years of denial, the Canadian government finally admitted to the testing, although they continue to drag their heels over compensation, even in cases where people worked with toxins directly and have multiple disorders. Additionally, although it is widely known that draft dodgers, deserters, and other so-called conscientious objectors sought refuge across the border, the Canadian government was never very happy about the trend and ultimately passed legislation that effectively stopped it. Not surprisingly, this is a topic seldom raised in Canada as it doesn't fit with our image of being nice.

The museum's pictures and exhibits were certainly stirring. Indeed, they were positively depressing. On the whole, however, the museum was amateurishly set up on top of being rather shabby. One of the viewing halls resembled an old garage, something I found inexcusable given the steady stream of ticket buyers. Also, rather than having a timetable of events or something in the way of a historical overview, the purpose seemed to be solely to shock, but this lost its effect after a while. Despite the fact that the war was over, Hanoi had *won*, the country was reunited, and foreign sentiment was overwhelmingly on their side, they just couldn't refrain from employing propaganda. I took particular issue with the garbled English explanations that were printed on uneven bits of paper and scotch taped to the displays. Lest you think me particular, these had the effect of making the interesting and tragic appear absurd and tragicomic. A photo of a windowless truck plowing through a jungle path was explained via the banner, "Truck Without Glasses On Road." More poignantly, a photo that could only be described as heartrending carried this caption: "Woman Selling Prawns In Market Killed By Stray Bullet. Her Surprising Husband Stands Beside Her." For such an important part of their history, you would have thought they would have gotten their act together. The millions who sacrificed their lives deserve no less.

By the time I finished viewing the exhibits, I felt thoroughly miserable. And right on cue, I emerged to discover that the sun, which had been present ever since the resort town of Nha Trang, was cloaked in a foreboding veil of grey. The humidity was stifling and an oppressive layer of exhaust hung disgustingly in the air.

What do foreign tourists feel like doing, after they've viewed pictures of atrocities their country may have helped commit? Why, spending money, of course. The sidewalk outside the museum was teeming with touts and drivers helping to relieve travelers of some of their guilt. I walked for a while before getting lost, after which I took a motorcycle to the Notre Dame Cathedral. The sky burst open, jettisoning buckets of water, and a long rumble of thunder ripped through the air just as I entered through the church's considerable wooden doors. Although not a Christian, I appreciate churches for their architecture, and this one was a fine example. I spent a contented half hour inside the structure examining the stained glass windows and high ceilings. This done, I relaxed on one of the pews and waited out the rain, all the while watching Japanese tourists take pictures of themselves.

That night, I ate at a place in the tourist district called Good Morning Vietnam. Located more or less in the middle of everything, it was an ideal spot to just sit and people watch. In the short time it took for my dinner to arrive, four women asked me if I wanted a massage, while another badgered me to buy a copied book from a string-bound stack of 67 books that she was lugging around with her. At the next table sat a faction of jabbering Koreans, while behind me a group of brightly dressed Africans blabbed away into their cell phones. Outside, on the neon strip, vendors were selling bananas, postcards, film, and junk jewelry, and an old man sauntered around playing horrible electric guitar to clusters of distressed looking foreigners. His wife followed behind him carrying the amplifier. It wouldn't have been so out of place to have seen a team of acrobats go somersaulting on by.

Saigon had the miraculous ability of appearing even dingier at night. The greenery of its boulevards and the colors of its shops and signs were gathered in and swallowed whole by an inky blackness made possible by a dearth of proper street lighting. After eating, I jumped in a cab and drove to Cholon, Saigon's Chinatown, only to realize that I had been duped yet again by my travel guide. From the description, you would have thought the place was the cultural heartbeat of Asia, with nightly dragon dances and martial arts displays, but alas, it was just another dismal, fume-choked section of town, distinctive only in the Chinese characters that adorned its shop and street signs.

My travel book seemed much more concerned with alliteration and effervescent phrases than on providing objective assessments. But, of course, nearly everything has to be hyped and hyped big, otherwise the books won't sell and the industries they indirectly support will suffer a loss. From a business perspective, this makes perfect sense. If a man is thinking of taking his family on holiday to, say, Greenland, then Greenland has to be trumpeted as a child-friendly paradise with facilities for kids at every turn. If not, Dad might decide not to take the trip, and, more to the point, put the book back on the shelf.

The next morning, I boarded my final minibus to the Cu Chi Tunnels. I had entertained the notion of touring the Mekong Delta, but gave up on the idea due to an irrational fear of contracting malaria. Also, I was looking forward to blowing off a few rounds from an AK-47. Our tour guide introduced himself as Mr. Binh, but said we could call him Mr. Bean. He didn't speak English, he told us, but rather American, so he apologized if we didn't understand him. Then he repeated himself. As it was, he repeated himself often. At first, I took him to be a kindly sort and even thought he had a wise air about him, but, of course, looks can be deceiving.

As it turned out, Mr. Bean had some pretty serious issues, and for the next hour and a half he used his microphone to impart these to us by way of an autobiography. His parents had divorced when he was young and this affected him deeply. As a young man, he had flunked out of medical school, went on to fail as a writer, and then fought on the side of the South and had failed miserably at that. This sad overview out of the way, he proceeded to test the passengers on their knowledge of the Vietnam War. As a lead in, he speculated that we probably didn't know anything.

"For example," he said. "Does anyone know when the war ended?"

There was no response.

"Come on. I know you read it in your travel books. What year did the Vietnam War end? It's OK. Just tell me what you think."

"1975?" a woman answered tepidly.

"No! Wrong! It was 1980! You see? You know nothing! Your travel book knows nothing!"

In fact, the woman was correct. Between 1975 and 1980 Vietnam battled it out with both the Cambodians and the Chinese, but those are considered to be separate events. As has been mentioned, the South surrendered in 1975. After berating us for our ignorance, he went on to explain how the Vietnam War had come within a hair of setting off World War III. Apparently, in 1967, all of the world's communist countries had their ICBMs trained on Washington and were on the verge of wiping that city off the face of the Earth. Why the communist nations failed to follow through, he failed to specify; but he assured us that it was true. He had read it in a book.

Something else he assured us of was that the Vietnam War was part of an international Jewish conspiracy orchestrated in part by Henry Kissinger, who, he said, was an Israeli. It's true that Kissinger is Jewish, but he was born in Germany and became an American citizen in 1943, and he only helped oversee the conflict in its final few years. But there was no point in arguing with him. After all, our guidebooks were wrong and so were the history books. We weren't to take any of this personally, mind you. He liked Westerners, especially Americans, although he wasn't too fond of the American women because they all had "big asses," a point he elaborated on for nearly a minute.

Arriving at the tunnels, we were treated to a grainy old black and white propaganda film in a drab viewing hall. Showing snippets of the American made devastation, the film was narrated by the same laconic female voice I had heard reciting the Leninist speech on the Reunification Express and announcing the closure dates at Hanoi's Ho Chi Minh Mausoleum Complex. "Like a pack of crazed devils, the Americans fired into villages, into rivers, into cows, into pigs, and into ducks," the voice droned. "They fired into homes, into schools, and even into Buddhist statues." Next, it showed a young woman smilingly blowing up an American tank with a rocket launcher. The tank had been sitting motionlessly and all alone in the middle of a dirt track. It was the first time she had used such a weapon, the voice stated, which you have to admit is impressive, especially seeing as how it was captured on film. Everyone on the screen was smiling; smiling as they cooked, smiling as they fought, smiling as they died.... It was all very strange and I counted the phrase "killing Americans" five times.

The tunnels were interesting, but not for their structural integrity, like those at Vinh Moc, but rather because of their scope and approximation to Saigon. This typifies the pattern of the war. While the Americans went on "search and destroy" patrols and bombed the smithereens out of the North and the Ho Chi Minh Trail in Cambodia, the enemy just kept infiltrating and circumventing them. The network of tunnels at Cu Chi extended from supply routes in Cambodia to within 30 kilometers of Saigon proper, making for a total length of 250 kilometers. The tunnels housed weapons factories, printing presses, field hospitals, headquarters, storage depots, and so on.

In order to deal with the tunnel complex and the trouble it caused in terms of logistics and surprise attacks, the Americans established a military base nearby. However, having vastly underestimated the network's scale, "nearby" turned out to be "directly on top of." Indeed, it took the Americans several months to put together just why they were being shot at over their morning coffee. Finally discovering a couple of tiny trap doors, they sent soldiers down to investigate, but few came back alive. After this, they tried sending trained dogs, but the VC caught them in traps. They also confused them by washing with American soap and hanging out uniforms of POWs. After discovering more trap doors and more of the tunnels they led to, additional men were sent down, and they became known as the "tunnel rats." Although brave to be certain, they were almost totally out of their element, or so I learned from an absorbing book entitled *The Tunnels of Cu Chi* written by two British journalists. Perhaps most interesting is the information garnered from Viet Cong soldiers who worked in the tunnels. To them, the Americans were noisy and predictable. They rumbled in on their tanks at the same time every morning and rumbled back to their base before it got dark. Whenever one of their "tunnel rats" was killed, they would focus a great deal of attention on recovering the body, thus allowing the VC time to regroup or retreat.

Realizing that tunnel warfare was a losing game, the US decided in the end to raze the entire area. For years, the Americans blasted, burned, bulldozed, bombed, and napalmed the tunnels of Cu Chi, all to little avail. Bombers returning from sorties were ordered to dump any unexpended ordinance on top of the place before landing in Saigon. Finally, on the brink of withdrawal, the entire region was cynically carpet bombed, causing the collapse of most of the network and killing hundreds.

Mr. Bean told us how the Americans had started out by building a defensive perimeter in the shape of a triangle. "Did we know what a triangle was?" he wanted to know. We did, we mumbled. Initially, they used a lot a lot of helicopters. "Were we familiar with helicopters?" he asked. We were, we nodded. Other words he used, and wanted to make sure we knew too, were "pilot," "Mexico," "root," "mice," and "cat." He still hated the North, he said, but he loved all Vietnamese people. Then, he said this again. He said almost everything again.

Halfway through the tour, we got to fire guns at a target range, and so I chose the AK-47 over the M-16 and spent $12 on 10 bullets, hitting everything but the target itself. Interestingly, only three weeks previous, a Korean tourist turned the gun on himself and committed suicide. The upshot of this was a jittery staff who quite literally breathed down the back of your neck as they made sure you kept your weapon in front of you. During the second half of the tour, Mr. Bean showed us a dozen or so very nasty booby traps. He also pointed out some of the miniscule trap doors and a blown up tank before indicating a spot where the remains of American soldiers had been discovered a decade earlier.

"Do you want to know how they could tell they were Americans?" he asked.

"Big asses?" responded an Australian man.

On the way back to Saigon, old Mr. Bean cracked open a beer and informed us that his job was done and that he would cease talking. He then prattled on for the better part of an hour. Just when we thought he had finally wrapped things up, he launched into a very long and incredibly bad joke that had to with a man having his watch stolen. When no one laughed, he asked, "Do you know what a watch is?" A couple of patient people in the front nodded that they did, but most of us just stared blankly out the window. For the *grand finale* he began begging us for a tip while pleading that no one complain about him to the travel agency. The idea of complaining never even crossed my mind. But, then again, neither did the notion of giving him a tip.

That night, I did a bit of shopping in the seedy tourist district and in doing so bumped into Jacques and Donny, the two Canadians I had met on the bus to My Son. In the midst of trading anecdotes, the Quebecois couple that I had met on the junk to Halong Bay walked over to say *Bonjour*. They wanted to know where they could find some good pizza. The man elaborated by saying, "We want, eh, how to say? Very big pizza, but for very small money?" Running into all four of them at once wasn't necessarily that much of a coincidence. As mentioned earlier, Vietnam is like a tourist corridor. It's not unusual to run into or see the same people a half a dozen times.

A more meaningful coincidence occurred the next morning at the airport. I had checked in and was making my way to the restaurant to order a cup of tea when a gentleman in his sixties intercepted me, and in a familiar accent, inquired, "Where are *you* from?"

"I'm from Canada," I replied.

"Yeah? Whereabouts?" he asked. This sounded like, "Wear boots?"

"New Brunswick."

"I know you are. So am I. I've seen you before. Are you from Woodstock?"

"No, I'm from Saint John."

"Really? My brother lives in Saint John. His name's Charlie Keenan. He's a lineman at Saint John Power."

"I know him," I said. "My father worked there, and so did I for four years as a student worker."

I had never been to the town he was from, and most likely had never met him before. He didn't know who my father was, and to be honest, I couldn't remember what his brother looked like. It had been a decade since I had left Canada, and yet somehow this man had instantly pegged me as a New Brunswicker in an airport in Vietnam. His name was Gary Keenan, and he invited me to join him and his friend for breakfast.

As it turned out, Gary's friend had lived across the street from him when he was a boy. The two had grown up together. "I'd never been to Asia before, and so one day I thought 'Why not Vietnam?'" he informed me, joking that he had brought his friend along in order to keep him out of trouble. He politely asked me if there was anyone I wanted him to say hello to back home. Then, he took my photo and offered to send it to my family. "And here," he said, reaching into his pocket. "I think you need a couple of these." He then produced two pins; one of the Canadian flag and one of the New Brunswick provincial flag. During our discussion, he told me how highly he thought of the Vietnamese. "They're wonderful people," he said, and I agreed with him. They certainly did seem friendly enough. "But the tourists..." he went on. "Now, *that's* another story," and then, in a hushed tone, he added, "It's mostly the Brits, eh? They're a bunch of jerks." This caused me to chuckle. People where I come from have a tendency of being somewhat ingenuous, so it isn't surprising that they would find, say, a Londoner, stand-offish. Despite their naïveté, propensity for taking the moral high ground, erroneous belief that foreigners everywhere would like nothing more than to have a Canadian pin to stick above the door of their wigwam, and even occasional war profiteering, I was reminded that Canadians generally are very nice. This chance encounter somehow seemed a fitting ending to my journey.

Back in "the other China," my plane touched down at Chiang Kai-shek International Airport at a little after nine. Two hours earlier, the grass all around the runways had been set ablaze by a flying lantern that was launched from a temple located a stone's throw from my apartment building. Three days later, the man who brought 51 years of Nationalist Party rule to an end, President Chen Shui-bian, characterized Washington-Taipei relations as being akin to the homosexual love portrayed in the Oscar winning film *Brokeback Mountain*. Just a few days after this, Chiang Kai-shek's grandson filed a lawsuit against President Chen and his government for more than $150 million for having libeled his grandfather. The defamation could supposedly be found within a government report accusing Chiang of overseeing the murder of more than 30,000 people shortly after his troops fled to Taiwan once it became clear they would soon lose the mainland, something that has long been historical fact.

Anti Chen Shui-bian sentiment reached its zenith several months later in the form of a massive crusade meant to bring about his resignation. The snappily named "Million Voices against Corruption, President Chen Must Go" campaign featured a series of large and occasionally unruly demonstrations, including a "siege" of the Presidential Building. Sporting red T-shirts and matching head-bands, the faction chose the English word "depose" for its motto along with a pair of Vs as its symbol. A spokesperson for the group explained that the emblem signified "Taiwan's Nazca Lines," a reference to Peru's Nazca Lines, which are depictions of giant animals that were carved into a plateau in that country by the Nazca Indians between 200 BC and AD 600. Visible only when viewed from the air, the images were presumably meant to facilitate communication with the gods. Likewise, the protestors in Taiwan were to assemble in imitation of the lines so as to communicate with their own gods, thereby summoning the power required to oust the president, although this never actually occurred. What did occur was general disorder. The largest demonstration saw more than 300,000 people, a fair number of which were children. Partaking in the festivities early one evening, I asked a total of 10 protestors what specifically President Chen had done to warrant such a reaction. Not one of them could give me an answer.

Indeed, despite investigations, the president was never found guilty of any wrongdoing (although his wife and son-in-law were) and he stayed on despite an enormous drop in popularity. Having survived the firestorm, Chen soon set out on a "name rectification campaign." This began by seeing the words "China" and "Chinese" removed from state-run enterprises. Later, the name Chiang Kai-shek was dropped from the aforementioned airport and not long after this a large statue of the former dictator was dismantled. Finally, President Chen went after the Nationalist crown jewel itself: Chiang Kai-shek Memorial Hall. This attractive building, with its signature blue-tile roof and whitewashed walls, was renamed National Taiwan Democracy Memorial Hall. Mr. Chen explained the change by stating that the previous memorial wasn't appropriate for a democratic nation. That may be so, but what the president failed to realize was that the new name effectively implied that democracy in Taiwan was dead. At the time of this writing, various branches of the government were engaged in vigorous dispute (read: chaotic wrangling) over the monument and just what to call it.

To celebrate the twentieth anniversary of the lifting of martial law (during which time, it should be mentioned, more than 90,000 "political dissidents" were disappeared for speaking out against government policy and at least half of them were executed), the government passed a commutation bill that immediately released 9,597 inmates. President Chen urged tolerance, adding that he hoped the public would see the act as "an asset rather than a liability." In just a little over two weeks, ex-convicts had committed crimes in nearly every major city and county throughout the country. Twenty-one died from drug overdoses and one attacked and killed a university professor who was riding his bicycle through a Taipei park — he considered Taipei's roads to be too dangerous. It was recently announced that between 2003 and 2006 there were 664 deaths and 27,000 injuries due to bicycle-related traffic accidents in this country. The government is considering passing a set of new right-of-way laws and laws prohibiting driving against the flow of traffic.

"May you live in interesting times," or so the enigmatic saying goes. If you happen to live in "the other China," or elsewhere in East Asia, you should be virtually assured of it.